Where to w

North
Spain

THE *WHERE TO WATCH BIRDS* SERIES

Where to watch birds in
North & East Spain

Michael Rebane

Christopher Helm

A & C Black · London

© 1999 Text and maps Michael Rebane
Line drawings by Stephen Message

Christopher Helm (Publishers) Ltd, a subsidiary of
A & C Black, 35 Bedford Row, London WC1R 4JH

0-7136-4700-0

Printed and bound in Great Britain by
Redwood Books, Trowbridge, Wiltshire

CONTENTS

Contents

Contents

ACKNOWLEDGEMENTS

A thank you to the many individuals, organisations and agencies who contributed to and assisted with the production of this book, including all the environment, agriculture and game departments of the 13 regions of north and east Spain, the offices of the national parks, Sociedad Española de Ornitologia and, in the UK, Robert Kirk. Finally, special thanks to Diana Mortimer for all her help and encouragement over the past two years.

FOREWORD

Spain is a huge country. Much larger than most first-time visitors ever imagine. Its vastness supports many spectacular, stunning and important wildlife habitats which in turn hold some of the most diverse bird communities in Europe. It is especially noteworthy for its raptors and steppe birds, but also has some extremely rich wetlands.

These habitats like many others in Europe have become threatened in recent years. Of all land uses, it is 'modern' farming practices that have been the most destructive and caused greatest losses. Agricultural intensification, driven by funding from the European Union's Common Agricultural Policy has had a significant impact on farming practices. Increased use of artificial fertilisers and pesticides, funding for irrigation, the introduction of new crop types, loss of fallow land and moves away from traditional forms of livestock farming have led to substantial declines in many species. Those hit hardest include Lesser Kestrel, Little Bustard, Great Bustard, Black-bellied Sandgrouse, Pin-tailed Sandgrouse, Scops Owl, all species of lark, Orphean Warbler and Woodchat Shrike. It is the more *extensive* traditional methods of food production that have actually created habitats and landscapes rich in wildlife. The black Iberian pigs continue to graze the open wooded dehesa, and from these is produced the high quality hams of Spain — the *Jamon Serrano* — and remarkable cheeses of high quality are still produced from the milk of sheep and cattle which graze the alpine and valley meadows of the mountains. Unfortunately recent farming practices have focused on high input production which have caused severe environmental problems — for example the widespread growing of tomatoes or strawberries.

It is not all gloom and doom, fortunately there is still much to see, and hopefully this book will encourage those interested in birds to explore the vastness of Spain, and discover new landscapes and experiences. The spectacle of Great Bustard stalking the cereal fields, the effortless flight of flotillas of Griffon Vultures as they drift across the deep gorges, and the spectacular sky-filling sight of thousands of Cranes as they leave their feeding grounds at dusk making their way to roost in the neighbouring wetlands at night, are but a few of the unforgettable sights to encounter.

If you feel there is little you can do personally to safeguard the future of these threatened landscapes and birds, then think again. At the very least take more interest in where your food comes from and how it is produced (that goes for food produced in the UK as well!), and at what cost to the environment and birds. And when you get back to the UK (or better still while you are on holiday) join the **Sociedad Española de Ornitologia at Ctra.de Húmera, nº 63-1; 28224 Pozuelo de Alarcón, Madrid, Spain (tel: +34-1-351 1045; fax: +34-1-351 1386)**, the Spanish equivalent of the RSPB. It will be a small price to pay out of the total price of your holiday.

VISITING NORTH AND EAST SPAIN

There is no shortage of both flight-only deals and all-in-one package holidays to Spain. Not all cater for the mass tourism market and possibilities now exist for organising accommodation and transport separately, or as part of a package to some of the less visited parts of the region, with a number of specialist companies that advertise widely. Scheduled flights are, however, more flexible if you want to stay for longer than the seven or 14 days that charter flights offer.

Iberia, Spain's national airline, offers the widest selection of scheduled flights to the country, flying to the more usual destinations such as Madrid and Barcelona as well as cities such as Santiago de Compostela. It is also possible with *Iberia* to fly in to one airport and back home from another, normally for the same return price, ideal if, for example, you want to fly into Bilbao and explore the north coast and mountains and fly back from Santiago. Out of season especially it is possible to pick up some bargains with both scheduled and charter, and increasing competition is bringing fares down even further.

Most of the charter flights, as you would expect, have as their destination one of the holiday resorts on the Mediterranean coast and they can offer good value if you prefer to stay in one region and explore the local area. Most companies fly into resorts such as Alicante, Valencia, Barcelona or Girona.

If you do not want to fly, and especially if you want to explore the north coast, the Picos de Europa or the Pyrenees, then the ferry is an alternative. There are two services: one from Plymouth to Santander, operated by Brittany ferries and which takes 24 hours and runs twice weekly for most of the year; P&O also operates a twice-weekly ferry service from Portsmouth to Bilbao. The journey takes a little longer at around 30 hours and leaves Portsmouth on Saturdays and Tuesdays. Driving down into Spain or taking the train or a combination of the two are other alternatives.

For general road maps, the 1:400,000 Michelin series is recommended — five cover the area described in this guide — although there are other equivalent scales. The relevant Michelin maps are numbers 441 (North West Spain), 442 (Northern Spain), 443 (North East Spain), 444 (Central Spain) and 445 (Levante).

For more detailed and larger-scale maps then opt for the Spanish Military Survey series. These are the equivalent of the British Ordnance Survey maps. Although dated, they give contour, road, building and vegetation detail. They are relatively small maps, approximately A2 in size.

There are also provincial maps, these being contour maps that come folded and show the whole of the province covered.

The whole of Spain is covered by maps at the following scales.

1:200,000	Provincial maps (good for cycling)
1:100,000	Military Survey
1:50,000	Military Survey (good for walking)
1:25,000	Miltary Survey (based on aerial survey and, although larger scale, have less footpath information)

These maps can be obtained from specialist map suppliers, for example Stanfords at 12–14 Long Acre, London WC2E 9LP (tel: 0171 836 1321; fax: 0171 836 0189).

When to go

Spain's size, geographical location and topography all make for extreme diversity in its overall climate, and the weather does vary enormously from region to region. Spring arrives early on the Mediterranean coast, but much later in the north in the Picos de Europa or the Pyrenees.

In the north, between the Atlantic coast and the Cantabrian mountains, is a narrow northern 'coastal' strip, where Euskadi (País Vasco), Cantabria, Asturias and Galicia are squeezed in. This coastal strip has a temperate or oceanic climate similar to the western coasts of northwest France, southwest England and west Wales. The proximity to the Atlantic causes depressions to roll in off the sea, creating mild winters and warm summers, but with the possibility of rain (at least outside the main summer months) never far removed.

To the south of the Cantabrian range lies dry Spain and the high plains of the centre of the country. A combination of altitude and distance from the sea together with the influence of the surrounding mountains makes it terrifyingly hot in summer, and bitterly cold and swept by freezing winds in winter. This is an area with a continental climate, scarce rainfall and in the summer a pitiless burning sun in an intensely blue sky, occasionally crossed by short-lived, fierce local thunderstorms.

The Mediterranean climate in the south and east is warm virtually all year round, and it can be very hot during the summer, although on the coast onshore breezes help to keep temperatures bearable. The hot dry summers contrast with the mild moist winters.

If you are planning to visit north and east Spain for a birdwatching holiday then, as you would expect, the most productive times are from the end of March through into June. For particular species or areas then you may need to focus your visit more accurately.

However, there is still much of interest outside the spring and early summer. Birds of prey display in the winter months; seaduck, auks and divers feed and shelter close to the shore and in the bays in winter; Wallcreeper and Alpine Accentor are found at low altitudes in the winter; and spectacular numbers of Cranes spend the autumn and winter in central Spain. All of this is on offer plus the return migration in autumn and the year-round presence of Spain's resident species. In the high summer especially, but also during certain times in the spring, heat haze can be a particular problem — not just over water but on the plains as well. The high-altitude plains, outside spring and autumn, have their own problems: bitterly cold in the winter and, in summer, unbearably hot.

Birdwatching in north and east Spain

What follows is a brief introduction to some of the main wildlife habitats in north and east Spain. It provides some guidance in seeking out some specialities and in the planning of a visit to this region of Spain. However, there are many species, as there are in the UK, that are more widely dispersed throughout the countryside. Traditionally managed olive groves, orange and lemon plantations and extensively managed farmland, for example, can support a wide range of species — many of which are distributed widely across the countryside, and these include species such as White Stork, Red Kite, Woodchat Shrike, Hoopoe, Bee-eater, Little Owl, Turtle Dove, Rock Sparrow, Spotless Starling and many others. Others are more localised in their distribution but may not be restricted to specialist habitats and these species do not always, therefore, find their way into special sites; examples of such species include Rufous Bush Chat and Olivaceous Warbler, both of which are found mainly in south Valencia and Murcia.

The mountains and forests

Apart from Switzerland, Spain is the highest country in Europe, with a mean altitude of 600 m, with the highest summits (outside the Sierra Nevada and Tenerife) in the Pyrenees. Pico de Posets is the highest peak at 3375 m, but the Spanish Pyrenees is best known for its Parque Nacional de Ordesa. There is more to mountainous Spain than the Pyrenees and there are a number of other significant mountain blocks in north and east Spain which include the following.

Cordillera Cantabrica: running across the length of the northern regions westwards to Galicia, with the most famous area being the Picos de Europa.

Sistema Iberico: forming the southern boundaries of La Rioja, Navarra and Aragón, containing the area known as La Demanda.

Sistema Central: comprising the Sierra Gredos and the Sierra Guadarrama to the west and north of Madrid.

Sierra Morena: forming the southern boundary of Castile-La Mancha with Andalucía.

In addition there are smaller blocks, still of considerable altitude and extent including the following.

Meastrazgo: on the border of Valencia, Catalunya and Aragón.

Montes de León: in the northwest of Castile-León.

Montes de Toledo: to the south of Toledo in Castile-La Mancha.

Serrania de Cuenca: in the east of Castile-La Mancha.

These mountain areas are characterised by more than high peaks and bare rocks and comprise an intricate mosaic of crags, cliffs, gorges, rivers and streams, cultivated valleys, hay meadows and alpine grasslands, scrub and woodlands.

Oak and chestnut forests are well developed in the Cantabrian mountains, although beech is the dominant forest tree in the Cantabrian mountains and the Pyrenees. Silver fir forms the highest forest zone in the more humid north-facing valleys of the Pyrenees; by contrast in the drier mountain areas silver fir is missing and the highest forests comprise Scots pine, with black and mountain pine.

For the greatest variety of montane bird species, then head for either the Pyrenees or the Cordillera Cantabrica. Both have a similar bird fauna, and species found in both include Alpine Chough, Snow Finch, Capercaillie, Black Woodpecker, Middle Spotted Woodpecker and Wallcreeper. The Cordillera does, however, lack five species that occur in the Pyrenees — Lammergeier, whose breeding sites are now restricted to the Pyrenees, although they did have a much wider distribution, Tengmalm's Owl, found mainly in the eastern Pyrenees, especially Catalunya (try the Parc Nacional d'Aigüestortes), White-backed Woodpecker (mainly in Navarra), Ring Ouzel and Ptarmigan.

All of the other upland areas in north and east Spain, apart from the top end of the Sistemo Iberico (La Demanda) generally lack all of these species. One mountain species, however, that is absent from the Pyrenees but is found in the western and central part of Cordillera Cantabrica and in the Sistema Central is Bluethroat, with the Sierra Gredos being a good area to explore, offering reasonable chances of success.

There are a number of additional species more widely found in the north of Spain (but the north of Spain only), not specifically confined to the mountains but typically found in the associated habitats of the upland blocks of the Pyrenees and the Cordillera, its woodlands, scrub and valleys. These include Grey Partridge, Treecreeper, Bullfinch, Yellowhammer, Woodcock, Marsh Tit and Red-backed Shrike.

In similar habitats, but more widely dispersed outside the north of Spain (occurring in the Sistemo Central and a few other places) are species such as Hen Harrier, Honey Buzzard, Citril Finch, Woodlark, Water Pipit, Alpine Accentor and Goldcrest.

The largest natural forests remaining in the Pyrenees are found in Navarra. The vast beech and silver fir forests of Irati and Quinto Real hold an extremely rich woodland bird fauna with seven species of woodpecker, along with Booted Eagle, Hobby, Pied Flycatcher and Hawfinch. There are of course many other woods and forests worthy of exploration across the length and breadth of Spain, including the extensive deciduous woodland within the Bosque de Muniellos in Asturias, one of the most important and largest mixed oak woods in Spain, and one of the finest in Europe.

Steppes and cereal plains

Between the mountain ranges and blocks are the three main plains.

Valle de Ebro: in the north of Spain, mainly found in Aragón (the most extensive areas being Los Monegros and the plains of Belchite), but spilling over into neighbouring Navarra and Catalunya.

Meseta Norte: to the north of the Sistema Central, and most of which is in Castile-León.

Meseta Sur: to the south of the Sistema Central and most of which is in Castile-La Mancha.

These characteristically wide open flat or gently undulating semi-arid plains are a patchwork of dry dwarf shrub steppes, grassland pasture (largely used for livestock grazing) and dry cereal cultivations (in rotation with fallow periods). This complex mosaic supports some of the most threatened birds in Europe including Montagu's Harrier, Quail, Great Bustard, Little Bustard, Pin-tailed Sandgrouse, Black-Bellied Sandgrouse and Dupont's Lark. Thekla Lark, Black-eared Wheatear and Spectacled Warbler are also key breeding species.

These are the three main areas for steppe birds. Not all of the sites hold the full complement of species, and some species are more common than others in particular areas. Some steppe species also occur in Murcia, including Dupont's Lark, and in the saltpans of south Valencia, notably Stone Curlew, Short-toed Lark and Lesser Short-toed Lark.

Castile-León, and the Meseta Norte are excellent for Great Bustard, while Little Bustard is relatively common in Castile-La Mancha. For Dupont's Lark it is probably better to go to the Ebro Valley (particularly Aragón) where the strongest population lies. This is also one of the best areas in north and east Spain for Black-bellied Sandgrouse and Calandra Lark.

Wetlands and the coast

Most of the Spanish coastline is fairly straight without inlets, as the mountain ranges lie parallel to the coast. The major exception is the Galician coast which more than makes up for the lack of inlets with many beautiful fjord-like estuaries. The Atlantic and Mediterranean coasts do have their physical differences — the north (particularly Galicia and Cantabria) being rockier. The north and south coasts also have a completely different bird fauna.

The Mediterranean coast generally has a much richer bird fauna, with internationally important coastal lagoons, marshes and saltpans. And it is this coast — with the familiar sounding names of the Costa Brava, Costa Blanca and the Costa del Sol — that is so well known to millions of British holiday-makers. In addition to the huge numbers of tourists, these coasts also attract a vast range and number of bird species. However, a large amount of natural coastal wetlands have been lost to tourist developments in the 20th century. Conversion to rice paddies has also taken its toll, and this has mainly occurred on the rich sediment of river deltas such as the Ebro. Interestingly, due to the reduction in their natural feeding habitat, breeding and wintering herons such as Little Egret, Squacco Heron and Night Heron have turned to rice fields for feeding, and some other species also find these areas attractive.

Some of the most important Mediterranean coastal sites are Aiguamolls de L'Empordà, with around 300 species of bird recorded and having some excellent viewing facilities; the Ebro Delta, one of the most important wetlands in Europe, with 90% of the world's Auduoin's Gull population, seven species of breeding tern, 1,500 Red-crested Pochard, 500 pairs of Slender-billed Gull and good numbers of Collared Pratincole, together with over 100,000 wildfowl in winter; and L'Albufera de València which has a large population of breeding herons and wintering species. There are a number of other coastal sites, particularly in the south of Valencia and in Murcia, notably Mar Menor, the largest coastal lagoon in Spain.

Other wetlands in south Valencia are important for two globally threatened species of duck, White-headed Duck and Marbled Teal. El Hondo is the most important site in Europe for the latter species. The saltpans in this area are also good for species typically associated with wetlands in dry inland steppes, such as Stone Curlew, Avocet, Black-winged Stilt, Kentish Plover, larks, and recently, good numbers of Greater Flamingo.

The Atlantic coast holds species with a northern European distribution, with small numbers of Oystercatcher, Shag, Curlew, scattered populations of Grasshopper Warbler and Savi's Warbler, and a concentration of Fan-tailed Warbler. Galicia has the only breeding Kittiwakes (just over 200 pairs) and the remaining handful of breeding Guillemots in the whole of Spain, together with the majority of the Shag population (c.3,000). The northern coast does also attract a good range of wintering birds and occasional American migrants (in Galicia) and there is notable Spoonbill passage in the spring.

Both Atlantic and Mediterranean coasts attract a range of winter visitors, the bulk of the duck and waders occurring in the south. Eider, Common Scoter, Velvet Scoter, divers, Red-breasted Merganser, auks, skuas, shearwaters and Gannet can be seen close to the coast and sheltering within the bays of both north and south coasts.

Many of the wetlands in inland Spain are reservoirs, and they are generally poor in bird life with the occasional Great Crested Grebe and little else, although there are some notable exceptions. Some of the best natural wetlands include the large group of small lagoons in the centre of the Castile-La Mancha, known as La Mancha Húmeda, the best known being Las Tablas Daimiel. This group of wetlands has important populations of Black-necked Grebe and Marsh Harrier, together with a diverse mix of other species including White-headed Duck, Black Tern, Whiskered Tern, Gull-billed Tern and Bearded Tit. Las Tablas Daimiel is also very important for wintering duck.

Worth a special mention in its own right is Laguna de Gallocanta, a large natural lake in the far southwest and of importance not only for large numbers of wintering duck but also as a major passage and wintering site for sometimes over 50,000 Cranes.

The rivers

The rivers of north and east Spain, even the major ones, have a very modest flow as they drain away only rainwater, and rainfall is scarce and irregular. There are nine major rivers: the Segura (325 km), the Jucar (498 km), the Turia (280 km) and the Ebro (910 km) drain into the Mediterranean; the Mino (310 km), the Duero (895 km), the Tajo (1007 km), the Guadiana (778 km) and the Guadalquivir (657 km) all empty into the Atlantic.

Much of the birdlife associated with the rivers is linked to the riverine woodlands with populations of Little Bittern, Night Heron, Purple Heron, Penduline Tit and Golden Oriole. The Ebro is one of Spain's greatest rivers and this system has some good examples of this very rare habitat. The area around Zaragoza in Aragón is particularly good, and has the added bonus of breeding Bittern, but there are other stretches along this and other rivers. For example, the Tajo and Tietar valleys to the west of Toledo include some large heron colonies, notably Night Heron and Cattle Egret, and also form part of an important wintering area for Cranes. The Duero Valley in Castile-León is a core area for Penduline Tit.

The other major habitat associated with rivers is that of deep gorges (for which Spain is renowned), with the typical bird fauna of vultures, Alpine Swift, Crag Martin and Blue Rock Thrush, and the gorges are not restricted to just one part of north and east Spain. There are some particularly spectacular gorges in the foothills of the Pyrenees, especially Navarra which has the largest Griffon Vulture colony in Spain at the Foz de Arbayun. Gorges are also well represented in Castile-León, such as those at Hoces del Río Duratón, and the Río Duero that forms the western boundary with Portugal has some very impressive high river cliffs. Almost all of the Western Palearctic population of Griffon Vulture occurs in Spain, and the habitat is also important for Egyptian Vulture, Peregrine and other birds of prey, including Eagle Owl.

Dehesas and pasture land

Dehesas are ancient wood pastures, unique to the Iberian peninsula and consisting of Mediterranean oak forest (holm oak and cork oak) with open grasslands, cereal cultivation and Mediterranean scrub. Most birdwatchers visit Extremadura to sample this particular habitat but there are both extensive and good examples in the far west of north and west Spain. In Castile-La Mancha, Cabañeros has some of the largest populations of Black Vulture in Spain, and in Castile-León and some parts of Madrid region have good areas of *dehesa*.

The availability of acorns in the autumn and winter supports both pigs and large numbers of wintering birds including most of the western

European population of Common Crane. The habitat also has important breeding populations of globally threatened birds such as Spanish Imperial Eagle and Black Vulture. The open woodland is also important for both insectivorous birds and scavengers such as Lesser Kestrel, Black-shouldered Kite and Azure-winged Magpie.

Forty species of European conservation concern found in north and east Spain

Forty species that are of conservation concern* within Europe have significant populations within north and east Spain.

Marbled Teal	*Mararonetta angustirostris*
Red-crested Pochard	*Netta rufina*
White-headed Duck	*Oxyura leucocephala*
Black-winged Kite	*Elanus caeruleus*
Lammergeier	*Gypaetus barbatus*
Egyptian Vulture	*Neophron percnopterus*
Griffon Vulture	*Gyps fulvus*
Black Vulture	*Aegypius monachus*
Spanish Imperial Eagle	*Aquila adalberti*
Golden Eagle	*Aquila chrysaetos*
Booted Eagle	*Hieraaetus pennatus*
Bonelli's Eagle	*Hieraaetus fasciatus*
Lesser Kestrel	*Falco naumanni*
Red-legged Partridge	*Alectoris rufa*
Baillon's Crake	*Porzana pusilla*
Crane (wintering population)	*Grus grus*
Little Bustard	*Tetrax tetrax*
Great Bustard	*Otis tarda*
Stone Curlew	*Burhinus oedicnemus*
Collared Pratincole	*Glareola pratincola*
Kentish Plover	*Charadrius alexandrius*
Audouin's Gull	*Larus audouinii*
Gull-billed Tern	*Gelochelidon nilotica*
Black-bellied Sandgrouse	*Pterocles orientalis*
Pin-tailed Sandgrouse	*Pterocles alchata*
Scops Owl	*Otus scops*
Dupont's Lark	*Chersophilus duponti*
Calandra Lark	*Melanocorypha calandra*
Short-toed Lark	*Calandrella brachydactyla*
Lesser Short-toed Lark	*Calandrella rufescens*
Thekla Lark	*Galerida theklae*
Tawny Pipit	*Anthus campestris*
Black-eared Wheatear	*Oenanthe hispanica*
Black Wheatear	*Oenanthe leucura*
Blue Rock Thrush	*Monticola solitarius*
Dartford Warbler	*Sylvia undata*
Orphean Warbler	*Sylvia hortensis*
Woodchat Shrike	*Lanius senator*
Red-billed Chough	*Pyrrhocorax pyrrhocorax*
Ortolan Bunting	*Emberiza hortulana*

* Species of European Conservation Concern, Categories 1–3. Species with an Unfavourable Conservation Status because their populations are small and non-marginal, declining, or localised (Tucker and Heath 1994).

HOW TO USE THIS BOOK

The layout and structure of this book will be familiar to those who have already consulted and used the other country guides in this series. Information on southern Spain covering the regions of Andalucía and Extremadura, together with Gibraltar is contained within the sister volume *Where to watch birds in Southern Spain* by Ernest Garcia and Andrew Paterson.

REGIONS OF NORTH & EAST SPAIN

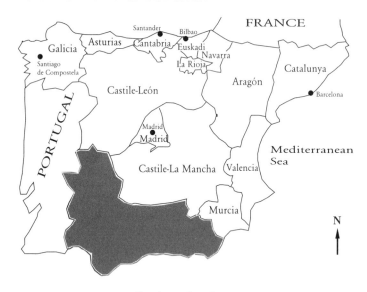

Region chapters
The 104 major sites and 73 additional sites that this guide describes are grouped by region. This book covers the following 13 mainland regions of Spain.

Aragón: 16 main sites, 12 additional sites.
Asturias: 6 main sites, 3 additional sites.
Cantabria: 7 main sites, 5 additional sites.
Castile-La Mancha: 16 main sites, 14 additional sites.
Castile-León: 11 main sites, 7 additional sites.
Catalunya: 9 main sites, 6 additional sites.
Euskadi (País Vasco): 2 main sites, 3 additional sites.
Galicia: 8 main sites, 5 additional sites.
Madrid: 3 main sites, 4 additional sites.
Murcia: 3 main sites, 2 additional sites.
Navarra: 7 main sites, 3 additional sites.
La Rioja: 5 main sites, 3 additional sites.
Valencia: 11 main sites, 6 additional sites.

Each of the 13 chapters gives a brief account of the geography of the region together with an overview of the main birds of interest that occur in the area, referring to some of the sites that then follow. A map of the region shows the position of both major and additional sites along with some of the major roads and main towns to assist in the location of sites and planning of itineraries. The sites are numbered on these maps and refer to their position within the site information.

A key to the names of both major and additional sites are given, and detailed individual site descriptions follow.

Site descriptions

The status of the site is given, but unlike the UK, few sites have nature reserve status, and many have little or no formal protection. Of the sites that do have this form of protection, e.g. *Reserva Natural* or *Reserva Ornitológica*, as with the UK, some are administered and managed by government agencies and some by voluntary bodies such as SEO. The small number of sites that are national parks (*Parque Nacional*) are similar in concept to those in England and Wales, with nature conservation only one of a number of land uses. There are many other designations, some regional, some local. The more commonly encountered examples include.

Parque Natural: similar to Country Parks in the UK but normally much larger with fewer visitors and fewer facilities.

Ramsar sites: internationally important wetlands recognised by the Convention on Wetlands of International Importance (especially waterfowl habitat) held at Ramsar, Iran in 1971.

Reserva Nacional de Caza: large areas which have been protected for the game (and hunting) interest.

ZEPA (Zonas de Especial Protection para las Aves): special protection areas for birds.

Site descriptions are consistent throughout and follow the familiar series format. Each major site is described in terms of its habitat, the species to be seen, best times to visit, access, and with a calendar listing the seasonal highlights throughout the year. A detailed site map complements the text.

Basic information is given on additional sites within the area that are also worthy of a visit if time permits.

Site map

These differ in scale and detail depending on the size of the site or area being described. The distances are approximate but give you an overall idea of the size of the area. Key features are noted on the maps (see below) and include location of observation hides and visitor centres, although the majority of the sites do not have these. More detailed site maps can be obtained for a small number of sites once in Spain, notably those with interpretative centres, or those areas covered by national park status, and areas which are popular with walkers.

Key to the maps

●	Village or town	ⅎ	Marsh	
⬠	Village or town	◆	Bridge or dam	
——————	Motorway or major road	★	Viewpoint	
——————	Secondary road	ⵣ	Lighthouse	
——————	Minor road	⚲	Monastery or church	
- - - - -	Unsurfaced road or track	⌂	Mountain refuge	
- - · - - -	Regional boundary	H	Observation hide	
+—+—+—	Railtrack	*i*	Information centre	
∿∿∿	River	Ⓟ	Car parking	
	Lake or reservoir	✈	Airport	
	Extent of reserve/park	⏥	Ferry terminal	
◮	Major peaks			

Site description

A brief indication of the extent of the site and the main habitats present is given. This section is subdivided to give details of key features within the larger sites.

Species

The main species of interest are listed, with, where information is available, details of the population sizes. Occasionally information is also provided on mammals present.

Timing

For most of the sites spring is the ideal time of year to visit. However, for many wetland sites the interest can be year round, with additional interest during migration and in winter. The same can be said for many coastal sites.

Heat haze can be severe problem in summer, and even in spring during the later part of the morning and throughout the afternoon. This affects not only the wetland sites but also the steppe areas on the plains, and can make searching for bustards and sandgrouse difficult.

Access

Information is given on how to get to the site, with additional details of access around the site including car parking areas, observation hides and visitor centres.

One should remember that many of the sites described in this guide are not nature reserves. Many sites are farmed land and care should be taken when exploring. There are normally enough tracks and paths to get you to parts of the site that appear interesting, but one should respect the land and not damage crops, and particular care should be taken in areas that are shot over!

Calendar

All species known from the site are not listed as space is limited and many species are ubiquitous and found widely throughout the country. Some sifting is done to list the most typical species for that site and the habitats it contains, those species that may be restricted in distribution, and those thought to be of likely interest to the birdwatcher. Generally, rarities that occasionally turn up on migration are not listed, although many of the coastal sites and some of the inland wetlands will have their fair share of these over the years.

Information on species occurrence and status is given under the following headings: *All Year*, *Breeding season*; *Winter*; *Passage periods*.

Some species are resident in Spain throughout the year but do move geographically within season. In winter, for example, when the mountain climate becomes very severe, high-altitude species such as Wallcreeper and Alpine Accentor occur lower down the valleys or even on the coast.

Other sites worth visiting

Some basic information is also provided on additional sites within the region that will be of interest to the birdwatcher and which may form part of an itinerary for the day or week. Only the briefest of information is given on the main ornithological interest of the site and access to the area.

GLOSSARY OF COMMON SPANISH
WORDS FOUND WITHIN THE TEXT

Bahía	bay
Barranca	gully/ravine
Bosque	wood
Cabo	cape/headland
Cañón	gorge
Castillo	castle
Costa	coast
Dehesa	open woodland, normally of oak
Dunas	dunes
Embalse	reservoir
Estación	station
Estepas	steppes
Galachos	ox-bow lakes
Foz	gorge
Hoz	gorge
Ibones	small glacial lakes
Lago	lake
Laguna	lake/lagoon
Llanos	plains
Marismas	saltmarshes
Monasterio	monastery
Muelas	isolated massifs
Parador	state run hotel of high quality
Pico	peak
Playa	beach
Puente	bridge
Puerto	port or mountain pass
Punta	headland
Río/ría	river
Saladas	brackish (seasonal) lagoons
Salinas	saltpans
Sierra	mountain range
Sotos	plantation or grove
Valle	valley

ARAGÓN

It is the Pyrenees that draw birdwatchers to Aragón, and if you have only limited time to sample this superb mountain chain then this is the region to head for. The mountains here are remarkably unspoilt — and much less exploited than further east in Catalunya or across the border in France. The region is best known for the Parque Nacional de Ordesa (AR4), the first national park to be designated in Spain, and a spectacular introduction to the birds and scenery of the Spanish Pyrenees. But there is much more to the Pyrenees than just this national park. Jaca is the only town of any real size, and is a good base from which to explore the Pyrenees and countryside around. It is not only birds that draw people here, as the mountains are a major attraction to everyone interested in climbing, walking, alpine flowers and bears, although sadly there are only a handful of these magnificent animals left.

At their lowest in the west, the height of the peaks slowly increases as you move eastwards, topping at over 3300 m with Monte Perdido, Posets and Maladeta. The high-level mountains of the Pyrenees are well known not only for their birds of prey — Lammergeier, Golden Eagle and Bonelli's Eagle — but also for their specialist upland birds such as Alpine Accentor, Snow Finch, Water Pipit, Ptarmigan, Alpine Chough and the elusive Wallcreeper. Lammergeier numbers are increasing gradually, and there are now 60–70 territories throughout the whole mountain range, although the main concentrations are found in the central area of the Pyrenees, with the core area being Aragón. The majority are found on the Spanish side, with around a dozen territories in France.

Other species of key interest include Honey Buzzard, Capercaillie, Tengmalm's Owl, Eagle Owl, Grey Partridge, Black Woodpecker and Citril Finch. The distribution of Capercaillie and Tengmalm's Owl is very restricted, both favouring open forest, particularly mountain pine. Both species are at the southwestern end of their European range here in Spain, and while Capercaillie is also found in the Cordillera Cantabrica, Tengmalm's Owl is restricted to the eastern part of the Pyrenees and also favours the higher-altitude forests. There are around only 100 pairs of Tengmalm's Owl in Spain, with the majority found in neighbouring Catalunya. Black Woodpecker is always an exciting species to find, and is relatively common in the right habitat across the Pyrenees, unlike White-backed Woodpecker, which also occurs in Aragón but is thinly dispersed. Grey Partridge here is the Spanish race, which is found in open wooded mountain habitats in Spain unlike the UK race which is more of a lowland farmland species.

A number of species that are relatively common in the UK are also found in the Pyrenees, but are noteworthy as they are at the southern limit of their range. These include Woodcock, Treecreeper, Bullfinch and Yellowhammer.

The lower valleys and towering gorges are a very appealing distraction to the Pyrenees proper, and the Ansó (AR1) and Hecho (AR17) valleys are two of the most attractive in the whole mountain range. In addition to good numbers of Red-backed Shrike and Wryneck, two species now largely lost from the UK, what is most impressive again is the healthy population of birds of prey, for example Black and Red Kite and the large colonies of Griffon Vulture.

The Pyrenees are hardly awash with people, yet the rest of the region is definitely overlooked and under-visited — fortunately so for those who prefer quietness and solitude. Those people visiting Aragón for its wildlife do so mainly for the Pyrenees, and most are unaware of the considerable interest of the rest of the region. Its southern mountain ranges, long river gorges, woodlands and meadows, and the River Ebro valley are little visited and little known and include some isolated and beautiful villages, for example in the district of El Meastrazgo.

Not only does Aragón lack tourists, but it also has few inhabitants, being the least populated region in Spain. The countryside is even emptier as half of the population now lives in the centrally located capital, Zaragoza, situated on the River Ebro, one of Spain's greatest rivers, and which bisects Aragón, dividing north and south. Zaragoza does have an airport some 20 km outside the city, and if you can get a flight here then it is very conveniently located to explore both the south and north of the region.

The Ebro Valley is more populated and cultivated, and best known for its steppe areas. Most birdwatchers interested in steppe birds head for Extremadura and miss out on the attraction of Los Monegros (AR13) and the nature reserves of La Lomaza and El Planerón (AR12) on the plains of Belchite. This is an area of low rainfall and open impressive landscapes which are the habitat for a number of threatened species including Montagu's Harrier, Great and Little Bustard, Pin-tailed and Black-bellied Sandgrouse, Stone Curlew, Tawny Pipit and larks. It is especially important for its populations of Black-bellied Sandgrouse, and is one of the best areas in Spain for seeing Dupont's Lark, having over 25% of the Spanish population. Calandra Lark, which has suffered some dramatic declines across Spain, also reaches some very high densities here. Intensification of agriculture through irrigation, however, still poses a serious threat to these important habitats and birds.

There is much more to the Ebro Valley than the steppe areas, and if time permits it is an area well worth exploring with its cliffs, woods and wetlands. The River Ebro itself supports a range of wetland species including Little Bittern, Night Heron and Purple Heron. The oxbow lakes near Zaragoza (AR11) are especially important as they form one of only a few remaining breeding sites in the country for Bittern, a species that is hanging on in Spain with now fewer than 35 breeding males.

South of the Pyrenees the sierras then become the dominant landscape feature, the most impressive and famous — for landscape, climbing and birds — being the huge towering sandstone pillars of Mallos de Riglos (AR6), one of the most northerly sites in inland Spain for Black Wheatear and Sardinian Warbler, and a regular site for Pallid Swift.

In southern Aragón, two mountainous regions are also of interest and have a great diversity of species. While not quite so rich as the Pyrenees they are largely unexplored territory for birdwatchers, but offer much with their considerable variety of upland habitats. West of Teruel, the Serrania de Albarracín (AR16) and part of the Montes Universales, have some excellent walking, and to the east is the isolated and remote region of El Maestrazago (AR27). This latter area has some striking landscapes of stark peaks, deep ravines and colourful and lush meadows.

Worth a special mention in its own right is Laguna de Gallocanta (AR15), a large natural lake in the far southwest and of importance not only for large numbers of wintering duck, but also as a major passage and wintering site for, on occasion, over 50,000 Cranes!

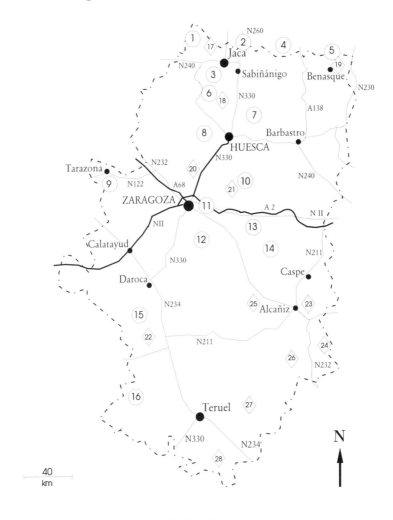

Main sites

1	AR1	Foz de Biniés y Valle de Ansó
2	AR2	High Valleys and Passes of the Central Pyrenees
3	AR3	San Juan de la Peña
4	AR4	Parque Nacional de Ordesa y Monte Perdido
5	AR5	Valle de Benasque y Parque Posets–Maldeta
6	AR6	Mallos de Riglos
7	AR7	Sierra y Cañones de Guara
8	AR8	Embalse de Sotonera
9	AR9	Sierra del Moncayo
10	AR10	Laguna de Sariñena

Other sites worth visiting

AR1 FOZ DE BINIÉS Y VALLE DE ANSÓ

Status: Part of the site is covered by the Reserva Nacional de Caza de los Valles (28,757 ha) which is also a ZEPA.

Site description

One of the most beautiful and spectacular valleys in the whole of the Pyrenees. The River Veral winds its way down from the high Pyrenees to join the River Aragón to the west of Berdún where the valley opens out into a broad plain. The valley can be narrow at times, especially so in its section through the rocky gorge and towering limestone cliffs of the impressive Foz de Biniés. A large part of the valley is covered in woodland of pine and beech, or mixed oak scrub. Higher up the valley the composition of the woodland changes with more silver fir set amongst the alpine pastures above the village of Zuriza. The lower part of the valley below the hilltop village of Berdún is also very attractive, with the village perched above a mosaic of cultivated land, riverside woodland and eroded slopes.

Species

A good chance of Montagu's Harrier and Quail in the cereal fields around Berdún, and species of birds of prey including some that are normally restricted to higher altitudes. Lammergeier, Griffon and Egyptian Vulture, Red and Black Kite, and Short-toed Eagle are regularly seen over the valley and the village of Berdún itself. The riverside woodlands hold Golden Oriole, Nightingale and Wryneck. The gorge of the Foz de Biniés begins at the first tunnel or arch, and from here onwards for the next 3 or 4 km are a range of cliff-nesting birds such as Blue Rock Thrush, Alpine Swift, House Martin, Crag Martin, Rock Sparrow and Rock Bunting, with Dipper and Grey Wagtail in the fast-flowing River Veral below. Eagle Owl breeds in this valley, and 30–50 pairs of Griffon Vulture nest in high cliffs above and in the side valleys. Spotted Fly-catcher, Firecrest and Bonelli's Warbler are common in the mixed and deciduous woodlands. Where the valley opens out higher up the valley, Red-backed Shrike is widespread.

In the woods and alpine pastures of the higher valley a range of different species of bird is possible with Black Woodpecker, White-backed Woodpecker, Citril Finch, Grey Partridge, and in the rocky terrain, Rock Thrush, Wallcreeper and Snow Finch. Red-billed Chough and Alpine Chough are abundant in the area and there are several pairs of Golden Eagle and Lammergeier. This is the western limit in the Pyrenees for a number of species found above Zuriza including Ptarmigan and Ring Ouzel. Snow Finch just sneaks into Navarra, but is also found in the Cordillera Cantabrica.

A number of mammals typical of high altitudes occur, the most interesting being brown bear which is now extremely rare in the Pyrenees.

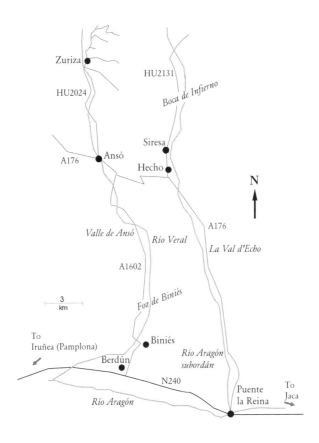

Timing

Late spring through into summer (mid-May to July) can be particularly productive. Take care with late snowfalls in the highest area; thunderstorms can also occur from time to time.

Access

Take the N240 from Pamplona eastwards towards Jaca, and at the hilltop village of Berdún (around 70 km), turn north off the N240 on a minor road (A1602) towards the villages of Biniés and Ansó. There is much of interest in the whole length of the valley, with the options of exploring the lower valley between Berdún and Biniés before exploring the gorges and valley higher up. Parking is not easy in the Foz de Biniés, and care should be taken with birdwatching from the roadside. It is easy to park along the roadside along the valley between the Foz, Ansó and Zuriza. From Zuriza a track leads out into woodlands and finally alpine pastures and can be followed by car for part of the distance, but care should be taken.

From Zuriza one can retrace the road back to Ansó, and then back to Berdún, or across the hillside to the Hecho Valley. Alternatively one can head westwards from Zuriza to join another Pyrenean valley from Roncal over into France.

Calendar

All year: Red Kite, Lammergeier, Griffon Vulture, Goshawk, Buzzard, Golden Eagle, Peregrine, Grey Partridge, Rock Dove, Scops Owl, Eagle Owl, Little Owl, Black Woodpecker, White-backed Woodpecker, Water Pipit, Grey Wagtail, Dipper, Alpine Accentor, Blue Rock Thrush, Cetti's Warbler, Dartford Warbler, Firecrest, Wallcreeper, Red-billed Chough, Alpine Chough, Raven, Spotless Starling, Rock Sparrow, Snow Finch, Citril Finch, Rock Bunting.

Breeding season: Honey Buzzard, Black Kite, Egyptian Vulture, Short-toed Eagle, Montagu's Harrier, Booted Eagle, Quail, Alpine Swift, Bee-eater, Wryneck, Crag Martin, House Martin, Nightingale, Rock Thrush, Ring Ouzel, Subalpine Warbler, Orphean Warbler, Spotted Flycatcher, Golden Oriole, Red-backed Shrike.

AR2 HIGH VALLEYS AND PASSES OF THE CENTRAL PYRENEES

Status: Monumentos Naturales de los Glaciares Pirenaicos occurs in the site. Part of the site is included within the Ordesa–Viñamala Biosphere Reserve (30,000 ha).

Site description

This large area stretches from the highest cols on the French border down through alpine meadows, mixed woodlands and pine forests, hay meadows and river valleys. Towards the central part of the Pyrenees is the area between the valleys of the Aragón and the Tena, and the adjoining mountain ranges. This large area is mostly unprotected but includes not only superb scenery but a considerable wealth of bird habitats, some of which are very important. This is a very high mountain area with extremely rugged scenery including several glaciers. Alpine meadows occur higher up either side of the France–Spain border, and are also commonly found in a mosaic of mixed and conifer woodland.

The Valle de Canfranc is occupied by the River Aragón leading to a high mountain area, where the steep valley sides are covered with pine woods, which give way to alpine pastures at higher altitudes and where there are many rock outcrops.

The Valle de Tena is occupied by the River Gállego with much forest of beech, oak, silver fir and pine, with hay meadows and pastures, rocky cliffs and tarns, known locally as *ibones*. This valley is surrounded by mountains rising to over 3000 m and many small lakes, meadows and thermal springs (at Panticosa) and picturesque side valleys.

A high limestone mountain range with alpine pastures separates the Aragón and Gállego rivers. The mountain area to the east of the Tena Valley is included within a Biosphere Reserve (Ordesa–Viñamala). This is another high mountain area with both limestone and granite rocks, numerous small glacial lakes *(ibones)* and pine woods giving way to mountain pastures at higher levels.

Species

Around half a dozen pairs of Lammergeier can be found in and above the two valleys, with similar but slightly higher numbers of Golden Eagle. Access by road is possible to the highest areas.

The border areas with their alpine meadows and rock outcrops at Col de Somport and El Portalet can be good for Rock Thrush, Alpine Chough and Alpine Accentor, Water Pipit, Snow Finch and Citril Finch, as well as marmot and chamois. Lammergeiers can sometimes be seen soaring between Spain and France here. Small numbers of Ptarmigan and Ring Ouzel are present.

It is worth spending some time exploring rock faces for Wallcreeper. Quarry faces are also worth checking, for example at the well-known site a few kilometres north of Villanúa on the road to Somport. This is not a regular site, however, and one mainly used outside the breeding season. Woodlands and meadows are common and time can be well spent looking for Honey Buzzard, Capercaillie, Grey Partridge, White-backed Woodpecker and Black Woodpecker, Tree Pipit and Whinchat.

Red-backed Shrikes are common at lower altitudes.

Timing

Best time for visiting is spring and summer. Road signs will indicate whether the roads are closed by snow, which is possible in the early part of the season.

Access

Valle de Canfranc Take the N330 out of Jaca towards Villanúa, the Canfranc ski resort, and the border with France at Somport. Various minor roads and tracks occur all up the valley and walking is easy across the alpine meadows at the border.

Valle de Tena The N260 runs the entire length of the Tena Valley, covering 44 km between the small town of Sabiñánigo and El Portalet on the French border. There are a number of possible stopping points worth exploring before you reach Formigal and El Portalet, including the Asieso Ravine, a wooded valley just to the north of Biescas and Escarra Forest, near Escarilla. Much of the main interest, however, is in the higher areas around Formigal, and the El Portalet pass, where there is a car parking area next to some shops and cafes.

There is easy walking all around the border point in flower-rich meadows. A track leads off to the left around 200 m before the shops and passes disused mine workings which can be good for Alpine Chough.

Various paths occur around Sallent de Gállego. From the La Sarra reservoir above Sallent there is a well-marked path to reach the *Ibóne de Respumoso*, a small lake. The spa of Panticosa is reached via the C136 to Sandiniés, from where you take the minor road (HU610) to Panticosa and the Balneario (or spa) which is around 10 km from the turning. Various tracks lead off from the spa including a popular route to the lakes at Bachimaña, but there are many others.

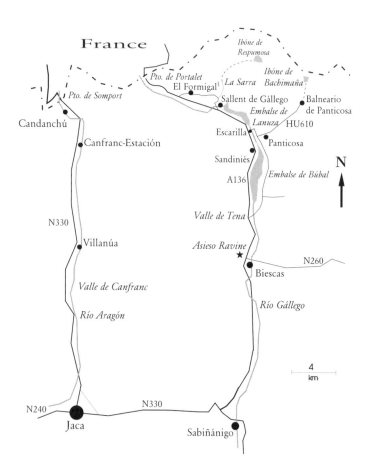

Calendar

All year: Red Kite, Lammergeier, Griffon Vulture, Goshawk, Golden Eagle, Peregrine, Ptarmigan, Capercaillie, Grey Partridge, Woodcock, Rock Dove, Eagle Owl, Tawny Owl, Black Woodpecker, White-backed Woodpecker, Crag Martin, Blue Rock Thrush, Dartford Warbler, Dipper, Alpine Accentor, Crested Tit, Marsh Tit, Wallcreeper, Treecreeper, Red-billed Chough, Alpine Chough, Rock Sparrow, Snow Finch, Citril Finch, Bullfinch, Yellowhammer, Cirl Bunting, Rock Bunting.

Breeding season: Honey Buzzard, Egyptian Vulture, Montagu's Harrier, Black Kite, Short-toed Eagle, Booted Eagle, Alpine Swift, Hoopoe, Tree Pipit, Water Pipit, Rock Thrush, Ring Ouzel, Whinchat, Melodious Warbler, Subalpine Warbler, Whitethroat, Spotted Flycatcher, Red-backed Shrike, Ortolan Bunting.

AR3 SAN JUAN DE LA PEÑA

Status: Sitio Natural (310 ha).

Site description

Essentially there is a flat-topped ridge covered in a pine plantation with cliff faces and ridges giving spectacular views and panoramas, with steep wooded slopes, and is the site of two, now unoccupied, monasteries. The lower and oldest (12th century) of the two monasteries is tucked under an impressive cliff overhang and above a steeply wooded slope, whilst the larger and more recent monastery (17th century) of San Juan is sited on top of the plateau in a large grassy clearing on the edge of the pine plantation. The surrounding area is well known for bird of prey populations, and many of these species can be seen from the ridges.

Species

Despite the apparent lack of old large trees, Black Woodpeckers are found in the plantation and woodland, and it is also good for Short-toed Treecreeper, Nuthatch, Crossbill and Crested Tit. The lower monastery has Alpine Swift and Crag Martin, while both have Red-billed Chough, and the open areas around the new monastery can have Rock Sparrow, Citril Finch and Mistle Thrush. Views from the ridges and on the journey up to the monastery can give Lammergeier, Griffon Vulture, Egyptian Vulture, Short-toed Eagle, Honey Buzzard and a number of other raptors. Blue Rock Thrush, Cirl and Rock Bunting are in the scrub and rock faces around. Alpine Accentor and Wallcreeper winter in the area.

Timing

Spring is by far the most productive, particularly through late May to early June. Early morning is the best time to go as the site can attract large numbers of visitors, including schoolchildren. Most, however, stay within the open grassy area around the upper monastery, although they can get a little boisterous!

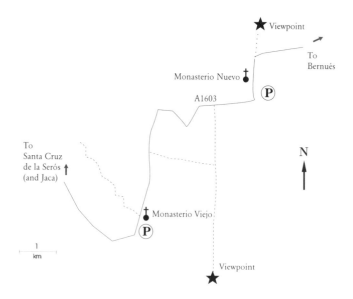

Access

The site is signed off the N240 from Pamplona to Jaca, around 9 km west of Jaca. A secondary road (A1603) climbs up towards the monasteries (12 km) and is well used by coaches. The road passes through the attractive village of Santa Cruz de los Serós, and on to the Monasterios de San Juan. It is well worth stopping between the village and the first monastery as there are several lay-bys from which to scan the cliff faces and skies for birds of prey. If you have time, then there is a footpath that leads from the village of Santa Cruz up to the monastery, but it is a steady climb. There is plenty of car parking at the new monastery at the top of the ridge where most time should be spent. There are various roads and tracks through the plantation, with a spectacular viewing area for birds of prey close to the eastern end of the monastery. In addition there is a track on the left, before the descent back down the road towards the old monastery, which takes you through woodland out onto a ridge towards a communications tower and provides stunning views on two sides; again this can be very good for birds of prey.

Calendar

All year: Red Kite, Lammergeier, Griffon Vulture, Goshawk, Golden Eagle, Peregrine, Black Woodpecker, Great Spotted Woodpecker, Black Redstart, Goldcrest, Firecrest, Blue Rock Thrush, Mistle Thrush, Crested Tit, Coal Tit, Nuthatch, Short-toed Treecreeper, Jay, Red-billed Chough, Rock Sparrow, Citril Finch, Crossbill, Bullfinch, Cirl Bunting, Rock Bunting.

Breeding season: Honey Buzzard, Black Kite, Short-toed Eagle, Booted Eagle, Alpine Swift, Crag Martin, Chiffchaff, Bonelli's Warbler, Spotted Flycatcher.

Winter: Alpine Accentor, Wallcreeper.

AR4 PARQUE NACIONAL DE ORDESA Y MONTE PERDIDO

Status: Parque Nacional (15,608 ha) and also part of the Ordesa–Viñamala Biosphere Reserve (30,000 ha).

Site description

This national park is one of nine Spanish national parks and was the first to be established (1918). At this time it only comprised Ordesa Valley itself, after which it is named. In 1982 it was extended to include the spectacular Añisclo and Pineta valleys, the Escuaín gorges, and the high peak of Monte Perdido (3355 m) which has one of the few remaining glaciers in the Pyrenees. Today this famous and important park now covers a much larger area of over 15,600 ha. As one might imagine in a park of this size, a great variety of habitats occur, the most important being the high mountain tops themselves with extensive grassy alpine pastures. Lower slopes are clothed in forests of Scots pine, black pine, beech and silver fir and rivers carve their way through a series of impressive valleys and gorges. Their are four valleys and each has its own individual characteristics. The River Arazas (Ordesa Valley), the River Aso (Añisclo Valley and ravine), River Yago (Tella Valley and Escuaín Gorge) and the River Cinca (Pineta Valley).

Species

On the highest ground where there are extensive alpine meadows and rocky outcrops are Ptarmigan, Alpine Accentor, Snow Finch (particularly around the screes) and Water Pipit. Rocky areas also have Rock Thrush, Ring Ouzel, Dunnock (which are often initially taken to be Alpine Accentor!), Wheatear and Black Redstart.

Cliffs and rock faces are common throughout the park and support Golden Eagle and Lammergeier, Peregrine, Raven, Alpine Swift, Crag Martin, Wallcreper, Red-billed Chough and Alpine Chough. Wallcreeper

Lammergeier

also occur at several other sites within the park. Egyptian Vulture breed at the lower altitudes.

In the mixed woodlands of beech, silver fir and pine are Goshawk, Sparrowhawk, Capercaillie, Black Woodpecker and White-backed Woodpecker, Crossbill, Crested Tit and Goldcrest. Grey Partridge and Citril Finch are found in the more open areas. A very rare bird in Spain, Siskin, breeds in these woods.

Chamois is abundant in the national park, and it is also home to genet, western polecat, pine marten, wild boar and otter. Of greatest interest perhaps is the Spanish ibex or wild goat ssp *pyrenaicus,* which is only found here in the central Pyrenees and nowhere else in the world.

Timing

May and June, but avoid weekends and public holidays whenever possible as the park can become very busy. There are quieter areas if one avoids the main access points to the mountain. Roads can be blocked by snow.

Access

There are several points of access to the national park and the general mountain area, including the four main river valleys. There are also numerous tracks and routes into the mountains, but some can be very difficult. There are several refuge huts inside the park as well as camping facilities.

Ordesa Valley (main park entrance) The focus of most visits to the park is Ordesa Valley, which is the main park entrance and has a visitor centre, a large car park and a number of trails, including the main one which starts off in the lower river valley of the Ordesa, climbs up

through beech and silver fir and pine forests and finally into the high alpine pastures. This trail leads eventually to Gavarnie on the French side of the border. Take the N330 east out of Jaca, or north from Huesca as far as Sabiñánigo, then turn northwards towards France on the N260 as far as Biescas. Take a right turn here, still along the N260 to Torla and the A135 to Ordesa and the park entrance.

Añisclo Valley and ravine From the main park entrance return to Torla and take the N260 south through Broto and Boltaña to Ainsa. If travelling from the south take the A138 northwards from Barbastro, which is sited on the N240 between Huesca and Lleida. From Ainsa the A138 continues north again towards Bielsa and the French border. At the village of Escalona take a left turning for Ereta de Bies and the Ermita de San Urbez where there is a car park, and where a walk along the gorge begins.

Tella Valley and Escuaín Gorge For this section of the park follow the directions as given above up to the village of Escalona. For Escuaín Gorge, take the same left turn here, but shortly afterwards take a right along a minor road to Escuaín. Tracks lead from the village.

For Tella Valley do not turn off at Escalona but carry on the A138 for a further 5–6 km taking a left turn shortly after San Juste. If you reach the village of Lafortunada you will have missed the turn! This minor road leads to the village of Revilla from which a track takes you up the Tella Valley.

Pineta Valley See above for details of getting to Ainsa. From Ainsa continue on the A138 road north as far as Bielsa. From Bielsa take a left turn to the Parador Nacional de Monte Perdido situated at the head of Pineta Valley. As well as the parador there is an information kiosk and a number of walks lead from nearby, including one to the Valle de Lalarri through beech woods and out onto alpine meadows.

Calendar

All year: Lammergeier, Griffon Vulture, Goshawk, Sparrowhawk, Buzzard, Golden Eagle, Kestrel, Peregrine, Ptarmigan, Capercaillie, Grey Partridge, Woodcock, Common Sandpiper, Rock Dove, Woodpigeon, Tengmalm's Owl, Eagle Owl, Tawny Owl, Black Woodpecker, Great Spotted Woodpecker, Water Pipit, Skylark, Grey Wagtail, Dipper, Dunnock, Alpine Accentor, Robin, Black Redstart, Goldcrest, Firecrest, Long-tailed Tit, Marsh Tit, Wallcreeper, Short-toed Treecreeper, Treecreeper, Jay, Red-billed Chough, Alpine Chough, Raven, Snow Finch, Siskin, Crossbill, Bullfinch.

Breeding season: Egyptian Vulture, Alpine Swift, Crag Martin, House Martin, Wheatear, Rock Thrush, Ring Ouzel, Whitethroat, Garden Warbler, Blackcap, Bonelli's Warbler, Chiffchaff, Spotted Flycatcher, Redbacked Shrike, Citril Finch, Yellowhammer, Ortolan Bunting.

AR5 VALLE DE BENASQUE Y PARQUE POSETS–LA MALADETA

Status: Parque Natural (33,267 ha), and also forms part of the Reserva Nacional de Caza–Benasque (50,000 ha).

Site description

Benasque Valley lies between the massifs of Posets and Maladeta. On these massifs are found the highest summits in the Pyrenees, the Pico de Aneto at 3404 m, and the Pico de Posets at 3375 m. This high mountain area of the Pyrenees is not restricted to the peaks as large areas are over 3000 m, with small glaciers, numerous mountain lakes, and many rocky areas. Interest is not restricted to the high mountains, and as is the case with many other valleys there is much to see between the 3400 m peaks and the foot of the valley at around 1500 m. There is a wide range of habitats, running from hay fields, woods of birch and silver fir to large pine forests growing at an altitude of up to 2200 m. On reaching the treeline, habitats change, giving way to alpine meadows, rock fields, lakes and some glacial cirques. The forests of Vallibierna and Atriga de Lin-Portillón are particularly exceptional.

Species

As you would expect this site has high-mountain bird communities including both Lammergeier and Golden Eagle, Ptarmigan, Snow Finch, Alpine Accentor, Alpine Chough and Water Pipit. This is one of the best areas in the Pyrenees for Capercaillie, and the forest has very good numbers of Black Woodpecker. Areas of extensive woodland also have Honey Buzzard, Goshawk, Tengmalm's Owl, Marsh Tit and Crossbill. In the more open woodland and in pastures and rocky slopes are Grey Partridge, Ring Ouzel, Rock Thrush, Whinchat and Red-billed Chough.

There are a number of side valleys, for example Estós Valley, where there are some huge rocky cliffs and where it is possible to get views of birds of prey.

Brown bear and chamois.

Timing

May and early June, with access difficult during periods of heavy snowfall late in winter.

Access

Benasque can be reached via the A139 from the south where it joins the N260 and is the main focal point for the area, particularly so for serious climbers and walkers. Benasque Valley splits the park in half. The western arm of the area can be approached along the Valle de Chistau (Gistain) which itself can be reached via a minor road off the A138 at Salinas de Sin, or from the east along a minor road off the N260 near Castejón de Sos.

There are a huge number of options for exploring the area in search of birds. Many mountain and hill routes have been shown on the ground with coloured markers. Details of these routes can be found in the villages, but particularly Benasque. There are five mountain refuges and numerous routes up many of the side valleys. There are also

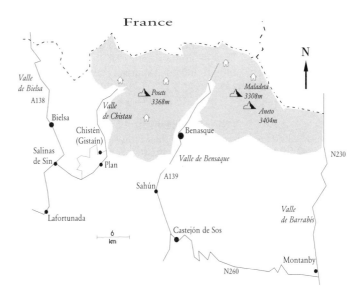

numerous forest tracks leading up the mountains from any of the villages along the A139 road.

There are large numbers of trails linking the villages of the Valle de Chistau.

Calendar

All year: Red Kite, Griffon Vulture, Lammergeier, Goshawk, Golden Eagle, Peregrine, Ptarmigan, Rock Dove, Long-eared Owl, Tengmalm's Owl, Black Woodpecker, White-backed Woodpecker, Crag Martin, Blue Rock Thrush, Dipper, Alpine Accentor, Marsh Tit, Crested Tit, Wallcreeper, Rock Sparrow, Red-billed Chough, Alpine Chough, Raven, Citril Finch, Snow Finch, Bullfinch, Yellowhammer, Rock Bunting.

Breeding season: Honey Buzzard, Black Kite, Short-toed Eagle, Alpine Swift, Water Pipit, Whinchat, Rock Thrush, Ring Ouzel, Red-backed Shrike, Ortolan Bunting.

AR6 MALLOS DE RIGLOS

Status: Unprotected.

Site description

Mallos de Riglos are part of the Sierra de Santa Domingo mountain range that includes the spectacular red sandstone rock formations immediately behind and dominating the village of Riglos. The site consists of towering perpendicular cliffs, known locally as *Los Mallos de Riglos,* together with a rocky scree base. Vegetation is sparse to nonexistent on the scree, with pockets of scrub in the gulleys, and with more scrub, river and cultivated land below the cliffs, scree and village. The local climate here is noticeably much warmer and drier compared to the rest of Pyrenean foothills further north. There are a number of other areas worth exploring in the general area around Riglos, including similarly impressive sandstone cliffs above the nearby village of Agüero. The general area is good for raptors.

Species

This is a well-known site for visitors to the Pyrenees for Black Wheatear, where it reaches its northern limit in Spain. It nests amongst the boulder-strewn cliff base but can be elusive, especially when the winds are strong at the foot of the cliffs. Black Redstart is very common here, and Rock Sparrow can be found around the church. The cliffs also support a good colony of Griffon Vultures and a range of other cliff-nesting species such as Egyptian Vulture, Crag Martin and Peregrine, despite disturbance from rock climbers. Although it is worth concentrating on the scree and cliffs habitats, it can also be fruitful searching the scrub immediately below for warblers, including Dartford, Spectacled and Subalpine. This is also a very northern, and inland site for Sardinian Warbler. The varied countryside below the cliffs and the river can have Orphean Warbler, Woodchat Shrike and Golden Oriole, and the mountain areas around have Lammergeier, Golden Eagle, Bonelli's Eagle and Booted Eagle. Pallid Swift also occurs.

Crag Martins

Timing

Good all year round, but best in April and May. However, also winter for Wallcreeper and Alpine Accentor. The cliffs are very popular with climbers and consequently can be very busy at weekends, and so this time should be avoided. On some days and at certain times of day there can be very strong winds and gusts at the foot of the cliffs, so care should be taken on the unstable slopes.

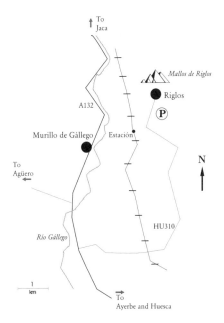

Access

Access is via the main road, the A132 from Pamplona to Huesca. Travelling south you will see the cliffs and village to your left but need to travel a few kilometres further south before turning left to cross the river, whereby you drive a further few kilometres back in the general direction from which you have come (on the HU310), but on the opposite side of the river, and up towards the village on a minor road. Car parking is immediately outside the village in a specially provided area for cars and coaches. Only cars owned by local people are allowed into the village as the streets are very narrow! There is a short walk up through the village towards the highest point, where the church is situated, and then along the foot of cliffs along rocky scree. Walking can be a little difficult in places, and care should be taken, especially when it is windy.

Calendar

All year: Red Kite, Lammergeier, Griffon Vulture, Golden Eagle, Bonelli's Eagle, Peregrine, Rock Dove, Eagle Owl, Blue Rock Thrush, Black Redstart, Black Wheatear, Sardinian Warbler, Red-billed Chough, Raven.

Breeding season: Black Kite, Egyptian Vulture, Short-toed Eagle, Booted Eagle, Alpine Swift, Pallid Swift, Crag Martin, Tawny Pipit, Rock Thrush, Dartford Warbler, Woodchat Shrike, Spectacled Warbler, Subalpine Warbler, Orphean Warbler, Golden Oriole, Rock Sparrow.

Winter: Wallcreeper, Alpine Accentor.

AR7 SIERRA Y CAÑONES DE GUARA

Status: Parque Natural and ZEPA (81,350 ha).

Site description

A huge upland limestone massif northeast of the city of Huesca, at the southern edge of the Pyrenees, and stretching for 40 km west–east. This is the largest of the 'pre-Pyrenean' ranges, where limestone countryside is cut through by rivers, and many deep gorges with high limestone walls that dissect the massif into 'mini-sierras' — Sierra del Águila between the rivers Isuela and Flumen; Sierra de Gabardiella between the rivers Flumen and Alcanadre; Sierra de Balces between the rivers Alcanadre and the Isuala de Balces; and the Sierra de Sevil between the Isuala de Balces and the Vero rivers.

The altitude within the park varies considerably from 430 m along the river Alcanadre to 2077 m at the highest point, Tozal (or Puntón) de Guara. It is a sparsely populated area with many abandoned small villages, and deep limestone ravines which have flowing torrents in the winter but are mainly dry during the summer months. Extensive areas of grassland and oak and juniper scrub cover the park, amidst mixed oak woods, beech and pine and yew.

Species

Extremely important for birds of prey, with around five pairs of Lammergeier, well over 200 pairs of Griffon Vulture, and smaller numbers of Egyptian Vulture. Red Kite, Honey Buzzard and Peregrine are fairly common and there are small numbers of Short-toed Eagle, Golden Eagle and Eagle Owl. Bonelli's Eagle is also widespread across the park. In the higher parts of the gorges and surrounding land in the winter are Wallcreeper, Alpine Accentor and Citril Finch.

In addition to Red Kite and Honey Buzzard, the woodlands also support both Sparrowhawk and Goshawk, Long-eared Owl, Black Woodpecker and Hawfinch, with Wryneck in the more open areas. Black Wheatear and Blue Rock Thrush are found scattered throughout the open rocky areas.

The grassy and scrubby areas have Red-backed Shrike and Cirl and Ortolan Bunting.

Timing

While winters are not so severe as in the high Pyrenees, spring does arrive relatively late to the area. April to June are the best months, with May onwards being especially good. Some species can be found throughout the year, especially birds of prey, and the high altitude species such as Wallcreeper and Alpine Accentor winter in the park

Access

There is a network of small roads leading north from the N240 Huesca–Barbastro road, or south from the A1604 which links the two major roads — the N330 in the west and the N260 in the east. Many lead to monasteries and chapels, which are interesting in their own right as well as good points of access to the wilder parts of the Guara. Three are particularly noteworthy: those of San Martín, San Cosme and la Virgen de Arraro. Numerous small roads and forest tracks lead into the inner parts of the park.

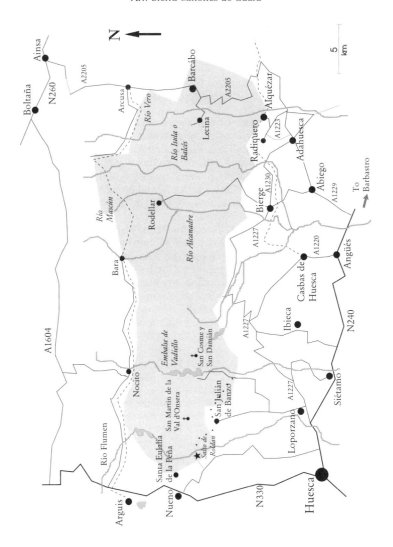

Salto de Roldán-San Martín de la Val de Onsera Take the N240 from Huesca towards Barbastro. After 7 km turn left onto the minor road for Loporzano, and left again to Barluengo and San Julián de Banzo. A signed forestry road leads to a path that takes you up to the ravine, waterfall and chapel of San Martín de la Val de Onsera.

Embalse de Vadiello As above as far as Loporzano and from there turn right after about 3–4 km towards Sasa del Abadiado, Castilsabas and finally to the Embalse de Vadiello, a reservoir. A track from the dam of the reservoir goes to the Chapel of San Cosme, through oak scrub woodland climbing towards the Huevo de San Cosme, a rocky outcrop. Other possibilities include a track which starts at the last road tunnel, across a ravine, the Barranco del Diablo, along the bank of the reservoir to Nocito.

Alcanadre and Gorges at Mascún From Huesca take the N240 towards Barbastro, after some 30 km, just after the bridge over the River Alcanadre, turn left onto a minor road (A1229 and A1227) taking you to Abiego, Bierge and Rodellar. In Rodellar, information and maps of the area are normally available. From Rodellar a path goes to Mascún Gorge and it is possible to climb up to the source of the River Mascún.

Sevil Range and Gorges at Balcés As above, but at the village of Abiego bear right to Adahuesca. Alternatively, in Barbastro take the minor road (A1232) towards Alquézar and, once through the village of Huerta de Vero, turn left for Adahuesca. In this village take the road to Radiquero and to San Pelegrín. From San Pelegrín a track leads up to the high point of Mesón de Sivil (1273 m), and along Balcés Gorge for about 8 km, ending at Sarsa de Surta.

River Vero and Forests at Barcábo Take the minor road (A1232) out of Barbastro for Castillazuelo, and from there continue to Alquézar. From the square in the village follow the base of Vero Gorge for cliff-nesting species. To reach other routes, 3 km before Alquézar take the A 2205 to Colungo, Lecina and Barcábo, from where there are numerous forest tracks for woodland species. Try also the road from Naval through Suelves to Barcábo.

There are further tracks worth exploring at Santa Eulalia de la Peña and the Embalse de Belsué, the Barranco de la Pillera near Nocito, and near Lecina. Long-distance trails are also possible to the north and south of the main massif.

Calendar

All year: Lammergeier, Griffon Vulture, Goshawk, Sparrowhawk, Golden Eagle, Bonelli's Eagle, Peregrine, Stock Dove, Long-eared Owl, Eagle Owl, Woodcock, Green Woodpecker, Black Woodpecker, Crag Martin, Dipper, Black Redstart, Black Wheatear, Blue Rock Thrush, Red-billed Chough, Raven, Hawfinch, Cirl Bunting, Rock Bunting.

Breeding season: Red Kite, Honey Buzzard, Egyptian Vulture, Short-toed Eagle, Booted Eagle, Hobby, Hoopoe, Wryneck, Alpine Swift, Tawny Pipit, Redstart, Wheatear, Black-eared Wheatear, Rock Thrush, Sub-alpine Warbler, Melodious Warbler, Spotted Flycatcher, Woodchat Shrike, Red-backed Shrike, Ortolan Bunting.

Winter: Wallcreeper, Alpine Accentor, Citril Finch.

AR8 EMBALSE DE SOTONERA

Status: Unprotected

Site description

This large reservoir was created by damming the Gállego river, and has a shallow indented shoreline and stands of tamarisk and willow intermixed with areas of reed and marsh. The northwest corner of the reservoir has the best developed and greatest expanse of marsh. During the year, considerable changes in water level occur which can flood out nests and drown vegetation, but which at other times can also leave exposed considerable areas of mud and emergent vegetation.

Species
The marshes are especially worth visiting, and this area is of greatest bird interest, with Purple Heron, Spotted Crake, Water Rail, Great Reed Warbler and a variety of waders and warblers, most especially during the spring and autumn. However, probably the site's real claim to fame lies in the large numbers of duck that winter on the reservoir and particularly for the number of Cranes that visit the site in late winter–early spring and which have reached in excess of 7,000 individuals.

There is further interest in the immediate areas surrounding Sotonera, in particular steppe species such as Black-bellied and Pin-tailed Sandgrouse, Little Bustard, Stonecurlew, Calandra Lark, and occasionally Great Bustard.

Timing
Winter for wildfowl and Cranes, and spring and autumn for passage migrants, waders, warblers and terns. The area can get very hot in late spring and summer, and the reservoir should be avoided in the heat of the day at these times of years as the heat haze can be a great problem.

Access
The Embalse de Sotonera can be reached off the N330 out of Huesca towards Zaragoza. Turn right at the village of Almudévar onto a minor

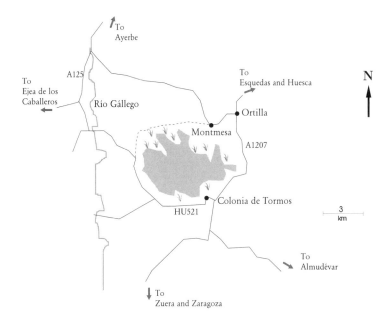

road (A1207) signed for Tormos. Alternatively on the Huesca to Pamplona road (A132), turn left shortly after the village of Esquedas towards the village of Montmesa, again onto the A1207. It is possible to follow tracks for some distance along the northern perimeter of the reservoir but it is not possible to drive very far, especially when muddy. A road does, however, go round the remaining edges of the reservoir, and there are a number of places where it is possible to get views over the lake. The wetland area between the northern track and the reservoir are the most productive, however, where well-developed marsh vegetation now occupies the site of a former reservoir.

Calendar

All year: Little Grebe, Great Crested Grebe, Mallard, Marsh Harrier, Water Rail, Moorhen, Coot, Little Bustard, Great Bustard, Kentish Plover, Lapwing, Redshank, Black-headed Gull, Black-bellied Sandgrouse, Pin-tailed Sandgrouse, Little Owl, Calandra Lark, Cetti's Warbler, Fan-tailed Warbler, Dartford Warbler, Corn Bunting.

Breeding season: Purple Heron, Black Kite, Spotted Crake, Black-winged Stilt, Little Ringed Plover, Common Sandpiper, Bee-eater, Yellow Wagtail, Reed Warbler, Great Reed Warbler, Melodious Warbler, Woodchat Shrike.

Winter: Wigeon, Teal, Pintail, Shoveler, Tufted Duck, Golden Plover, Grey Plover.

Passage: Little Egret, Grey Heron, Red-crested Pochard, Garganey, Osprey, Crane, Avocet, Ruff, Black-tailed Godwit, Whimbrel, Spotted Redshank, Black Tern.

AR9 SIERRA DEL MONCAYO

Status: Parque Natural–Dehesa del Moncayo (1389 ha). The sierra is around 45,000 ha in total.

Site description

An isolated and sparsely populated mountain massif in the far west of the region, rising in altitude from 800 m to the peak of Cerro de San Miguel (2315 m), the highest mountain in Aragón south of the Pyrenees, and covered with snow for up nine months of the year. The spectacular limestone scenery of crags and gorges is impressive, and although the area is largely deforested there are a few relict oak, beech and pine woods on the northern slopes of the sierra that now comprise the parque natural.

The habitats and vegetation are, however, surprisingly varied, and apart from woodlands and gorges also include alpine pastures and scrub.

Species

The highest ground around the Sanctuario del Moncayo provides excellent views for scanning the surrounding countryside for Griffon Vulture, Golden Eagle, Alpine Swift, Raven and other birds of prey. The open ground of pasture, scrub and rock has Rock Thrush, Blue Rock Thrush, Rock Sparrow, Water Pipit, Citril Finch, Red-billed Chough, Grey Partridge and Alpine Swift. The area is important for Griffon Vulture with over 100 pairs, and there is also Golden Eagle and Eagle Owl.

The oak woods have Short-toed Eagle, Honey Buzzard, Woodcock, Tree Pipit and Bonelli's Warbler with Turtle Dove, Nightjar, Bee-eater, Subalpine Warbler and Dartford Warbler in the lower scrubby and more open wooded areas.

Crested Tit, Crossbill and Goldcrest are found in the pine woods

Timing

Best times of year are May and June.

Access

Take the N232 or the A68 motorway west of Zaragoza. 45km from Zaragoza at the Gallur junction turn left onto the N122 for Soria. After 24 km, turn left onto the minor road for Vera de Moncayo. When you reach Vera de Moncayo, there are two options: (1) Continue in the direction of Tarazona, passing through Trasmoz, until you reach San Martín de Moncayo and then Agramonte, where there are car parks and an information centre. (2) Drive in the direction of Añón (Z373) until you reach the monastery of Veruela and on to Agramonte. From Agramonte a road climbs up the hillside to the Sanctuario de la Virgen del Moncayo, passing a number of springs on the way and a mountain refuge. A path leading from the sanctuary takes you up through pine woods and areas of scree to the peak, and is well marked and relatively easy to follow.

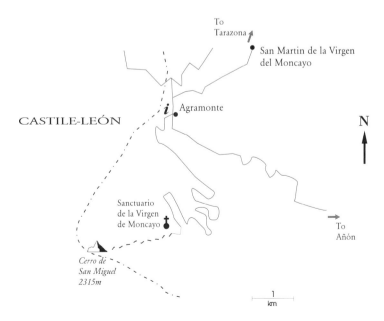

45

Calendar

All year: Goshawk, Sparrowhawk, Golden Eagle, Grey Partridge, Woodcock, Eagle Owl, Long-eared Owl, Woodlark, Grey Wagtail, Dipper, Dunnock, Blue Rock Thrush, Song Thrush, Chiffchaff, Firecrest, Goldcrest, Crested Tit, Great Tit, Nuthatch, Short-toed Treecreeper, Red-billed Chough, Raven, Rock Sparrow, Citril Finch, Crossbill, Serin, Cirl Bunting.

Breeding season: Honey Buzzard, Short-toed Eagle, Booted Eagle, Nightjar, Crag Martin, Tree Pipit, Water Pipit, Rock Thrush, Subalpine Warbler, Garden Warbler, Orphean Warbler, Bonelli's Warbler, Red-backed Shrike, Ortolan Bunting.

AR10 LAGUNA DE SARIÑENA

Status: Refugio de Fauna Silvestre and ZEPA (604 ha).

Site description

This is a large shallow lagoon with a well-developed fringe of marsh vegetation situated in a steppe area between the valleys of the rivers Alcanadre and Flumen. The lake and surrounding land have a high salt content which has developed through evaporation during periods of high summer temperatures, and in addition to a reed fringe the lake also has saltmarsh communities.

A great deal of the area immediately around the lake has been agriculturally improved by cultivation and irrigation, and much land has been put down to large areas of rice paddies. The water level of the lake was, until relatively recently, subject to considerable variations but now remains constant throughout the year because of the construction of irrigation channels for the rice industry. The lagoon provides a stark but welcome contrast within the dry steppe landscape.

Species

The lagoon has a good variety of wetland birds including Black-necked Grebe, and breeding herons and waders, notably Little Bittern. The site is also important as a passage site for waders and terns, and can hold over 10,000 wildfowl over winter. A range of species also uses the irrigated surrounding land as feeding areas while using the lake to breed or roost.

Timing

Spring and autumn, but winter also produces large numbers of duck.

Access

The lake is immediately northwest of the town of Sariñena, around 70 km from Zaragoza along the A129, or south from Huesca on the A131. The lake is signed from the village and a track leads up to the edge.

Paths are located along much of the shore, although as irrigation channels are now present these have to be crossed and care should be

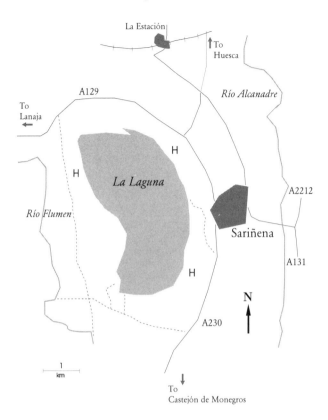

taken in doing so. Viewing can sometimes be difficult over the reed fringe to the lake, but there are three main viewing areas around the lake, with the northernmost shore the best place for waders.

Calendar

All year: Little Grebe, Great Crested Grebe, Black-necked Grebe, Cattle Egret, Grey Heron, Marsh Harrier, Water Rail, Lapwing, Black-headed Gull, Kingfisher, Cetti's Warbler.

Breeding season: Little Bittern, Night Heron, Little Egret, Purple Heron, Black-winged Stilt, Little Ringed Plover, Kentish Plover, Redshank, Great Spotted Cuckoo, Roller, Sand Martin, Reed Warbler, Great Reed Warbler, Penduline Tit.

Winter: Cormorant, Greylag Goose, Wigeon, Teal, Mallard, Pintail, Shoveler, Grey Plover, Dunlin, Snipe.

Passage periods: Osprey, Little Crake, Little Stint, Curlew Sandpiper, Ruff, Spotted Redshank, Greenshank.

AR11 LOS GALACHOS DEL EBRO

Status: Reserva Natural and ZEPA (777 ha).

Site description
These oxbow lakes or *galachos* are situated 12 km downstream of Zaragoza between Pastriz and Pina de Ebro. There are three *galachos*, Alfranca de Pastriz to the north of the Ebro and two to the south, La Cartuja and El Burgo de Ebro. These are now unconnected with the river, and fed entirely from underground supplies. Much of the area has been planted with poplar in recent years, but there is also well-established associated fringe vegetation and extensive scrub.

Species
These oxbow lakes are important for breeding herons, particularly Bittern, a very rare species that has suffered severe declines in most European countries and now only numbers around 35 males in the whole of Spain. There are also around five pairs of Little Bittern, 40 pairs of Night Heron and several pairs of Little Egret and Purple Heron.

The poplar plantations or *sotos* are good for Wryneck, Nightingale, Penduline Tit, Golden Oriole and Woodchat Shrike, and are also be important for migrating passerines, including warblers and flycatchers, and roosting hirundines and wagtails. This is a very rich and diverse site and a total of around 200 species has been recorded.

Timing
March to May, and again September and October can be outstanding for falls of small migrants, roosting hirundines and wagtails.

Access
Take the NII eastwards from Zaragoza towards Bujaraloz. Turn right at the village of Puebla de Alfindén to Finca de la Alfranca, where there is

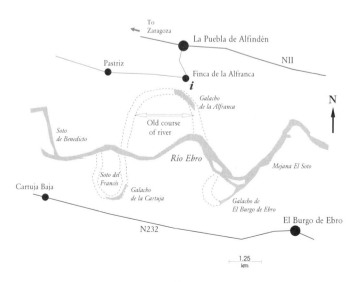

an interpretative centre. It is also possible to reach the area along a minor road off the NII, immediately right after the road crosses over the River Gállego, to Pastriz. Full details of access around the reserve are available at the visitor centre.

Calendar

All year: Little Grebe, Great Crested Grebe, Bittern, Little Egret, Marsh Harrier, Water Rail, Coot, Kingfisher, Green Woodpecker, Penduline Tit, Cetti's Warbler, Fan-tailed Warbler, Sardinian Warbler.

Breeding season: Little Bittern, Night Heron, Purple Heron, White Stork, Black Kite, Scops Owl, Bee-eater, Wryneck, Sand Martin, Nightingale, Great Reed Warbler, Melodious Warbler, Spotted Flycatcher, Golden Oriole, Woodchat Shrike.

Passage periods: Grey Heron, Booted Eagle, Swallow, House Martin, Wood Warbler, Willow Warbler, Spotted Flycatcher, Pied Flycatcher.

AR12 LAS ESTEPAS DE BELCHITE

Status: Mostly unprotected (40,000 ha), although part of the area is a ZEPA and there are two important reserves (1) Refugio de Fauna Silvestre de la Lomaza de Belchite (961 ha); (2) La Reserva Ornitológica El Planerón (600 ha), which is run by SEO.

Site description

The area to the south and southeast of Zaragoza forms one of the most important steppe landscapes, not only in the Ebro Valley, but the whole of Spain. Sadly, substantial area of steppe have been destroyed through ploughing and cultivation and the area is further threatened by more proposals for agricultural irrigation. The low hills and plains of the Ebro Valley and associated valleys are now a mosaic of steppe, cereal fields, and irrigated areas with occasional wooded hillocks and gullies and cliffs formed by the rivers that cross the steppe.

The general area is extensive if a little fragmented, and stretches from the west of Muel to Azaila in the east. Most is unprotected and the focus of attention is the two reserves of La Lomanza and El Planerón, although there are other areas worth visiting including the steppe area lying either side of the road running from Belchite to Azaila and known as El Saso.

La Lomaza was created in 1987, while El Planerón is a bird reserve owned by SEO.

Species

The whole area is of great importance for steppe birds and one of the most critical areas in Spain for Black-bellied Sandgrouse (with up to an estimated 1,000 pairs) and Dupont's Lark (800 pairs). This is probably the best place in Spain to see the latter species. There are similar numbers of Pin-tailed Sandgrouse (1,000 pairs), but few Great Bustards

Black-bellied Sandgrouse

(around 30) and only small numbers of Little Bustards, which are mainly found in the Alfamén plains area west of Muel. Most of the remaining species typical of steppe bird communities are present with around 150 pairs of Stone Curlew, and at least 2,000 pairs of Lesser Short-toed Lark. Other species present include Tawny Pipit, Short-toed Lark, Calandra Lark and Black-eared Wheatear.

The other species of note is Dotterel, which can be found at certain areas on the plain, but are most commonly encountered in late summer–autumn, from late August towards the end of October around the area known as Corral de Monís, which can be found near the 50 km marker post on the C221 road.

Las Estepas de Belchite is not only well known for its steppe birds, it is also an important area for birds of prey, especially Golden Eagle, Short-toed Eagle, and Eagle Owl.

Timing
Spring for steppe birds, early autumn for Dotterel. The evening, and particularly the morning, are good times to visit the open water areas to view sandgrouse coming down to drink.

Access
Take the N232 out of Zaragoza towards Alcaniz and after 20 km turn right onto the A222 for Belchite, continue past Mediana, and La Lomanza de Belchite lies 11 km north of Belchite.

There is a car park at the site, but visits to the area require a permit which can be obtained from the Departmento de Agricultura, Ganaderia y Montes, Seccion de Conservacion del Medio Natural, Vasquez de Mella, No 10, 50071, Zaragoza.

The reserve of El Planerón can be reached from Belchite (see directions above) or by continuing along the N232 out of Zaragoza until you reach Quinto. Take a right here onto the minor road for Codo and Belchite. Coming from Belchite the reserve is on the left-hand side about halfway between Belchite and Quinto, around 15 km from Belchite. Turn right onto a track taking you to the Balsa de Planerón, a small

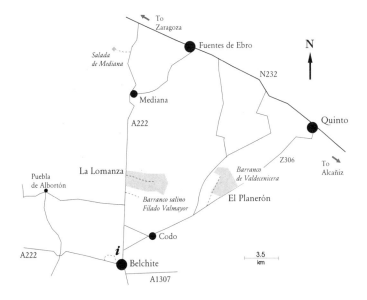

reservoir visible from the road and about 6 km beyond Codo. It is clearly marked. You can stop anywhere along the track and there are a number of other smaller footpaths. Higher vantage points also occur in this area and can give good views over adjoining areas of steppe. Unlike La Lomanza, permission is not required to visit the site.

On the outskirts of Belchite there is a small information centre, run by SEO, where you can obtain additional information. The Centro de Informacion 'Estepas del Valle del Ebro' also organises guided visits to the reserve, but is normally closed during the middle part of the day.

Other places worth investigating are the El Saso area alongside the C221 road from Belchite to Azaila; the area immediately west of Muel on the N330 south of Zaragoza, and other sites in the immediate Belchite area such as Salada de Mediana, Barranco salino Filada Valmayor, Barranco de Valdecenicera, and a route near the SEO visitor centre (Sendero al Olivar).

Calendar

All year: Golden Eagle, Peregrine, Little Bustard, Great Bustard, Stone Curlew, Black-bellied Sandgrouse, Pin-tailed Sandgrouse, Eagle Owl, Dupont's Lark, Calandra Lark, Lesser Short-toed Lark, Thekla Lark, Black Wheatear, Blue Rock Thrush, Sardinian Warbler, Rock Sparrow.

Breeding season: White Stork, Black Kite, Short-toed Eagle, Egyptian Vulture, Montagu's Harrier, Lesser Kestrel, Bee-eater, Red-necked Nightjar, Short-toed Lark, Tawny Pipit, Black-eared Wheatear, Spectacled Warbler, Subalpine Warbler, Orphean Warbler, Woodchat Shrike.

On passage: Dotterel.

AR13 LOS MONEGROS

Status: Unprotected

Site description

Los Monegros is an area almost twice the size of La Estepas de Belchite, with a similar landscape and similar conservation problems. This huge region to the east of Zaragoza occupies the central and driest area found in the whole Ebro Valley, lying north of the Ebro itself and stretching from Zaragoza eastwards almost as far as Lleida. The main area of interest lies either side of the main roads A2 and NII from Zaragoza and Lleida, although it does extend south as far as Sastago and north to Alcolea de Cinca. The area you should concentrate on if time is short is the steppe and series of brackish lagoons to the southwest of Bujaraloz.

As with Belchite, these huge plains are now a mosaic of steppe with sparse vegetation, hillsides, cereal fields, deep gullies and cliffs and land under irrigation. This is not a new threat as irrigation has destroyed much steppe land over the last 60 years, but encroachment has not stopped and threats from new irrigation schemes are still present. The main differences from Belchite are the surviving areas of juniper and pine woodland and seasonal brackish lagoons, *saladas*, which contain extremely saline water due to high evaporation rates in the summer, but which are bone dry in the summer months. The *saladas* are present at Belchite, but they are more numerous in Los Monegros and mainly concentrated in the area between Sastago and Bujaraloz.

Species

The whole area is important for steppe birds, although Great Bustard is now very rare with similar numbers to the Belchite steppe area (around 30 pairs), and can be very difficult to find. Interest is spread throughout, but as the area is large it can sometimes be difficult to locate certain species. Having said that, species typical of steppe are well represented with both Pin-tailed and Black-bellied Sandgrouse, Dupont's Lark and Lesser Short-toed Lark all relatively common. Spectacled and Dartford

Dupont's Lark

Warbler are also widespread as is Black-eared Wheatear. Lesser Kestrel still hangs on in the area, and although the population has declined substantially, small colonies still remain in some villages.

There are numerous small brackish lagoons between Bujaraloz and Sastago, and the largest of the lakes, Laguna de la Playa, can hold wildfowl in winter (if water levels hold up), and the area around La Playa can be good for bustards, sandgrouse, Lesser Short-toed Lark and Dotterel on passage in March and April. The area to the north of Osera is a well-known site for Dupont's Lark.

Birds of prey and other species associated with cliffs and rocky faces such as Egyptian Vulture, Peregrine, Alpine Swift, Crag Martin and Rock Sparrow are present, and are found near or alongside watercourses such as the Ebro at Alforque and Sastago, or the River Cinca between Alcolea de Cinca and Fraga.

White Stork nest in many of the villages.

Timing

There is much of interest from autumn through to spring, although the winters can be bitterly cold. Later in the season birdwatching becomes much more difficult as the heat haze can be dramatic and the crop and vegetaion height can make picking out ground birds such as larks very difficult.

Access

Much of the Los Monegros area is uninhabited, but is crossed by good roads and linked west–east from Zaragoza to Lleida by two major roads (A2 and NII). There are three main areas to concentrate efforts on within the large expanse of Monegros.

Osera Take the NII towards Lleida, and at Osera turn left northwards towards Monegrillo into an area of steppe about 5–6 km along this road. On the left-hand side there is a rough track that leads off left under some electricity pylons. Other areas of steppe along the main road are also worth searching, and the landscape is very impressive.

Steppes and brackish lagoons south of Bujaraloz Bujaraloz is just under 70 km from Zaragoza on the NII. Turn south onto the A230 towards Caspe when you reach Bujaraloz, and shortly afterwards turn right onto a minor road (A2105) for the village of Sastago. There are numerous tracks off this road which should be explored. It is certainly worth spending some time around Laguna de la Playa, the largest of the lagoons which can be located relatively easily as it is situated near some ruined buildings. A number of routes south are possible to the Ebro with its cliffs at Alforque and Sastago along unsurfaced but well-used tracks. These take you a number of other small lagoons.

Ballobar area Continue along the NII from Zaragoza through Bujaraloz as far as Candasnos. Turn left on the A2214 northwards towards Ontiñena which is around 20 km to the north. This stretch of steppe is very good for sandgrouse and larks, as is the road to Ballobar which is a right turn about 8–9 km out of Candasnos. There are some good areas to search along this road. Dupont's Lark is well known from this area. The seasonal ponds are worth searching for sandgrouse, and the saline steppe areas around here are normally full of larks. One should also

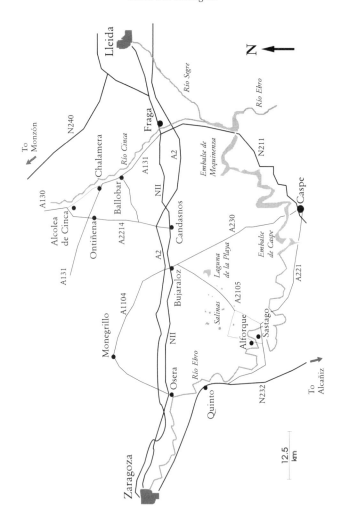

investigate the area north of Ontiñena to Alcolea de Cinca, where there are some huge sandstone cliffs with Egyptian Vulture and other cliff-nesting species on the road back south to Chalamera.

Calendar

All year: Golden Eagle, Peregrine, Little Bustard, Great Bustard, Stone Curlew, Black-bellied Sandgrouse, Pin-tailed Sandgrouse, Dupont's Lark, Calandra Lark, Lesser Short-toed Lark, Crested Lark, Thekla Lark, Black Wheatear, Blue Rock Thrush, Rock Sparrow.

Breeding season: White Stork, Egyptian Vulture, Montagu's Harrier, Lesser Kestrel, Great Spotted Cuckoo, Red-necked Nightjar, Bee-eater, Hoopoe, Short-toed Lark, Tawny Pipit, Black-eared Wheatear, Spectacled Warbler.

Passage periods: Dotterel and other waders.

AR14 SALADAS DE CHIPRANA

Status: Ramsar site (162 ha).

Site description
These are three small natural lagoons to the south of the Ebro, in the
Ebro Valley west of the town of Caspe in the province of Zaragoza. The
lakes have only limited shoreline fringes of reed and other emergent
vegetation with scattered tamarisk and other shrubs and are set in a
landscape of intensively cultivated land including cereal fields, irrigated crops and olive groves. The lagoons are of varying size and
degrees of salinity and depth. La Salada Grande (La Laguna de la
Estanca) occupies the lowest depression adjoining the Ebro. This
lagoon and La Salada de Roces (La Laguna Salada) are both permanent
water features. The third, El Prado del Farol and El Campo de Saladas
(Saltirosa) is seasonal.

Species
Breeding Purple Heron and Little Bittern, and a good selection of
waders on migration, and wildfowl in winter. The immediate countryside can also have a good range of typical open-country species
such as Great Spotted Cuckoo and Bee-eater, and Shoveler has
recently colonised the area but is still a very rare breeding bird in
Spain.

Timing
Spring months for herons and for a wide range of both wetland and
open-country species. Winter for wildfowl. Summer can be very hot,
and heat haze can be a problem from late morning well into the afternoon, even in spring.

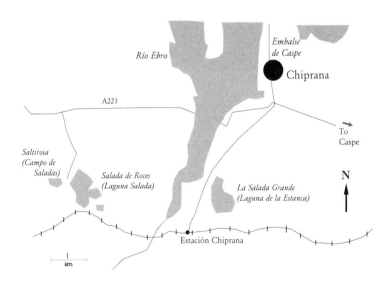

Access

Caspe is 25 km north of Alcañiz and the lagoons are found to the west of Caspe. Take the C221 from Caspe for 12 km to Chiprana. Take a left turn immediately before crossing an arm of the Ebro to the railway station (Estación Chiprana). The lake is some 3 km down this road, and turn left onto a track leading to some houses and the lake.

To reach La Salada, continue on the C221 towards Escatrón. The lagoon is on the left hand side of the road and next to the railway line again. At the 113 km marker post, turn left onto a track leading to the lake. The third seasonal lake is next to La Salada and is approached by taking a right turn before the Casa de la Salada.

Calendar

All year: Little Grebe, Black-necked Grebe, Mallard, Shoveler, Red-crested Pochard, Marsh Harrier, Water Rail, Black-headed Gull, Sardinian Warbler.

Breeding season: Little Bittern, Purple Heron, Shelduck, Black Kite, Spotted Crake, Black-winged Stilt, Avocet, Little Ringed Plover, Kentish Plover, Great Spotted Cuckoo, Bee-eater, Black-eared Wheatear, Reed Warbler, Great Reed Warbler, Golden Oriole, Woodchat Shrike.

Passage periods: Little Crake, Ringed Plover, Little Stint, Dunlin, Ruff, Redshank, Greenshank, Common Sandpiper, Black Tern, Whiskered Tern.

AR15 LAGUNA DE GALLOCANTA

Status: Refugio de Fauna Silvestre, Ramsar site and ZEPA (6720 ha).

Site description

The largest natural lake in Spain covering around 1500 ha of open water within a total area of some 6720 ha. The lake is fed mainly by rainwater, giving rise to dramatic changes in water level from year to year. In wet years the lake can be vast while in dry years during the hot summers the lake dries out completely. As the lake is at an altitude of 1000 m there can be some very low temperatures in winter. The water of the lake is saline but freshwater springs allow for localised patches of reeds and reedmace. This is one of the most important bird sites in Spain.

The surrounding fields are steppe in character, although much is now under agricultural production (mainly cereals).

Species

Cranes that breed in Fennoscandia and the Baltic states (and parts of Russia) take the west European migration route to their wintering grounds. It is thought that the total number of birds migrating along this route is now in the order of 70,000, and most of these, some 50,000–60,000, winter mainly in Spain, with smaller numbers in Portugal

Cranes

and North Africa. Gallocanta attracts the Cranes on migration both in the autumn and spring, stopping off to use the lake and surrounding land to feed and rest for varying periods before continuing their journey. However, the Cranes also appear to be using the area increasingly to overwinter. Gallocanta has by far the greatest concentration of Common Crane in Spain, and is also the largest 'wintering' concentration in Western Europe with numbers regularly reaching over 20,000, but sometimes peaking at over 50,000. Spring has the greatest concentration of birds and they can cover the sky in huge numbers, one of the ornithological spectacles of Europe.

The Cranes almost eclipse interest in other birds, but these are also worthy of a special trip. Another species of conservation concern in Europe is the Red-crested Pochard. Spain has an important breeding population in its own right, but it is also important as a wintering ground for this short-distance migrant. The bird winters in two main areas in the Western Palearctic, the western Mediterranean, centred around Spain and the Camargue in southern France, and the Black Sea. Gallocanta now has up to 75% of the Western Palearctic population, with 8,000 regularly wintering but numbers as high as 35,000 have also been recorded here. Huge numbers of other species of wildfowl use Gallocanta, with maximum counts of 3,000 Gadwall, 80,000 Pochard and 40,000 Coot, for example.

Around 220 species have been recorded here, and over 90 species breed including Black-winged Stilt, Lapwing, Avocet, Kentish Plover, Whiskered Tern and Gull-billed Tern; and the drier parts of the site have resident steppe birds including both Pin-tailed and Black-bellied Sandgrouse and Stone Curlew. While much of the steppe has been lost, a very rich area to the southeast of Gallocanta also has Little Bustard and good numbers of Dupont's Lark.

Timing

There is much of interest all year round, although high summer is to be avoided as there can be little water and heat haze is fomidable. For Cranes and wildfowl the best times of year are autumn and winter, although temperatures can be extremely low.

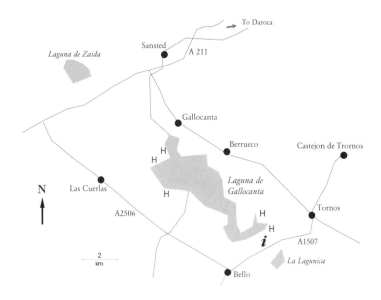

The migration of Cranes south in the autumn lasts from the end of October into early December, with peaks in November. The return migration north runs through February into March and peaks at the end of February or occasionally early March, and it is at this time of year that numbers are concentrated and at their highest. Increasingly, Gallocanta is also being used as a wintering site. During the day the Cranes are more dispersed and feed on the surrounding fields but use the lake as a roost and fly in during the evening. The evening fly-ins are spectacular. Weekends can be very busy.

Access
Laguna de Gallocanta lies approximately halfway between Madrid and Zaragoza and about 100 km southwest of Zaragoza beyond Daroca. Take the N330 as far as Daroca, and here turn right onto the A211 towards Cillas and Molina de Aragón. This road takes you to the north of the lake, and you should turn left onto the minor road (around 18 km) that takes you to Gallocanta.

Minor roads follow the periphery of the site and there are many tracks across the area with some hides and an information centre at the south of the lake in between Bello and Tornos. While Cranes can be seen from all around the site, it is the southeastern side that normally provides the best views.

Calendar
All year: Little Grebe, Shelduck, Mallard, Gadwall, Red-crested Pochard, Pochard, Marsh Harrier, Coot, Little Bustard, Great Bustard, Stone Curlew, Lapwing, Black-headed Gull, Black-bellied Sandgrouse, Pin-tailed Sandgrouse, Dupont's Lark, Calandra Lark, Lesser Short-toed Lark, Thekla Lark.

Breeding season: Black-necked Grebe, White Stork, Black Kite, Short-toed Eagle, Montagu's Harrier, Lesser Kestrel, Little Bustard, Black-

winged Stilt, Avocet, Little Ringed Plover, Kentish Plover, Collared Pratincole, Gull-billed Tern, Whiskered Tern, Red-necked Nightjar, Bee-
eater, Short-toed Lark, Tawny Pipit, Yellow Wagtail, Wheatear, Reed
Warbler, Great Reed Warbler.

Winter: Wigeon, Teal, Pintail, Shoveler, Tufted Duck, Crane.

Passage: Greylag Goose, Spotted Crake, Crane, Avocet, Ringed Plover,
Knot, Sanderling, Curlew Sandpiper, Ruff, Black-tailed Godwit, Bar-
tailed Godwit, Whimbrel, Marsh Sandpiper, Greenshank, Green Sandpiper, Wood Sandpiper, Common Sandpiper, Common Tern,
Whiskered Tern, Black Tern, Sand Martin.

AR16 SERRANIA DE ALBARRACÍN

Status: Part of the Montes Universales Reserva Nacional de Caza (59,260 ha).

Site description

This is a large mountainous area, just shy of 2000 m and tucked into
the far southwest corner of Aragón in the province of Teruel. It is covered by substantial areas of ancient pine forest, oak forest and
juniper scrub, along with broom, mixed oak scrub and many meadows, pastures and gorges. The Serrania de Albarracín extends from
the border of Cuenca province in Castile-La Mancha eastwards to the
town of Gea de Albarracín on the River Guadalaviar, running northwest to southeast and made up of a number of isolated massifs or
muelas with slate valleys between. The mountain complex consists of
high mountain plateaux of limestone, between 1500 and 1800 m, such
as Los Llanos de Pozondón, Ródenas and Monterde in the north of
the Sierra and Los Llanos de Villar del Cobo Griegos in the south.
Also worthy of mention are the quaking bogs of the Sierra del
Tremedal.

Especially outstanding are the forests at the mountain passes of
Noguera, Orihuela and Bronchales which also have a number of natural
meadows.

In addition to normal forest management practices there is a tradition
of collecting aromatic plants, mushrooms and truffles. The area is also
famous for its Levantine style cave paintings. The town of Albarracín
should be visited, a well-preserved medieval walled city.

Species

The massif is especially important for birds of prey including Griffon
Vulture, Egyptian Vulture, over ten pairs of Golden Eagle, Bonelli's
Eagle, Peregrine and Eagle Owl.

The mountains have extensive pine and oak forests with a corresponding range of typical forest birds and a rich bird of prey population
with at least 20 pairs of Booted Eagle, Short-toed Eagle, Sparrowhawk, Goshawk, Buzzard, Tawny Owl, Pied Flycatcher, Crested Tit and
Bonelli's Warbler.

Wolf became extinct here at the end of the last century, but otter and wild cat still survive in this area, together with beech marten, polecat, badger and red squirrel. Local place names are full of references to red deer, roe deer and ibex (eg. Ciervo, Corzo and Cabra montales) and red and fallow deer were reintroduced in the 1960s.

Timing
The best time of year is from April through to late June, although there are interesting flowers and butterflies at other times of year. Birds of prey are present throughout the year.

Access
The sierra is about 35 km northwest of Teruel. Take the N234 north out of Teruel and after 10 km turn left onto the A1512 towards Albarracín. There are many roads and forest tracks throughout the area, one of many possibilities includes taking the road towards the passes at Noguera, Bronchales and Orihuela, all of which have excellent areas of woodland and pasture.

Calendar
All year: Griffon Vulture, Goshawk, Buzzard, Golden Eagle, Peregrine, Eagle Owl, Tawny Owl, Blue Rock Thrush, Black Redstart, Crested Tit, Great Grey Shrike, Raven, Rock Sparrow, Rock Bunting.

Breeding season: Honey Buzzard, Black Kite, Egyptian Vulture, Short-toed Eagle, Booted Eagle, Hoopoe, Red-rumped Swallow, Black-eared Wheatear, Rock Thrush, Bonelli's Warbler, Woodchat Shrike.

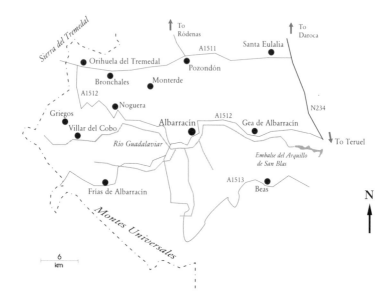

OTHER SITES WORTH VISITING

AR17 Valle de Hecho

A very attractive Pyrenean valley running parallel, but to the east of Valle de Ansó (AR1). It has a similar range of habitats and species, with a well-known, but not always productive breeding site for Wallcreeper at the Boca del Infierno, a gorge above the village of Hecho. Reached off the main N240 at Puente la Reina, where you take the minor road (A176) for Hecho.

AR18 Castillo de Loare

Worth a visit for its castle alone, one of the finest in Spain. Very rich with mixture of habitats, including pine forest, scrub, rocky areas and pasture. Birds of prey, Hoopoe, Woodlark and Rock Bunting. Take A132 to Ayerbe from Huesca then a minor road (A1206) to Loarre. Castle above the village.

AR19 El Turbón

Limestone mountain area in the Pyrenees with Lammergeir, Golden Eagle and high-altitude birds including Alpine Accentor and Wallcreeper. Take the N240 east from Huesca, turning left at Barbastro on the N123, and then A139 to Graus and Benasque. Take the minor road right at Campo to Vilas de Turbon.

AR20 Montes de Zuera

Pine woods and juniper scrub on hillsides in the Ebro Valley with Short-toed Eagle, Orphean Warbler, Firecrest and Ortolan Bunting. Take the N330 north out of Zaragoza towards Huesca and Zuera. Turn left at Zuera (22 km) on the A124 towards Las Pedrosas. There are various tracks off this road.

AR21 Sierra de Alcubierre

Mountain area with pine woods and juniper scrub, and cliffs. Birds of prey, Red-necked Nightjar, Black Wheatear, Black-eared Wheatear and Rock Sparrow. Take A129 northeast to Alcubierre from Zaragoza. Forestry tracks into sierra.

AR22 Estepas de Blancas

High-level steppe area with Little Bustard, Stone Curlew, Black-bellied Sandgrouse, Dupont's and other larks. From Zaragoza take the N330 south to Monreal del Campo, then N211 towards Molina de Aragon. Turn right after 10 km to the village of Blancas, and use various tracks cross the area to the north of the village.

AR23 Saladas de Alcañiz

Seasonal brackish lagoons in steppe area. Passage waders and Crane, wintering duck and steppe birds including sandgrouse, bustards, larks, Tawny Pipit and Spectacled Warbler. Take N232 to Alcañiz from Zaragoza. Lagoons immediately to the west of the town on either side of the main road.

AR24 Puertes de Beceite

Massif area with mixed woodlands and many impressive ravines in far eastern part of Aragón. Birds of prey, vultures, Crag Martin, Blue Rock

Thrush, Bonelli's Warbler, Crested Tit. N232 from Zaragoza to Monroyo (via Alcañiz) then the A1414 to Valderrobres and the A2412 to Beceite.

AR25 Río Martín

Cliffs along the river with large colony of around 200 pairs of Griffon Vulture; also Egyptian Vulture, Blue Rock Thrush and Red-billed Chough. From Zaragoza take the N232 towards Alcañiz. At Hijar (70 km) turn right on the A 224 to the village of Albalate del Arzobispo.

AR26 Río Guadalope

River gorge with vultures, Bonelli's Eagle, Alpine Swift and Dipper. Take the N211 south off the N232 out from Alcaníz, and at Calanda take a minor road left (A226) for Mas de las Matas and Castellote. From here there is a road along north shore of reservoir and beyond, to village of Ladruñan. Tracks beyond.

AR27 El Maestrazgo

Series of sierras, greatly eroded by rivers with tall cliffs and needle-shaped rocks. Unspoilt and beautiful area, little visited with vultures and birds of prey and otters. Difficult to reach: take A226 from Teruel to Allepuz, then continue on the same road to the heart of area and Cantavieja.

AR28 Sierra de Javalambre

High mountain massif with pine and beech woods, pastures and many valleys and ravines. Honey Buzzard, Goshawk, Booted Eagle, Eagle Owl and Dartford and Subalpine Warblers. Take N234 south of Teruel and turn right after Sarrión towards Manzanera and Torrijas along A1514.

ASTURIAS

A stunning region in northern Spain, best known for the Picos de Europa (AS6), a large national park shared with Cantabria and Castile-León that, under its veil of mists and snow and heavily wooded mountain slopes, offers much to those with an interest in birds — and dramatic landscapes. The colourful displays of its hay meadows, now a rarity in Britain, the richness of its butterflies, with over a third of all European species, and the last stronghold in Spain, albeit a very tenous one, for brown bear and wolf make it extremely alluring. Its remoteness has its advantages not only for these large mammals but also for visitors who prefer to birdwatch in isolation with the only backdrop a natural one.

Asturias is one of the four regions of Spain, together with Galicia, Cantabria and Euskadi (País Vasco), that make up *Espana Verde* — Green Spain — or, if you are spending a holiday on the coast, the *Costa Verde*. This remarkably lush northern part of the Iberian peninsula has mild temperatures throughout the year and is pleasantly warm, not hot, in the summer months — a southern European equivalent of Cornwall or the Lake District. Its mountains are, however, another matter with considerable snowfall and very low temperatures in the winter. Warm clothes are even needed in the summer if visiting the highest peaks. The region is, however, very attractive to those visitors who find the heat of the southern Mediterranean coast a little too much.

Much of the interest to birdwatchers is concentrated in the mountains, although the coast (some 345 km long with rocky cliffs, wide beaches, picturesque fishing villages, small coves and small intimate estuaries, for example Ría del Eo o Ribadeo (AS1)) also offers a diversity of waders and ducks in the winter and spring. Another estuary in the east of the region, Ría de Villaviciosa (AS5), is very attractive, and is one of the few breeding sites for Curlew in Spain. During rough weather in winter months one can also come across species sheltering in the relative calm of estuaries, for example Great Northern Diver, Red-breasted Merganser, Guillemot and Razorbill.

Although these coastal sites do not hold huge numbers of birds, they do attract a good variety of species and the scenery is incredibly beautiful and provides stunning backdrops for a day's birding. Seawatching can also be productive with Gannet, shearwaters and skuas. While the coast is of less importance for breeding birds, there are nevertheless species found here that are rare in the rest of Spain including Shag, Oystercatcher, Grasshopper Warbler, Savi's Warbler, Moustached Warbler and Reed Bunting.

The immediate hinterland has comparatively less to offer but is still very attractive, and Cuckoo, Turtle Dove, Wryneck, Woodlark and Red-backed Shrike are not uncommon here and in the lower valleys of the mountains.

Efforts are, however, best concentrated in the mountains. The lower and middle slopes of the mountains and valleys are extensively wooded with oak and beech, and the very important forested area, the Bosque de Muniellos (AS2), definitely requires a detour. These forests have a very rich avifauna: key species include Black and Middle

Spotted Woodpeckers, Capercaillie, and the Spanish race of Grey Partridge. Other more common but distinctly northern species include Pied Flycatcher, Treecreeper, Goldcrest and Bullfinch. The Capercaillie population of Asturias is one of the most important in Spain, with around 300 territories, as is the population of Middle Spotted Woodpecker whose core area is southeast Asturias and the adjoining forested mountains of Cantabria and Castile-León.

The Cordillera Cantábrica or Cantabrian mountains run inland parallel to the north coast of Spain, from the Pyrenees to the Portuguese border, and forms the southern boundary to Asturias, cutting it off from the rest of the country. The Cantabrian mountains are one of the least well known montane areas in Spain, and certainly the least visited, despite the popularity of the highest peaks — the Picos de Europa. Although the Picos attract mountaineers, walkers and other visitors from all over the world, the rest of Asturias sees few foreigners. Serious walking in the Picos is really only practical from the end of May to October, but even then you may get a soaking, as the Picos are only 32 km from the rainy Atlantic seaboard. The eastern parts are the most accessible and most visited and the very popular sites should be avoided at peak times (weekends and during the summer).

While the mountains of Asturias are the stronghold of brown bear and wolf in Spain, birdwatchers also have plenty to keep them occupied. They are home to the mountain specialities that are found in few other parts of Spain — Alpine Accentor, Wallcreeper, Alpine Chough and Snow Finch — all at the western edge of their range. Rocky outcrops, cliffs and gorges have Golden Eagle, Griffon Vulture, Egyptian Vulture, Peregrine, Eagle Owl, Rock Thrush and Red-billed Chough.

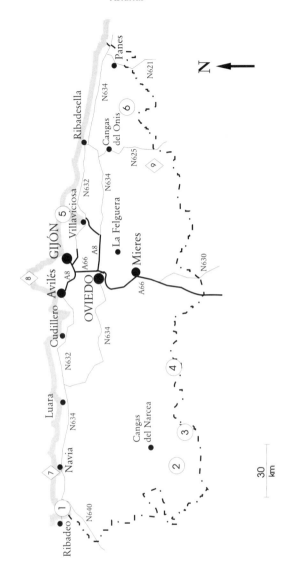

Main sites

1	AS1	Ría del Eo o Ribadeo
2	AS2	Bosque De Muniellos
3	AS3	Degaña–Hermano
4	AS4	Somiedo
5	AS5	Ría De Villaviciosa
6	AS6	Picos De Europa

Other sites worth visiting

7	AS7	Río Barayo
8	AS8	Cabo de Peñas
9	AS9	Parque Natural de Redes

AS1 RÍA DEL EO O RIBADEO

Status: Reserva Natural, ZEPA and Ramsar site (1740 ha).

Site description

One of the most important coastal wetlands in the north of Spain, found in the far west of Asturias where it straddles the regional boundary with Galicia. A medium-sized estuary of 1740 ha, most of which is covered by water at high tide, although large areas of mud-flats and sandbanks are exposed at low water. Reedbeds, saltmarsh and wet fields, along with underwater beds of *Zostera* (eel-grass) are also present. The surrounding countryside can be very attractive, but it is far from natural with areas of cultivation, eucalpyt trees and pine plantations.

Species

The estuary is one of the most important sites on the north coast for passage and wintering duck breeding in northern Europe. It has some of the highest concentrations in Spain with up to 5,000 individuals in total, including up to 900 Pintail and 2,500 Wigeon. It is, however, its range of species of wader and duck that make it important including Shoveler, Teal, Shelduck, Lapwing, Golden Plover, Snipe, Spotted Redshank and Curlew, and a number of other less common species such as Spoonbill.

Otters breed in the estuary.

Timing

The largest concentrations of wildfowl occur during the winter months, but the area can hold interesting birds all year round, and is particularly good in the spring and autumn passage periods.

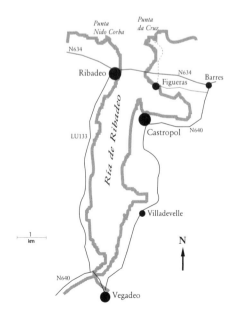

Access

The main coast road N634 crosses the estuary near its mouth and other roads complete the circle to the west (LU133) and eastern sides (N640) of the estuary and consequently there are many opportunities for views across the water and mudflats. Exposed mudbanks are more in evidence from the eastern shores, particularly near Figueras, Castropol and Villadevelle where inlets join the main bulk of the estuary. The mouth of the estuary can be particularly good in the winter when duck, divers and auks seek shelter in the calmer waters.

Open land to the north of Figueras between the road bridge and the mouth of the estuary is worth searching for migrant passerines, and headlands are good in the winter for seawatching, with the chance of shearwaters, skuas and auks.

Calendar

All year: Mallard, Water Rail, Moorhen, Oystercatcher, Yellow-legged Gull, Barn Owl, Kingfisher, Green Woodpecker, Crested Lark, Grey Wagtail, White Wagtail, Great Grey Shrike, Carrion Crow.

Breeding season: Hobby, Little Ringed Plover, Turtle Dove, Swift, House Martin, Yellow Wagtail, Reed Warbler, Great Reed Warbler, Melodious Warbler, Whitethroat, Woodchat Shrike.

Winter: Great Northern Diver, Cory's Shearwater, Yelkouan Shearwater, Gannet, Cormorant, Grey Heron, Greylag Goose, Wigeon, Pintail, Shoveler, Teal, Tufted Duck, Eider, Common Scoter, Red-breasted Merganser, Merlin, Lapwing, Golden Plover, Curlew, Redshank, Snipe, Great Skua, Common Gull, Great Black-backed Gull, Guillemot, Razorbill, Puffin, Fieldfare, Redwing, Brambling, Snow Bunting.

Passage periods: Little Bittern, Night Heron, Spoonbill, Black-winged Stilt, Ringed Plover, Dunlin, Ruff, Black-tailed Godwit, Bar-tailed Godwit, Curlew, Spotted Redshank, Greenshank, Wood Sandpiper, Green Sandpiper, Little Gull, Sandwich Tern, Common Tern, Tawny Pipit, Whinchat, Wheatear, Grasshopper Warbler, Willow Warbler.

AS2 BOSQUE DE MUNIELLOS

Status: Reserva Natural and ZEPA (2975 ha). This reserve has since been increased by the addition of Monte Valdebueyes and Monte Vallina de Abradeo, an extra 1623 ha, and Monte La Villiella (1224 ha). The whole area also lies within the Parque Natural - Fuentes de Narcea y del Ibias.

Site description

A mountainous area with extensive deciduous woodland, with the Bosque de Muniellos one of the most important and largest mixed oak woods in Spain, and one of the finest in Europe. The area is located in the western interior of Asturias within the Natural Park of Fuentes de Narcea y del Ibias. Most of the forest is made up of ancient stands of sessile and pedunculate oak, and areas of beech. The reserve lies at a height of 675 m in the valley bottom and stretches up the mountain sides to almost 1700 m. At around 1300 m silver birch becomes abundant, whilst in the valleys hazel, maple, ash, holly, alder, rowan and yew are component species of the woodland complex. Muniellos is also rich in mosses, liverworts and lichens with over 1,000 species present, and around 500 species of moth and butterfly have also been recorded.

Species

An excellent forest for its woodland bird communities with three species of eagle — Golden, Short-toed and Booted; and four species of woodpecker — Black, Great Spotted, Middle Spotted and Lesser Spotted which all breed here. Capercaillie and Honey Buzzard also occur. The site includes a number of species at the western edge of their range.

The area is also good for larger mammals with chamois, wild boar, roe deer, wildcat, otter and wolf all present. Bears are occasionally spotted here, but they are always elusive. Pyrenean Desman is found in valleys, although you are unlikely to see them.

Timing

Spring and summer are best, although the colours and scenery in October can be spectacular.

Access

Visits can only be made with prior permission, and a maximum of 20 people only per day are allowed access to the reserve. It is best to apply early to: Cosejería de Medio Ambiente y Urbanismo. Dirección Regional de Recursos Naturales, C/Asturias 8, 33004 Oviedo (tel: 98/527 61 73).

Take the AS15 from Cangas del Narcea south to Ventanueva. At Ventanueva take a right turn along the AS211 towards the village of Moal, where a track takes you to the visitor centre and car park 4 km away.

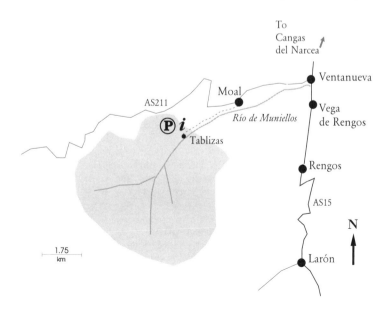

Calendar

All year: Goshawk, Sparrowhawk, Buzzard, Golden Eagle, Kestrel, Capercaillie, Grey Partridge, Woodcock, Eagle Owl, Tawny Owl, Black Woodpecker, Great Spotted Woodpecker, Middle Spotted Woodpecker, Lesser Spotted Woodpecker, Water Pipit, Dipper, Goldcrest, Firecrest, Treecreeper, Marsh Tit, Blue Tit, Great Tit, Raven, Bullfinch.

Breeding season: Honey Buzzard, Short-toed Eagle, Hen Harrier, Booted Eagle, Hobby, Nightjar, Tree Pipit, Redstart, Whinchat, Pied Flycatcher.

AS3 DEGAÑA–HERMANO

Status: Reserva Nacional de Caza (8657 ha) and part of Parque Natural de las Fuentes del Narcea. ZEPA (11,659 ha).

Site description

This site comprises deciduous woodlands, particularly beech, with heaths and meadows on lower mountain slopes, and rocky habitats found at an altitude of between 650 and 1924 m in a very remote, little visited and mountainous part of Asturias. It has much in common with Somiedo (AS4) with similar habitats and species. The area is substantially wooded, mainly with oak and beech, although higher up birch becomes common. Holly, hazel, yew, ash and alder are found in the valleys.

Species

Of special interest for Capercaillie, which has a very healthy population here, the Spanish race of Grey Partridge, Black Woodpecker and Middle Spotted Woodpecker. Another stronghold of wolf and brown bear, with otter, roe deer, wild cat, beech, pine marten and Pyrenean desman.

Capercaillie

69

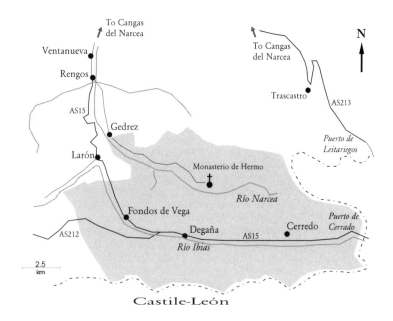

Timing
Late spring and summer.

Access
From Oviedo take the N634 to Sals, then left onto the AS226 to Soto de los Infantes, and right onto the AS15 to Cangas del Narcea. From Cangas continue on the AS15 to Ventanueva and Rengos. A local road follows the Narcea Valley to the left from Rengos through Gedrez to the beech forests of Degaña and the Monasterio de Hermo. Alternatively continue on the AS15 towards the border with Castile-León (Puerto de Cerrado).

Calendar
All year: Golden Eagle, Goshawk, Griffon Vulture, Peregrine, Capercaillie, Grey Partridge, Woodcock, Eagle Owl, Black Woodpecker, Middle Spotted Woodpecker, Crag Martin, Blue Rock Thrush, Crested Tit, Red-billed Chough, Crossbill, Bullfinch, Rock Sparrow, Cirl Bunting, Rock Bunting.

Breeding season: Black Kite, Honey Buzzard, Short-toed Eagle, Hoopoe, Subalpine Warbler, Melodious Warbler, Bonelli's Warbler, Rock Thrush, Red-backed Shrike, Ortolan Bunting.

AS4 SOMIEDO

Status: Parque Natural and ZEPA (29,122 ha), and forms part of the Reserva Nacional de Caza (87,900 ha).

Site description

Lying southwest of Oviedo, the capital of Asturias, and straddling the crest of Cordillera Cantábrica on the borders with Castile-León, is the rugged Parque Natural de Somiedo. The Reserva Nacional de Caza, of which it forms part is, at 87,900 ha, one of the largest hunting reserves in Spain.

Somiedo is a very large mountainous area, ranging from 800–2417 m in altitude, with narrow fertile valleys, many small villages, traditional thatched 'cabins' and cultivated areas. Extensive areas are covered by native deciduous woods of oak, beech and birch, scrub, and grasslands with rocks and subalpine grasslands in the highest areas, and mountain tarns. One of the most famous parts of the area is formed by the glacial lakes of Saliencia, lying at a height of between 1500 and 1700 m and sandwiched between the twin peaks of the Peña de la Cueva and El Canto de la Almagrera.

Somiedo is one of the most important areas for brown bear in Spain with just under half of the Spanish population of 100 individuals.

Species

Important in particular for Short-toed Eagle, Capercaillie (120 males), the Spanish race of Grey Partridge, with a minimum of 50 pairs, Black Woodpecker and Middle Spotted Woodpecker; also Honey Buzzard, Golden Eagle and Snow Finch.

The absence of roads in Somiedo has ensured that the typical vertebrate fauna of the Cordillera has remained undisturbed and Somiedo reserve is one of the last strongholds of Iberian brown bear with around 30–40 individuals. At the beginning of the century there were an estimated 1,000 bears in Spain, but a dramatic reduction of around 90% has seen the population fall to only 100. Other species which are typical of Somiedo include red and roe deer, chamois, wild boar, wolf, otter, badger and wildcat.

Timing

Late spring and summer. The pass at Somiedo (Puerto de Somiedo) tends to be closed for around three months in the winter.

Access

The visitor centre of the Parque Natural de Somiedo is situated in Pola de Somiedo (tel: 576 36 49/fax: 576 37 04), and details of tracks in the area are available here if you are interested in undertaking some serious exploration of the area on foot; there being many opportunities to do so.

From Oviedo take the N634 west past Grado, and before reaching Cornellana turn right inland on the AS15 for around 10 km, then left on the AS227 towards the border with Castile-León. From the south, approach along the C623 from León, as far as Piedrafita and then turn right towards the pass and the north.

Various opportunities exist for exploration once at Somiedo. For the Lago del Valle, a minor road at Pola de Somiedo leads up to the village of Valle de Lago, and the lake is beyond. For the Lagos de Salencia,

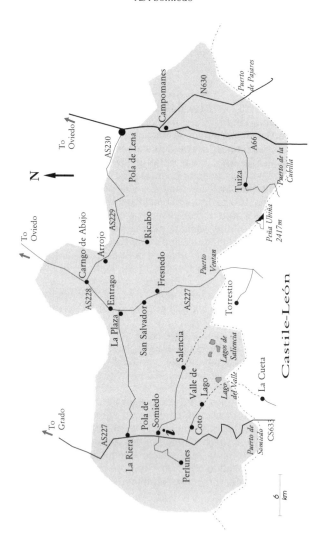

before Pola de Somiedo, a minor road leads to Salencia and beyond, followed by a walk to the lakes. Other possibilities exist along the Pol de Somiedo to Perlunes road, and at the pass, Puerto de Somiedo.

Calendar

All year: Griffon Vulture, Peregrine, Capercaillie, Grey Partridge, Black Woodpecker, Middle Spotted Woodpecker, Water Pipit, Black Redstart, Blue Rock Thrush, Song Thrush, Marsh Tit, Raven, Snow Finch, Citril Finch, Bullfinch, Yellowhammer, Rock Bunting.

Breeding season: Honey Buzzard, Egyptian Vulture, Short-toed Eagle, Hen Harrier, Booted Eagle, Alpine Swift, Wryneck, Crag Martin, Tawny Pipit, Tree Pipit, Whinchat, Bonelli's Warbler, Garden Warbler, Spotted Flycatcher, Red-backed Shrike.

AS5 RÍA DE VILLAVICIOSA

Status: Reserva Natural.

Site description

This relatively small but beautiful estuary or ría lies in the eastern part of Asturias and is set in the heart of cider-making country. The area is undeveloped, with an attractive backdrop of low wooded hills that clothe the slopes running down to its shores. As well as intertidal mud-flats and sand, the area around the mouth of the estuary has now stabilised and a sandy beach (Rodiles) with restricted areas of dunes occupies the river mouth. There are also areas, known locally as *porreos,* that were once part of the estuary but have now been reclaimed as pasture. Although reclaimed, they do have intrinsic interest as they still tend to be wet and form a matrix of complementary wetland habitats with scattered ponds and reedbeds and should be scanned for waders, herons and migrants.

Species

Main interest is during passage and at certain times in winter when you can get Great Northern Diver, Black-necked Grebe and a range of duck and waders. Numbers are generally modest but there is a very good variety of species, with peak counts of 7,500 Lapwing, 1,000 Dunlin, 700 Golden Plover, 600 Teal and 100 Wigeon. The marshy fields around the estuary can support over 600 Snipe and 250 Curlew. The site is also good during passage.

Breeding interest in the area is modest but includes Marsh Harrier, Hobby, Little Ringed Plover, Kentish Plover and a number of warblers, some of which are uncommon in the rest of Spain, although breeding may not occur each year. This is one of the few breeding sites for Curlew in Spain.

Timing

Passage and winter. Largest concentrations of duck and wader tend to be in January.

Access

Take the N632 east from Gijón towards Santander and to Villaviciosa, a small town at the head of the estuary. Roads follow the outline of the estuary, both the east and west shores. The mouth of the estuary has good views from both banks, either from the El Puntal harbour or the Rodiles Beach area. The road from Villaviciosa to Rodiles can be particularly good and gets close to the estuary and inlets at various points, including the bridge over the inlet at Espina.

Calendar

All year: Mallard, Hen Harrier, Moorhen, Coot, Water Rail, Curlew, Common Sandpiper, Yellow-legged Gull, Kingfisher, Grey Wagtail, Stonechat, Fan-tailed Warbler.

Breeding season: Marsh Harrier, Hobby, Little Ringed Plover, Kentish Plover, Turtle Dove, Cuckoo, Swallow, Grasshopper Warbler, Savi's Warbler, Whitethroat.

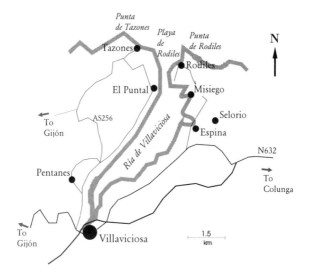

Winter: Great Northern Diver, Black-necked Grebe, Cormorant, Guille-mot, Razorbill, Grey Heron, Greylag Goose, Barnacle Goose, Wigeon, Pintail, Shoveler, Shelduck, Pochard, Eider, Oystercatcher, Golden Plover, Grey Plover, Lapwing, Dunlin, Snipe, Redshank, Herring Gull, Great Black-backed Gull, Black-headed Gull, Mediterranean Gull, Lesser Black-backed Gull.

Passage periods: Little Egret, Teal, Garganey, Ringed Plover, Knot, Sanderling, Curlew Sandpiper, Ruff, Bar-tailed Godwit, Black-tailed Godwit, Whimbrel, Spotted Redshank, Greenshank, Green Sandpiper, Turnstone, Sandwich Tern, Common Tern, Swift, Sand Martin, Wheatear, Wood Warbler, Red-backed Shrike.

AS6 PICOS DE EUROPA

Status: Parque Nacional (64,660 ha) including the Montaña de Covadonga which is a ZEPA (16,925 ha); 24,560 ha of the national park is in Asturias.

Site description

The Picos de Europa is the most impressive, breathtaking and rugged part of the Cordillera Cantábrica — the mountain chain that runs parallel to the whole length of the coast of northern Spain from the Basque Country (Euskadi) to Galicia. It rises to heights of more than 2600 m and yet is only some 25 km from the sea. Full of superlatives and records, Picos de Europa National Park is immense, originally covering almost 17,000 ha (when the Montana de Covadonga was designated as the first national park in Spain in 1918) it now covers some 64,660 ha, almost 650 sq km, and is shared among three regions — Asturias, Cantabria and Castile-León, making it the largest of all the Spanish national parks, and the largest national park in Western Europe.

A limestone massif, the Picos de Europa, reaches 2648 m at its highest, with the peak of Torre Cerredo, and stretches for 40 km from Covadonga in the west, almost to Panes in the east, and 20 km deep into Spain's interior. The landscape is spectacular with huge rocky outcrops and steep cliffs, the most famous being the impressive gorge cut out by the river Cares in the heart of the massif, 12 km long and rising up to 1000 m, closely followed by the deep gorge at La Hermida. There are also glacial lakes, the two most famous being Enol and Ercina above Covadonga.

The massif of the national park is carved into three separate regions by rivers that flow through very deep and narrow gorges. The Sella, Cares, Duje and Deva rivers mark the boundaries of these three massifs. The Cornión, or the western massif, in Asturias and León, can be found on the west side of the famous Cares Gorge. Its highest peak is Santa de Castilla (2596m). The central massif, Urrieles, is divided among Cantabria, Asturias and León and brings together the highest summits including the legendary, jagged Narnajo de Bulnes (2519 m), known locally as Picu Urriellu. The eastern massif, Andara, situated between the Deva and Duje rivers, belongs almost entirely to Cantabria and the high summits rise sharply above Liébana Valley. This massif is not so well known or visited as the others.

The park is not only made up of summits, peaks, gorges and glacial lakes. There are many alpine pastures, and within the valleys colourful hay meadows are common with some 40 species of orchids recorded. The Picos also are home to around a third of all the butterflies found in Europe. Meadows and pastures may predominate, but in the lower areas especially, woods and forests are extensive.

Species

The Picos hold most of the montane specialities of the Pyrenees, but in many cases they are far more accessible here. Three specialists of high altitudes — Wallcreeper, Snow Finch, and Alpine Accentor — are found along with other montane species such as Rock Thrush, Red-billed Chough and Alpine Chough throughout the three massifs that

Snow Finches

make up the Picos. One of easiest climbs up in search of these species is via the Teleférico at Fuente Dé.

Golden Eagle, Short-toed Eagle, Griffon Vulture, Egyptian Vulture, Booted Eagle, Kestrel and Peregrine are all possible over the many rocky limestone cliffs and gorges found throughout the park. Cares Gorge, La Hermida Gorge and cliff faces up at the Covadonga lakes can all produce these species along with Crag Martin, Alpine Swift, Black Redstart and Eagle Owl in these and other rocky valleys and gorges.

There are extensive beech and oak woods where Black Woodpecker and Middle Spotted Woodpecker are not uncommon, the latter are widespread throughout the park and are sometimes seen in and around villages. Great and Lesser Spotted Woodpecker are also present here, along with the Spanish race of Grey Partridge, and that rare Spanish bird, the Capercaillie. Bonelli's Warbler, Tree Pipit, Nuthatch and Short-toed Treecreeper also occur, and in the more mixed habitats where meadows form a matrix then Red-backed Shrike, Wryneck and Spotted Flycatcher all make regular appearances.

Bee-eater and Golden Oriole are found in the southern and eastern part of the Picos de Europa.

Timing

Late May to early July is an ideal time for a visit to the Picos. At week-ends throughout the year, and throughout the months of July and August, parts of the Picos can be extremely busy when accommodation can be very hard to find without prior booking, and certain roads can be clogged up by coaches. Long queues can form at Fuente Dé to use the Teleférico at weekends and in summer, so try to arrive early, even at times of year when visitors are few on the ground.

Access

As the national park is so large, it is not surprising that there are several points of entry, but most visitors enter the park from the north and the coast. The main roads in and around the Picos de Europa circum-navigate the mountains and are generally confined to the river valleys. There are no surfaced roads for vehicles crossing the three separate massifs.

1 Eastern approach, Liebana Valley, La Hermana Gorge and Fuente Dé Take the N634 from Santander and head inland after Unquera (on the N621 to Panes and Liébana Valley to Potes). At Potes take a minor road to Camaleño, Cosgalla, Espinama and Fuente Dé.

La Liébana Valley and La Hermida Gorge. La Liébana is a large valley at the foot of the eastern part of the Picos de Europa supporting a considerable variety and area of woodland. The high ground, impressive for its ruggedness and enormous rock faces, is dominated by mountain scrubland and alpine pastures. A striking feature of the valley, and one that is encountered soon after leaving Panes, is La Hermida Gorge, cut by the water of the River Deva. This narrow, steep-walled limestone gorge is 19 km long and, in stretches, 600 m deep, and the only means of access from the north and Panes into Liébana Valley proper. The gorge and immediate surrounds have breeding Griffon Vulture, Golden Eagle, Short-toed Eagle, Crag Martin, Red-billed Chough and Alpine Swift. There is a good network of roads in the valley, along with an extensive system of forestry tracks.

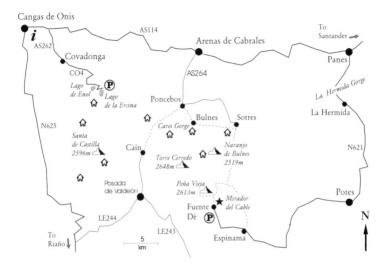

Fuente Dé. There is a cable car at Fuente Dé at the upper end of the Camaleño Valley, only 2 km beyond Espinama and 20 km west of Potes which, although crowded at weekends and throughout the summer, provides excellent views, quick access, and probably the easiest montane birdwatching. The trip in the Teleférico up the 800 m sheer cliff to the Mirador del Cable is breathtaking and lasts for less than five minutes. The Mirador del Cable, which is suspended over the drop below, provides stunning and panoramic views of the Picos de Europa and the Cantabrian mountain range. Once at the top, a walk back to Espinama, via the Refugio de Aliva, is easily possible. The mountains are good for Alpine Accentor and Snow Finch, and Wallcreeper is also possible. After leaving the cable car follow the path to the left to cliffs to the left hand-side the main path, this is the Wallcreeper site. However, to walk down to Espinama, follow the path to the right where the path forks, and right again past the cafe and back down to the valley road via a track through meadows and scrub which are good for Red-backed Shrike, Wryneck and Middle Spotted Woodpecker.

2 Western approach, Montana de Covadonga y Lagos de Covadonga

Reached from Oviedo, by following the N634 as far as Arriondas. From there take the N635 to Cangas de Onis. The visitor centre for the park is located in Cangas (Casa del Dago, Avda. de Covadonga 43, 33550 Cangas de Onis (tel: 584 86 14). From Cangas take the AS114 eastwards to Soto, then a right turn on the AS262 to Covadonga, and then left up to the lakes of Enol and La Ercina. There is a car park and cafe at the top lake, but it can get busy at weekends. Numerous walks are possible including one that can take you around La Ercina where one should see Griffon Vulture, Egyptian Vulture, Peregrine, Raven, Water Pipit, Black Redstart, Crag Martin, Red-billed Chough, and there is the possibility of Rock Thrush.

3 Central approach and Cares Gorge

Take the AS114 eastwards from Cangas de Onis or westwards from Panes to Las Arenas de Cabrales where you turn south into the mountains on the AS264 to Poncebos. The road comes to an end, and from here a track goes down to the the most spectacular gorge in the Picos de Europa. Cares Gorge, or the *Gargant Divina* as it is locally known, was formed by the fast-flowing Río Cares, and has sheer walls rising in places to over 2000 m. This is one of the most famous walks in Picos de Europa, 12 km (24 km if you walk the return!) along a narrow mule track that has been carved from the wall of the gorge and which eventually emerges at the village of Caín at the foot of the gorge. The gorge is a traditional site for Wallcreeper, along with species that are more easily encountered including Rock Bunting, Red-billed Chough, Alpine Chough, Crag Martin and Alpine Swift, and there is the strong likelihood on the walk of sightings of eagles and vultures.

Calendar

All year: Little Grebe, Mallard, Griffon Vulture, Goshawk, Sparrowhawk, Buzzard, Golden Eagle, Bonelli's Eagle, Peregrine, Kestrel, Capercaillie, Coot, Grey Partridge, Woodcock, Eagle Owl, Tawny Owl, Green Woodpecker, Black Woodpecker, Great Spotted Woodpecker, Middle Spotted Woodpecker, Crag Martin, Woodlark, Blue Rock Thrush, Stonechat, Crested Tit, Goldcrest, Firecrest, Dipper, Wren, Dunnock, Alpine Accentor, Nuthatch, Wallcreeper, Treecreeper, Jay, Red-billed Chough, Alpine Chough, Raven, Citril Finch, Snow Finch, Rock Sparrow, Bullfinch, Siskin, Linnet, Crossbill, Cirl Bunting, Rock Bunting.

Breeding season: White Stork, Black Kite, Honey Buzzard, Egyptian Vulture, Short-toed Eagle, Booted Eagle, Nightjar, Alpine Swift, Bee-eater, Hoopoe, Wryneck, Tree Pipit, Water Pipit, Rock Thrush, Melodious Warbler, Subalpine Warbler, Bonelli's Warbler, Whitethroat, Garden Warbler, Blackcap, Spotted Flycatcher, Pied Flycatcher, Red-backed Shrike, Ortolan Bunting.

OTHER SITES WORTH VISITING

AS7 Río Barayo

This small estuary with beach, dunes, extensive reedbeds and woods can attract a variety of wintering and passage birds, especially waders and herons. Take the coastal N632 east from Navia, and 2 km after Villapedre take a left to Vigo.

AS8 Cabo de Peñas

Sea cliffs and promontaries which can be good for seawatching and for migrants. Take the AS238 northeast out of Aviles towards Luanco, then one of the left turns towards Ovies and Ferrero.

AS9 Parque Natural de Redes

Upland hay meadows, cliffs and well-wooded areas. Brown bear and wolf, eagles, Capercaillie and woodpeckers. Take the A8 out of Ovieda, then AS17 to La Felguera/Langreo, following the valley of the Río Nalón into the park, from the Embalse de Tanes up to the border with Castile-León at the Tarna pass (Puerto de Tarna).

CANTABRIA

Extending west across the northern Spanish seaboard from the Basque region (Euskadi), Cantabria has much in common with its western neighbour Asturias. This is hardly surprising given the continuing dominance of the Cordillera Cantabrica mountain range, and the straddling across the shared regional boundaries of the huge Picos de Europa National Park (AR6). Far off the beaten tourist track, the Cordillera Cantabrica is one of the largest areas of wild terrain remaining in Europe, extending inland into the foothills of the Meseta, and like the Pyrenees, forming a barrier that is almost inpenetrable.

Cantabria through its port Santander, is normally the point of entry for those who travel to Spain by ferry, arriving on the north coast of Spain after a journey south down through the Bay of Biscay. The coast between Bilbao and Santander, the *Costa Emeralda*, is the busiest stretch in northern Spain. However, this is soon left behind as one travels westwards and inland to the mountains.

For those who do make the journey by sea, the birdwatching starts on the ferry, and like all other birdwatching what you see will depend on the time of year, the weather patterns and the weather on the day. It will always be somewhat of a lottery as to whether you are lucky enough to have passerines land on the boat, or whether you are able to see any waders. It is likely however, that if you put the time in then you may see at least some of the following depending on the season: Fulmar, Storm Petrel, Cory's Shearwater, Great Shearwater, Sooty Shearwater, Manx Shearwater, Yelkouan Shearwater, Gannet, Arctic Skua, Great Skua, Kittiwake and terns. If you make your journey outside the breeding season then it is also possible to pick up on various sea-duck such as Eider, Common Scoter and Velvet Scoter, divers, especially Great Northern Diver, although Red-throated and Black-throated are also possible, Red-breasted Merganser, and the auk family — Guillemot, Razorbill and Puffin. If you are really lucky then you may see a whale or dolphin.

While Cantabria is a small region in Spain, it has a relatively long coastline hiding a number of unexpected gems of dunes, beautiful beaches and key estuaries. Even the bay at Santander (CAN5) is worth a visit at the end or beginning of the holiday, especially the headland immediately to the west of the city and marshes and dunes across the mouth of the bay to the east. This is one of a number of estuaries found along the north coast, the most important being Santoña (CAN7), sometimes called the 'Doñana of the north'. Large numbers of waders and duck gather in the autumn and winter, and in the spring Spoonbill regularly stop off on their migration to breeding grounds in Holland and other parts of northern Europe. Most stop off at Santoña, but the estuaries all along this coast can expect to see a Spoonbill or two during the spring. One of the most typical of coastal species along the whole length of coast is Fan-tailed Warbler. Adjoining one of the estuaries, 10 km to the west of Santander, is the most extensive stretch of dunes, indeed the most extensive along the whole of the northern coast of Spain, the Dunas de Liencres (CAN4).

Seawatching can also be very fruitful along the northern coast, especially during or after periods of poor weather. The ferry obviously offers the best opportunities given the right weather conditions, but time spent on some of the headlands such as Cabo Mayor (CAN5) near Santander, between Santander and Santoña near Isla, or Cabo de Oyambre (CAN1) in the west of the region, can produce a similar list of species with luck.

Cantabria along with Catalunya is one of the strongholds in Spain of the introduced Pheasant, a bird which is thin on the ground in other parts of the country. A species you are unlikely to go in search of on holiday, but at least if you do manage to see one you will appreciate how lucky you have been!

Apart from beach holidays, the main focus of interest to visitors for Cantabria is its mountains, and more especially the Picos de Europa, the most visited, spectacular and highest area of the Cordillera Cantabrica, with the national park straddling the boundaries of Asturias, Cantabria and Castile-León (AS6 — a full description is found in the section on Asturias). The high ground of the Picos is easily visited for specialities such as Alpine Accentor, Wallcreeper, Snow Finch, Alpine Chough and Water Pipit, given the operation of the Teleférico at Fuente Dé, which transports you to the mountain tops within minutes, although queues can be severe at weekends and during holidays and high summer.

The woodlands have Black and Middle Spotted Woodpecker, and Capercaillie, while the gorges (such as La Hermida) can have breeding Golden Eagle and Bonelli's Eagle, Griffon and Egyptian Vulture. For those interested in exploring the region then the neighbouring valleys of Nansa (CAN9) and Saja-Besaya (CAN2) have a similar range of birds but are much less visited by tourists. Small populations of both brown bear and wolf hang on in the more remote corners of Cantabria's mountains, and the Cordillera is a national stronghold for chamois.

White Stork occur in Cantabria but only in the south, and breed beyond the Embalse del Ebro (CAN3), a reservoir in the far south of the region, where the climate has elements of both the Atlantic and Mediterranean. The Río Ebro, Spain's longest river, spills into the reservoir and is a post-breeding site for Red-crested Pochard. The area around and south of the reservoir becomes more steppe-like and Stone Curlew, and sometimes Dupont's Lark and Little Bustard, occur in small numbers.

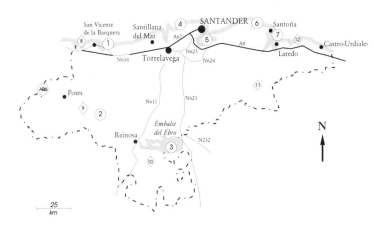

Main sites

1	CAN1	Oyambre
2	CAN2	Saja–Besaya
3	CAN3	Embalse del Ebro
4	CAN4	Dunas de Liencres
5	CAN5	Bahía de (Bay of) Santander
6	CAN6	Marismas del Joyel y de la Victoria
7	CAN7	Marismas de Santoña

Other sites worth visiting

8	CAN8	Tina Mayor and Tina Menor Estuaries
9	CAN9	Nansa Valley
10	CAN10	Valderredible
11	CAN11	Sierra del Hornijo
12	CAN12	Oriñon Estuary

CAN1 OYAMBRE

Status: Parque Natural (9000 ha).

Site description

A complex of coastal habitats between, and including, two estuaries — the relatively small Ría de la Rabia to the west, and the larger Ría de San Vicente to the east. Both estuaries have well-developed salt-marsh and fringe vegetation including mud- and sandbanks. While the main interest is focused on the estuaries, the coast between the two should also be visited and is included within the boundaries of the Parque Natural Oyambre. The coastline here has cliffs, sand dunes and beaches, while the headland at Cabo de Oyambre can be an excellent seawatching site.

Species

During the autumn and winter months, the estuary, especially San Vicente can hold good numbers of duck and waders, including Wigeon, Teal, Shoveler, Whimbrel and Grey Plover. During periods of rough weather, the estuaries and immediate coast attract auks and divers in search of shelter. Raptors such as Short-toed and Booted Eagle breed and hunt over the general area.

Timing

Good throughout the year, with autumn and winter especially productive in and around the estuaries, although a visit in spring can also produce migrants not only in the estuaries but along the whole coast and coastal hinterland.

Access

Situated in the far west of Cantabria, the western part of the site lies next to the attractive fishing village of San Vicente de la Barquera on the main N634 between Santander and Oviedo. The two estuaries are linked by the C6316. Minor roads lead off the C6316 towards the coast including one to the Casa de Jera, the nearest access by car to the Cabo de Oyambre. The estuary at San Vicente can be viewed from a number of locations including the causeway or from the minor road to the south. The C6316 also crosses Ría de la Rabia and allows viewing. Access on foot is also possible around most of the Ría de San Vicente, the western and southern banks of the Ría de la Rabia, and along the whole coastline between these two, including the Playa de Merón and Playa de Oyambre. The site is a large one overall and the direct distance between the two estuaries is around 10 km.

Calendar

All year: Little Grebe, Shag, Grey Heron, Peregrine, Common Sandpiper, Yellow-legged Gull, Barn Owl, Kingfisher, Grey Wagtail, White Wagtail, Stonechat, Chiffchaff, Garden Warbler, Spotless Starling, Great Grey Shrike, Serin, Cirl Bunting,

Breeding season: Black Kite, Short-toed Eagle, Booted Eagle, Hobby, Little Ringed Plover, Cuckoo, Swallow, House Martin, Fan-tailed Warbler, Red-backed Shrike.

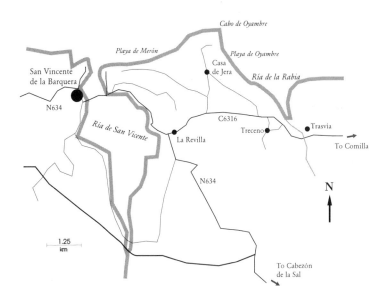

Winter: Great Northern Diver, Cory's Shearwater, Cormorant, Little Egret, Greylag Goose, Wigeon, Teal, Shoveler, Oystercatcher, Golden Plover, Grey Plover, Knot, Whimbrel, Great Skua, Guillemot, Razorbill, Puffin, Fieldfare, Redwing, Brambling.

Passage periods: Gannet, Marsh Harrier, Osprey, Avocet, Spoonbill, Greenshank, Ruff, Common Tern, Little Tern, Black Tern.

CAN2 SAJA–BESAYA

Status: Parque Natural (24,500 ha). Also forms part of the Reserva Nacional de Caza (180,186 ha).

Site description

This is a mountainous area with extensive deciduous forests, the largest in Spain. The parque natural forms only part of the immense Saja Game Reserve, an area which extends from the Besaya river to the Picos de Europa thus covering practically the whole of the western half of Cantabria, and making it the largest game reserve in Spain.

The area covered by the parque natural itself is focused around the long, steep-sided Saja Valley where substantial areas of oak and beech woodland still remain, grading into birch woodland, scrub and pastures at higher altitudes. A traditional 'extensive' type of cattle farming still exists where sections of pasture land, locally called '*brañas*', can be found within this protected area. This type of cattle farming has played an important role in the conservation of the Tudanca cow, a race native to this area.

Alpine Chough and Red-billed Chough

Almost 70% of the total area is woodland. The beech forest is normally found in shaded valleys at between 500 and 1300 m, the oak forest lies at a height of 600 m–700 m, with mixed forest along the riverbanks including many species, the most important being ash, elm, blackthorn, lime and willow. The beech forest of the Monte de Saja and the oak forest of the Monte de Ucieda are the most important areas.

Species
Excellent for birds of prey with Golden Eagle, Bonelli's Eagle, Short-toed Eagle, Booted Eagle, Honey Buzzard, Goshawk, Sparrowhawk and both Griffon and Egyptian Vulture. Alpine Accentor at high altitude and Capercaillie, Black Woodpecker and Middle Spotted Woodpecker. There is also the possibility of Bluethroat. Brown bear and wolf are rare, but badger, beech marten, polecat, weasel, fox and genet are all common. Otter and wild cat also occur in the park.

Timing
Late spring and summer; the pass can be blocked by snow in the winter.

Access
From Santander head west along the A67/N634 main coastal road as far as Cabezón de la Sal. Turn inland (and left) here along the C625. The C625 runs along the length of the valley of the River Saja up to the Puerto de Palombera, the mountain pass into Castile-León.

There are a number of routes into the different parts of the park. The main points of access to the heart of the park are via Ucieda or Bárcena Mayor. There is a campsite about 1 km from Bárcena Mayor and from there a track follows the course of the Argoza river through ancient oak and beech forest to La Arbencia pool.

There are also various places to pull off the road in between Saja and the pass, and you may explore the forests for Capercaillie. For easy access to the birds of higher altitude, continue up to the pass for Alpine Chough and Golden Eagle. Another alternative is to continue over the pass down into the adjoining region to Espinilla and then right along the C628, to the ski resort at Braña Vieja in the Alto Campóo.

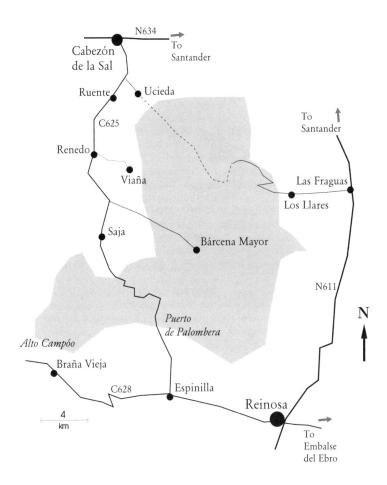

At the beautiful village of Carrejo, about 1 km from Cabezón de la Sal, is the Cantabrian Nature Museum (tends to be open late morning and afternoon but closed all day Monday and Sunday afternoon).

Calendar

All year: Griffon Vulture, Goshawk, Sparrowhawk, Golden Eagle, Grey Partridge, Tawny Owl, Black Woodpecker, Middle Spotted Woodpecker, Crag Martin, Dipper, Alpine Accentor, Robin, Bluethroat, Goldcrest, Treecreeper, Red-billed Chough, Alpine Chough, Bullfinch, Yellowhammer.

Breeding season: Honey Buzzard, Egyptian Vulture, Short-toed Eagle, Wryneck, Tree Pipit, Water Pipit, Rock Thrush, Whinchat, Bonelli's Warbler, Spotted Flycatcher, Pied Flycatcher, Red-backed Shrike.

CAN3 EMBALSE DEL EBRO

Status: No special protection (6000 ha).

Site description

The Embalse del Ebro is a large reservoir situated on a plain and sand-wiched between mountain ranges in the south of Cantabria. The longest river in Spain, the Ebro, has its source close by at Fontibre, and eventually finds its way into the Mediterranean via the reservoir, through a long journey across the breadth of Spain. Built in 1945, when three villages were abandoned and disappeared beneath the water, it not only collects water from the Ebro but also from some of its tributaries. It is the largest freshwater site in Cantabria and one of the largest in Spain with a surface area of roughly 5000 ha, 20 km in length with a perimeter of 90 km, and now makes possible the irrigation of land downriver in other regions. The reservoir is quite shallow and has well-developed aquatic vegetation, but the surrounding shores are dry grazed pasture, although there are some stands of trees and scrub.

Species

The shallow waters and the shores provide attractive roosting and feeding areas. It is a very important site for Red-crested Pochard with the reservoir supporting a large post-breeding population of over 2,000, numbers peaking in July. There are also good numbers of breeding Great Crested Grebe and Gadwall, and it is also important as a wintering site for other wildfowl.

The general area holds the only significant White Stork population in the area, but this is decreasing.

Timing

Late summer and winter.

Access

Two main roads can be taken deep into the mountains of Cantabria where the reservoir is situated. The N623 which follows the Pas Valley

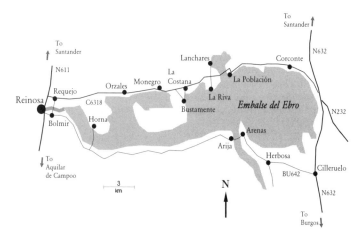

to the eastern side of this large reservoir. Go past Puerto del Escudo and take a right turn along the C6318 which follows the northern shores, through Corconte and La Costana towards Reinosa. Alternatively take the western arm down Besaya Valley, the N611 to Reinosa then eastwards along the same C6318. Further access is also possible to the southern shores.

Calendar

All year: Little Grebe, Great Crested Grebe, Gadwall, Mallard, Pochard, Red Kite, Griffon Vulture, Buzzard, Kestrel, Moorhen, Coot, Red-legged Partridge, Little Owl, White Wagtail, Cetti's Warbler, Dartford Warbler, Rock Sparrow.

Breeding season: White Stork, Red-crested Pochard, Honey Buzzard, Black Kite, Egyptian Vulture, Short-toed Eagle, Marsh Harrier, Hen Harrier, Booted Eagle, Hobby, Quail, Little Ringed Plover, Kentish Plover, Common Sandpiper, Cuckoo, Nightjar, Hoopoe, Yellow Wagtail, Whinchat, Great Reed Warbler, Melodious Warbler, Whitethroat. *Winter:* Grey Heron, Wigeon, Teal, Pintail, Shoveler, Tufted Duck.

Passage periods: Spoonbill, Greylag Goose, Marsh Harrier, Little Stint, Ruff, Black-tailed Godwit, Bar-tailed Godwit, Redshank, Common Tern, Black Tern, Grasshopper Warbler.

CAN4 DUNAS DE LIENCRES

Status: Parque Natural (194.5 ha).

Site description

These are the most extensive stretch of sand dunes on Spain's northern coast, forming the Playa de Valdearenas. This very important dune system adjoins the mouth of the Pas and Mogro estuaries and was designated as a natural park in 1986. Some pine planting has been undertaken in an attempt to stabilise the dunes.

Species

There is a good variety of birds and the interest of the site does vary from season to season, with seabirds, including auks, divers and seaducks particularly to the fore in the winter, and with the chance of Snow Bunting. It can be excellent during migration and has breeding Hobby and Fan-tailed Warbler.

Timing

Throughout the year for interest associated with the estuary and coastal seas, although the high summer can be quiet. Spring is the best time for the dunes, pine plantations, deciduous woodlands and scrub, especially so for migrant passerines. The nearby hill of Picota can be popular with paragliders and mountain-bikers at weekends.

Access

Very close to Santander, around 15 km to the west of the city and just beyond Liencres. Although one could take the A67 motorway out of Santander, a more agreeable approach is to take the local road (S463) to Liencres via the fishing village of Soto de la Marina. Carry on through Liencres and take a right turn to Valdearenas Beach where there is a large car park. The popular hill of Picota offers excellent views over the park and estuaries and can be reached by a track from the car park.

Views over the estuary are had by following the beach southwestwards, turning left once the beach has been reached. Alternatively, views are possible on the western side of the estuary from La Unquera (now a golf course) or Punta del Águila, a nearby headland.

Calendar

All year: Shag, Sparrowhawk, Buzzard, Peregrine, Kestrel, Common Sandpiper, Kingfisher, Stonechat, Fan-tailed Warbler, Crested Tit, Short-toed Treecreeper, Serin, Cirl Bunting.

Breeding season: Hen Harrier, Hobby, Little Ringed Plover, Kentish Plover, Whinchat, Spotted Flycatcher, Golden Oriole, Red-backed Shrike.

Winter: Great Northern Diver, Cory's Shearwater, Yelkouan Shearwater, Great Shearwater, Sooty Shearwater, Comorant, Little Egret, Grey Heron, Eider, Common Scoter, Velvet Scoter, Red-breasted Merganser, Grey Plover, Golden Plover, Curlew, Redshank, Guillemot, Razorbill, Snow Bunting.

Passage periods: Gannet, Little Bittern, Osprey, Marsh Harrier, Greylag Goose, Knot, Sanderling, Dunlin, Whimbrel, Turnstone, Short-eared Owl, Tawny Pipit, Tree Pipit, Wheatear, Grasshopper Warbler, Moustached Warbler, Sedge Warbler, Wood Warbler, Woodchat Shrike.

CAN5 BAHÍA DE (BAY OF) SANTANDER

Status: No special protection.

Site description

A large estuary on the shores of which lies the capital of Cantabria, Santander, which now dominates the bay. It is the first taste of the northern coast of Spain for those making the journey from the UK by sea. The estuary sees three rivers, Cubas, San Salvador and Bóo, joining here before they reach the sea. The estuary itself stretches from Cabo Mayor in the west to Cabo Ajo in the east, and supports extensive areas of mudflats with varying amounts of saltmarsh and intertidal vegetation around the periphery of the bay. Sand dunes are present at the eastern mouth of the bay at the Playa el Puntal and Playa de Somo.

Species

Most important for waders, ducks, divers and auks in the winter, plus other seabirds such as skuas, scoters and cormorants.

Timing

Of greatest interest in the autumn and winter, but not of great interest to the summer visitor, although it is possible for some interesting species to pass through in spring and early autumn.

Access

The bay is not especially attractive, although there are a few exceptions to this: the Peninsula de la Magdalena, Cabo Menor and Cabo Mayor and its lighthouse. To get to these areas turn right out of the port, and right again onto Paseo de Pareda, following the bay to the sea along

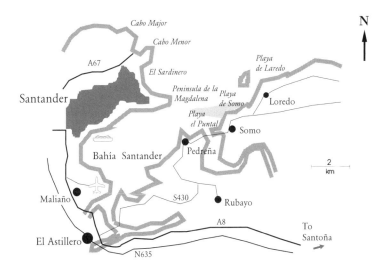

Castelar, Avenida de la Reian Victoria, and turning due east through the outskirts of the city and the beach of El Sardinero and on to Cabo Menor and Cabo Mayor.

If you are on your way east towards other sites such as Santoña, then try the mouth of the River Cubas and dunes on the eastern shores between Pedrena and Somo. Take the dual carriageway (A8) out of the city towards Bilbao, turning off at El Astillero (8 km from Santander) to follow the eastern shores of the bay towards Pedrena and across a bridge over the River Cubas to Somo.

Calendar

All year: Shag, Little Grebe, Buzzard, Yellow-legged Gull, Collared Dove, Kingfisher, White Wagtail, Cetti's Warbler, Fan-tailed Warbler.

Breeding season: Oystercatcher, Little Ringed Plover, Black-headed Gull, Common Tern, Swift.

Winter: Great Northern Diver, Black-necked Grebe, Cormorant, Grey Heron, Merlin, Common Scoter, Red-breasted Merganser, Grey Plover, Purple Sandpiper, Whimbrel, Guillemot, Razorbill.

Passage periods: Great Northern Diver, Manx Shearwater, Gannet, Spoonbill, Shoveler, Red-breasted Merganser, Marsh Harrier, Dunlin, Curlew Sandpiper, Ruff, Redshank, Greenshank, Sandwich Tern, Little Tern, Hoopoe, Sand Martin, Tree Pipit, Wheatear, Red-backed Shrike.

CAN6 MARISMAS DEL JOYEL Y DE LA VICTORIA

Status: Reserva Natural, ZEPA and Ramsar site. Part of the larger site that includes Marismas de Santona with the whole area totalling 6907 ha.

Site description

Protected as part of the larger reserve which includes Santoña (CAN7), but which is geographically separated from it. This area comprises two small estuaries with a variety of wetland habitats located within farmed countryside with hay meadows and areas of eucalyptus. To the west, Marisma del Joyel comprises rough grass, rushes, reedbed, brackish lagoon and saltmarsh. To the east, Marisma de la Victoria is a much larger area of reedbed surrounding a small freshwater lake. Just to the west of Noja, the coastline rises to the impressive cliffs of Cabo Quejo.

Species

An excellent range of species reflecting the variety of habitats present in the area. Purple Heron, Spoonbill, Black-tailed Godwit, Cetti's Warbler and Great Reed Warbler are found on the margins of the estuary. In the pools are Little Grebe, Little Bittern, Pochard and Shoveler. Marsh Harrier also breed and surrounding land has Tawny Pipit, Sardinian

Warbler and Fan-tailed Warbler. Black Kite and Peregrines living around the cliffs regularly visit the marismas, and Red-billed Chough and Raven breed on the cliffs.

Timing
Throughout the year, but best from September through to June.

Access
About 10 km west of Santona and sited immediately to the west of the village of Noja. Reached via the N634 from Santander or Bilbao, taking the minor road for Isla from the town of Beragga. Footpaths from Isla skirt the estuary until you reach the reedbeds and pools at the head of the estuary. The headland is reached from the resort via a footpath, while there is a coast path between the two estuaries that passes through a small area of scrub and mixed conifer and eucalyptus woodland. Both estuaries can be observed from roads and paths around their fringes.

Calendar
All year: Little Grebe, Cormorant, Grey Heron, Marsh Harrier, Peregrine, Water Rail, Scops Owl, Kingfisher, Crag Martin, Black Redstart, Cetti's Warbler, Fan-tailed Warbler, Dartford Warbler, Firecrest, Red-billed Chough, Raven, Spotless Starling, Serin, Cirl Bunting.

Breeding season: Little Bittern, Purple Heron, Black Kite, Hoopoe, Tawny Pipit, Great Reed Warbler, Grasshopper Warbler, Melodious Warbler.

Winter: Black-necked Grebe, Wigeon, Pintail, Gadwall, Red-breasted Merganser, Snipe, Curlew, Razorbill.

Passage periods: Grey Heron, Spoonbill, Hobby, Spotted Crake, Redshank, Spotted Redshank, Redstart, Orphean Warbler, Pied Flycatcher, Red-backed Shrike.

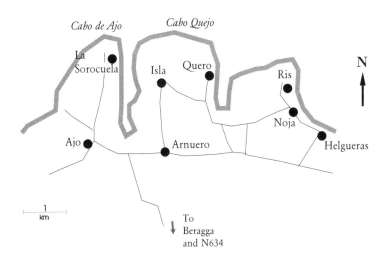

CAN7 MARISMAS DE SANTOÑA

Status: Reserva Natural, ZEPA and Ramsar site. Total area of 6907 ha includes nearby site of Marismas del Joyel y de la Victoria (CAN6).

Site description

The most important coastal wetland on the north coast of Spain and known as the 'Doñana of the North' after the Coto Doñana in Andalucia. The reserve was created in 1992 to safeguard this area from proposed developments that would have threatened the integrity of the site. The designated areas also include the adjacent smaller estuaries near Noja, Marismas del Joyel y de la Victoria (CAN6).

The estuary, at the mouth of the River Asón, has extensive mudflats and saltmarshes that are exposed at low tide, along with sand dunes and sand bars. Cliffs are covered with coastal holm oaks and scrub woodland as is Mount Buciero — a 'tombolo' — an island joined ot the mainland by a bank of sand. Montehano, a coastal peak also falls within the protected area.

It is also worth visiting the remains of the traditional tidal watermills conserved in the area, notably the Jado mill in Ancillo (Argoños) and the Santa Olalla mill in the Joyel marshland (CAN6).

Traditional activities such as shellfish fish harvesting and fishing take place within the reserve although they are subject to controls.

Species

A large number of species of birds has been recorded from the site, with many thousands overwintering here, including around 5,000 Wigeon that feed in the saltmarshes. An important site for passage Spoonbills with over 50 or so present at peak times, although many more pass through in the course of a season. There are important numbers of waders in spring and autumn, including up to 700 Curlew and 350 Whimbrel. Santoña is also one of the few breeding sites in Spain for Shelduck.

Spoonbills

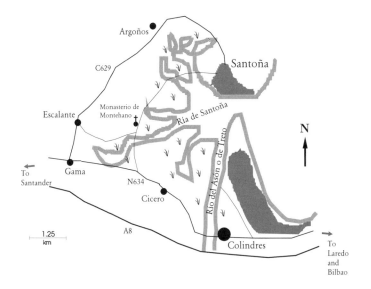

Timing

The weather in spring can sometimes be inclement on this Atlantic coast but can attract good numbers of birds on passage with late August to November the best period for migrants at the back end of the year. Wildfowl arrive in late October and stay until March. The best time to visit is between September and June.

Access

Around 60 km from Santander via the local coastal road or around 50 km via the more direct N634 or E70. Take the turning off the N634 at Gama, or at Cicero, where you then take the minor road across the saltmarsh towards Santoña. From Bilbao it is half as far again at around 75 km. There are a number of viewing places and small lay-bys across the bay from the N634 between Santoña, Cicero and Colindres.

Santoña is separated from Noja by the headland of El Brusco.

Calendar

All year: Little Grebe, Shelduck, Red Kite, Buzzard, Marsh Harrier, Goshawk, Coot, Yellow-legged Gull, Kingfisher, Stonechat, Song Thrush, Cetti's Warbler, Fan-tailed Warbler, Firecrest, Great Grey Shrike, Raven, Serin, Cirl Bunting, Reed Bunting.

Breeding season: Shag, Little Egret, Black Kite, Honey Buzzard, Short-toed Eagle, Hobby, Little Ringed Plover, Sand Martin, Yellow Wagtail, Tree Pipit, Whinchat.

Winter: Red-throated Diver, Great Northern Diver, Black-necked Grebe, Little Egret, Grey Heron, Wigeon, Teal, Pintail, Shoveler, Eider, Common Scoter, Red-breasted Merganser, Hen Harrier, Oystercatcher, Dunlin, Snipe, Curlew, Ringed Plover, Grey Plover, Golden Plover, Black-headed Gull, Lesser Black-backed Gull, Razorbill, Guillemot.

Passage periods: Osprey, Spoonbill, Avocet, Knot, Sanderling, Curlew Sandpiper, Black-tailed Godwit, Ruff, Whimbrel, Redshank, Spotted Redshank, Greenshank, Turnstone, Hoopoe, Wryneck, Golden Oriole Red-backed Shrike.

OTHER SITES WORTH VISITING

CAN8 Tina Mayor and Tina Menor Estuaries
In the far west of Cantabria next to border with Asturias. Smaller versions of other estuaries in the region, pretty and well wooded behind. Good range of waders including occasional Spoonbill. Reached via N634 coast road.

CAN9 Nansa Valley
Rugged and beautiful but little known and little visited by tourists. Well wooded. Capercaillie and Black Woodpecker. Road follows follows River Nansa deep into the mountains south from the estuaries at Tina Mayor and Tina Menor (CAN8). From the main coast road (N634) take the S223/S224 up the valley through Puentenansa into the mountains.

CAN10 Valderredible
Southern extremity of Cantabria with a more Mediterranean-like climate. Upper Ebro valley with limestone gorges, birds of prey and best area for White Stork in the region. N611 south from Santander to Reinosa, then minor road off to left halfway between Reinosa and Matamorossa to Arroyo, Arroyal and Polientes.

CAN11 Sierra del Hornijo
Limestone massif with world famous caves. Area of limestone crags with some outstanding woods and pastures. Birds of prey in southeastern corner, and sierra encircled by road. Head for Ramales de la Victoria via the S629/S521 off the coastal road at Colindres, or for Arredondo along the S533/S531 off the coastal road at Solares.

CAN12 Oriñon Estuary
The beautiful estuary lies below the two limestone massifs of Candina and Cerreda. The whole area is worth exploring. Monte Candina to the western side of the estuary supports the only coastal Griffon Vulture colony in Spain. Situated in the far east of Cantabria off the N634 coast road next to the village of Oriñon.

CASTILE-LA MANCHA

Although being enclosed by and surrounded by mountains, Castile-La Mancha is most famous for the huge flat plain that covers much of the central part of this dry inland part of Spain — the 'sun-baked Arabic wilderness'. This, the most extensive plain in Spain, has changed much since the times of Miguel Cervantes, no longer wilderness but a landscape of castles, cereal fields, vines and windmills that most visitors closely associated with Don Quixote and his companion Sancho Panza. Certainly the tourist boards make the most of that connection and you will certainly pass, if you are indeed not on the road itself, the *Ruta de Don Quixote*.

This immense sea of agricultural production stretches right across La Mancha and is yet another part of Spain that is little visited by birdwatchers from the UK — most favouring the adjoining region of Extremadura to go in search of birds of steppe or *dehesa*.

For those birdwatchers that do visit La Mancha, it is the plains and the *dehesa* that are the focus of the attention. Most of the steppe specialities are in evidence: Great and Little Bustard, Black-bellied and Pin-tailed Sandgrouse, Stone Curlew, Montagu's Harrier and Quail, whilst not forgetting larks with Calandra and Short-toed also present. Dupont's Lark does breed in La Mancha but there are better sites to visit, especially in Aragón and the Ebro Valley. While the population of the Little Bustard has undergone a dramatic reduction in Spain, it is still relatively common in Castile-La Mancha. The plains also have a number of breeding species that have a fragmented distribution in the UK but which are relatively common here, such as Tree Sparrow and Corn Bunting.

Head westwards from Toledo and southwest past Ciudad Real, and you encounter further steppe areas, but this time with a backdrop of low hills and *dehesa* holm oak woodland. These areas should figure on any birdwatcher's itinerary, having most of the species that birdwatchers come to Spain for. In addition to the steppe species there are also Spanish Imperial Eagle, some of the largest Black Vulture colonies in Spain such as at Cabañeros (CLM13) and the Sierra de la Canalizas (CLM14), Black Stork, Lesser Kestrel, Azure-winged Magpie, Black-shouldered Kite and Spanish Sparrow. Typical birds of Extremadura, but in Castile-La Mancha!

The area to the west of Toledo has the added advantage of river valleys, reservoirs and marshes with some large heron colonies, especially Night Heron and Cattle Egret at Valle del Tiétar (CLM1), Embalse de Azután (CLM3) and Embalse de Castrejón (CLM4). These wetland areas to the west of Toledo also have Purple Gallinule — a little known and important inland breeding population well away from the core area in Andalucía. The general area also has a large concentrations of wintering Cranes that feed on the acorns in the *dehesa* and cereal fields and roost around the reservoirs in the evening. There are also some reservoirs to the east of Madrid such as Embalse de Buendia (CLM8) that are regular passage sites for Cranes on their way further west.

It is La Mancha Húmeda (CLM11), however, that is the focus of attention for wetland sites. The Castilian arid plains can get a little too much at some times, even for the most avid birdwatcher, especially in the heat of the afternoon sun after a long and dusty morning searching for Great Bustard and Black-bellied Sandgrouse. This is the time to have a siesta and plan the evening's birdwatching itinerary (or the following morning's) by planning the visit to the wetlands and marshes found along the valleys of the Río Cigüela and Río Guadiana. Although nowhere near so good as they once were, mainly through the damage caused by large-scale irrigation, this group of more than 100 seasonal lagoons is still collectively one of the most important wetlands in Spain and provide some excellent birdwatching opportunities. In addition to some of the more widespread species, this wetland complex has one of the largest breeding populations of Black-necked Grebe in Europe. It is also a key area for breeding Red-crested Pochard, White-headed Duck, Black Tern, Whiskered Tern, Gull-billed Tern, Bearded Tit, Penduline Tit and Savi's Warbler. Marsh Harriers are also common, and Castile-La Mancha has the highest population of Marsh Harriers in Spain. The lagoons are of interest throughout much of the year although many are dry throughout the summer. Two of the best lakes to visit are Laguna de Manjaracas and Laguna de Pedro Muñoz.

Part of La Mancha Húmeda, but physically separated from the bulk of the lagoons, is Tablas de Daimiel (CLM12) — the most famous of all wetlands in the region — and a national park, the smallest in Spain. Like the other wetlands, Tablas de Daimiel has also suffered from irrigation but it still of great importance as a breeding site, for migrants and as a wintering site for birds holding up to 50,000 wildfowl, including peaks of 1,000 Red-crested Pochard.

But back to the mountains — the wooded limestone ground to the east of the region in the Serranía de Cuenca, the gorges of the River Tajo and the sparsely populated Sierra Moreno in the southwest. Griffon and Egyptian Vulture, Bonelli's Eagle, Alpine Swift, Crag Martin and Rock Thrush are all present, and the heights of the Sierra de Ayllón in the far north have one of the densest populations of Golden Eagle in Spain. If you are lucky then it is perfectly possible to come across Eagle Owl and, in the south, wolf!

Main sites

1	CLM1	Valle del Tiétar y Embalses de Rosarito y Navalcán
2	CLM2	Llanos de Oropesa
3	CLM3	Embalse de Azután
4	CLM4	Embalse de Castrejón
5	CLM5	Sierra de Ayllón
6	CLM6	Río Dulce
7	CLM7	Alto Tajo
8	CLM8	La Alcarria
9	CLM9	Serranía de Cuenca
10	CLM10	Las Lagunas de Ruidera
11	CLM11	Lagunas de La Mancha Húmeda
12	CLM12	Las Tablas de Daimiel
13	CLM13	Cabañeros
14	CLM14	Sierra de la Canalizas
15	CLM15	Valle y Sierra de Alcudia
16	CLM16	Sierra Madrona

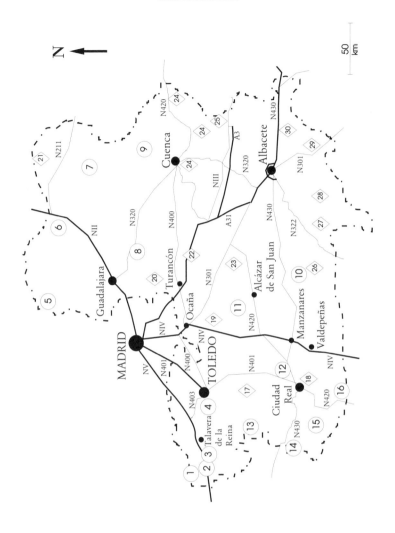

Other sites worth visiting

CLM1   VALLE DEL TIÉTAR Y EMBALSES DE ROSARITO Y NAVALCÁN

Status: Reserva Natural (26,000 ha) and ZEPA (29,000 ha).

Site description

This is a valley to the south of the Sierra de Gredos, with other fertile valleys flooded when the reservoirs were constructed. There is some concern for the future of the area as plans for a third reservoir have been proposed.

The area of interest is much greater than just that protected by the reserve, and adjoins Llanos de Oropesa (CLM2). The Tiétar Valley contains an extremely diverse mixture of habitat with a corresponding diversity of birds. The main focus of interest is the river valley itself, which is quite steeply banked, and the two reservoirs of Rosarito and Navalcán. The area between is a mixture of *dehesa* oak woodland, grassland, cereals and *Cistus* and lavender scrub.

The river follows the border between the provinces of Toledo (Castile-La Mancha) and Ávila (Castile-León), winding through beautiful scenery on its way to the Tajo, and riverine alder and willow woods. The reserve also includes the small isolated range of low hills to the east known as the 'Sierra de San Vicente'.

Species

This is an excellent site that is very important for a whole range of species both breeding and wintering, and as the habitat is very varied a long list of species is easily possible in a day's birdwatching. Birds of prey can be particularly good with Black-shouldered Kite and Spanish Imperial Eagle, but there are also Short-toed Eagle, Booted Eagle and numerous Black Kite. There are also small numbers of breeding Black Stork, although larger post-breeding concentrations. White Stork is also present and this is excellent countryside for Spanish Sparrow.

The *dehesa* also has Azure-winged Magpie, and in winter holds large numbers of Cranes which come to feed on the acorns in the open woodland.

The reservoirs have resident Great Crested, Little and Black-necked Grebe. Cattle and Little Egret and other herons can be seen around reservoir shores and also in the river valley itself. Baillon's Crake and Purple Gallinule also occur and Rosarito reservoir is one of the few breeding sites in Spain for Tufted Duck. Both reservoirs support wintering duck, including Wigeon, Pintail, Shoveler and Teal, Pochard and Ferruginous Duck. Crane also roost at the reservoirs in the winter after feeding during the day in the surrounding countryside, and large numbers of Cormorant (over 2,000) also overwinter. Osprey and Black Tern are found on passage.

Riverside trees hold Golden Oriole and Melodious Warbler, and Cetti's Warbler, Dartford Warbler and Orphean Warbler are also present. Bee-eaters nest in sections of the riverbank. The valley holds a good population of otters and is a stronghold of both lynx and wildcat.

Timing

November to February is a good time for raptors, Cranes, and wintering duck and Cormorant. Breeding birds and passage in spring. Also some passage in autumn.

Access

Take the NV road out of Madrid towards Cáceres. Before reaching the regional border with Extremadura take a right turn on the CM5102 at Oropesa. Almost immediately there is a left turn (CM5105) which takes you to the Embalse de Rosarito (Madrigal de la Vera), the main road (CM5102) takes you to Navalcán reservoir. This also leads to the valley itself and the village of Candeleda.

Other parts of the area can be explored by taking a variety of roads northwards from the town of Talavera de la Reina. Alternatively, a minor road to the north of the valley, the C501 between Piedravales and Madrigal de la Vera can be taken which follows the route of the river. This road also follows the foothills of the southern slopes of the Sierra de Gredos (CAS6) in Castile-León and a diversion into these mountains is recommended for another day. Minor roads to the south across the river occur from time to time.

Access around the both reservoirs is limited, although Rosarito reservoir can be very popular with visitors during the summer and at weekends when swimming, fishing and boating occurs. Cars can be parked on the western shores. A track follows the southern shore after reaching a campsite.

An information centre is situated on the northern shores about 2 km west of Candeleda, turn off the C501 south. The road between the two reservoirs can be very good, particularly the stretch between Candeleda and Navalcán.

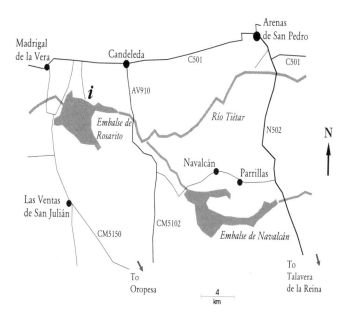

Calendar

All year: Great Crested Grebe, Little Grebe, Black-necked Grebe, Cattle Egret, Grey Heron, Gadwall, Tufted Duck, Black-shouldered Kite, Red Kite, Griffon Vulture, Black Vulture, Goshawk, Spanish Imperial Eagle, Purple Gallinule, Little Bustard, Stone Curlew, Eagle Owl, Long-eared Owl, Lapwing, Hoopoe, Crag Martin, Dartford Warbler, Firecrest, Crested Tit, Azure-winged Magpie, Spanish Sparrow, Cirl Bunting.

Breeding season: Night Heron, Little Egret, Black Stork, White Stork, Honey Buzzard, Black Kite, Egyptian Vulture, Short-toed Eagle, Booted Eagle, Hobby, Baillon's Crake, Black-winged Stilt, Common Sandpiper, Little Ringed Plover, Great Spotted Cuckoo, Red-necked Nightjar, Bee-eater, Roller, Melodious Warbler, Orphean Warbler, Bonelli's Warbler, Woodchat Shrike, Golden Oriole.

Winter: Cormorant, Grey Heron, Wigeon, Pintail, Shoveler, Crane, Golden Plover, Lapwing, Snipe, Lesser Black-backed Gull.

Passage periods: Purple Heron, Spoonbill, Osprey, Black Tern.

CLM2 LLANOS DE OROPESA

Status: Reserva Nacional de Caza (44,000 ha).

Site description

These are sparsely populated plains found in the Tajo Valley to the west of Talavera de la Reina, covering some 44,000 ha of land wedged in between the Tajo and Tiétar rivers. These cereal-covered plains contain important old *dehesa* woodland — open evergreen oak woodland. The general area is extensively grazed and in winter there are some parts that are frequently flooded. The plains are of great ornithological significance because of their strong populations of Great Bustard — the so-called Iberian Ostrich — and other steppe birds.

Species

The cereal and grassland plains of Llanos de Oropesa are important for steppe birds, with good numbers of both Great Bustard and Little Bustard. There are also at least 20 pairs of Montagu's Harrier. White Storks are common in the villages of the area and there are over 40 breeding pairs. Lesser Kestrels are also often seen in the villages and feeding in small groups over the plains. An important and well-known colony of Spanish Sparrow also occurs here.

Good views of typical *dehesa* birds are easy and species to be seen include Black-shouldered Kite, Spanish Imperial Eagle, Black Stork, Azure-winged Magpie and Great Spotted Cuckoo. Winter roosts of Red Kite occur in the area, and are well known locally, including a large one in woodland on the road north out of Oropesa towards the village of La Corchuela.

Lesser Kestrels

Depending on the amount of winter rain, small seasonally flooded areas can occur scattered throughout the plain and attract many species. Some hold concentrations of waders including large numbers of Golden Plover and Lapwing.

In the winter Cranes and Cormorants can also be seen in the area where they roost on the nearby reservoirs of Valdecanas, Azután, Rosarito and Navalcán. The wintering Cranes from northern Europe feed during the day amongst the *dehesa* and cereals.

Timing

There is something of interest throughout the year — Cranes, Red Kite roosts and Golden Plover in the winter with breeding *dehesa* and steppe birds in the spring and summer.

Access

Oropesa is located on the NV (Madrid–Cáceres) road between Talavera de la Reina and Navalmoral de la Mata. Much of the area is privately owned farmland and care should be taken when walking over the area, although it is perfectly possible to view from the road and the many tracks.

Take the road that runs north of Oropesa to Corchuela (CM5102) or Las Ventas de San Julian (CM5150) for good views of the plains, before exploring the *dehesa* of Monteagudo and the Tiétar Valley (CLM1). A smaller road southeast from Oropesa to Calera y Chozas runs through both *dehesa* and steppe-type habitat. Take the CM4100 south from Oropesa to El Puente del Arzobispo, and then left along the CM4101 to Calera y Chozas.

Many of the species can be seen from the roads north of Oropesa, and which also have a number of tracks leading from them. Take care if birdwatching from the busy main road, which is not recommended. Some of the small towns and villages in the area, such as Oropesa itself, Lagartera, La Calzada de Oropsea, are not only worth visiting for a cold beer or chilled fino, but also in search of the older buildings, especially the churches, which can have breeding White Stork and Lesser Kestrel.

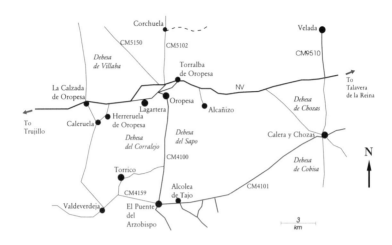

Calendar

All year: Cattle Egret, Black Stork, Black-shouldered Kite, Black Vulture, Griffon Vulture, Little Bustard, Great Bustard, Stone Curlew, Black-bellied Sandgrouse, Pin-tailed Sandgrouse, Barn Owl, Little Owl, Calandra Lark, Crested Lark, Thekla Lark, Dartford Warbler, Great Grey Shrike, Azure-winged Magpie, Raven, Spotless Starling, Spanish Sparrow.

Breeding season: White Stork, Egyptian Vulture, Montagu's Harrier, Lesser Kestrel, Hobby, Turtle Dove, Great Spotted Cuckoo, Cuckoo, Red-necked Nightjar, Bee-eater, Roller, Hoopoe, Short-toed Lark, Red-rumped Swallow, Black-eared Wheatear, Spotted Flycatcher, Woodchat Shrike.

Winter: Cormorant, Red Kite, Merlin, Lapwing, Golden Plover, Short-eared Owl, Fieldfare.

CLM3   EMBALSE DE AZUTÁN

Status: Reserva Nacional de Caza (6800 ha); the reservoir covers 1600 ha of this.

Site description

The stretch of the River Tajo, between Talavera de la Reina and El Puente del Arzobispo was flooded to form the Azután reservoir. The dam was completed in 1969, and flooded large areas of farmland lying in the floodplain.

In addition to the marshy vegetated margins and wooded islands, there are also some important riverside woods, especially the area known as 'Enebrales de Talavera', an important juniper wood on chalky ground on the banks of the Tajo.

102

Species

One of the most obvious features of the reservoir is an established heronry with around 100 pairs of Night Heron and over 2,000 pairs of Cattle Egrets. There is also enough cover to support a wide range of other species including Little Egret, Purple Heron and Little Bittern. Bittern also breeds occasionally, as does Water Rail and Purple Gallinule.

Marsh Harrier quarter the reservoirs, marshes and surrounding land throughout the year. The bankside vegetation and trees have breeding Great Reed Warbler, Penduline Tit, Reed Warbler, Golden Oriole and Scops Owl.

Winter interest focuses on Osprey, with Cranes using the reservoir as a roost, alongside Cormorant. The reservoir also supports reasonable wintering populations of duck and waders.

Timing

Interest all year round. The heronry is used throughout the year by breeding and roosting birds. Heat haze can be a problem during the summer.

Access

Located south of the NV Madrid–Cáceres road, immediately south and west of Talavera de la Reina. At Talavera de la Reina turn south onto the N502. That part of the reservoir closest to Talavera itself has well-developed fringing vegetation, bankside trees and wooded islands with heron colonies, including one close to the old bridge in the town.

Views over the reservoir can be obtained by leaving Talavera south on the N502 and turning right to Las Herencias, although there are no paths down to the river here. The local road (CM4160) from Calera y Chozas to Alcaudete de la Jara is another alternative, where the road crosses the Tajo at Puente de Silos bridge.

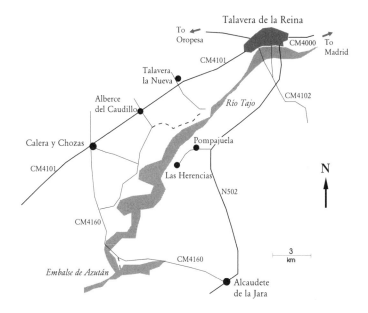

103

Calendar

All year: Cattle Egret, Gadwall, Teal, Mallard, Marsh Harrier, Water Rail, Purple Gallinule, Stone Curlew, White Wagtail, Cetti's Warbler, Fantailed Warbler, Penduline Tit, Reed Bunting.

Breeding season: Bittern, Little Bittern, Night Heron, Little Egret, Purple Heron, White Stork, Scops Owl, Roller, Sand Martin, Nightingale, Savi's Warbler, Reed Warbler, Great Reed Warbler, Melodious Warbler, Woodchat Shrike, Golden Oriole.

Winter: Great Crested Grebe, Cormorant, Grey Heron, Wigeon, Pintail, Shoveler, Snipe, Black-headed Gull, Lesser Black-backed Gull.

Passage periods: Osprey, Crane, Little Crake, Black-winged Stilt, Avocet, Ruff, Black-tailed Godwit, Wood Sandpiper, Moustached Warbler.

CLM4   EMBALSE DE CASTREJÓN

Status: Reserva Natural (1900 ha).

Site description

This medium-sized reservoir lies on the Tajo river some 25 km downstream from the city of Toledo, and provides water for irrigation. The river winds through a series of old alluvial riverine meanders between steep sandstone banks, with marshes, several small islands and old woods along its banks.

The reservoir itself extends for some 750 ha and is surrounded by grazing land with holm oak woods, and cliffs that are known as 'Las Barrancas'.

Night Heron

Species

The reservoir has a breeding colony of around 150 pairs of Night Heron (around 10% of the total Spanish breeding population), 75 pairs of Cattle Egret and small numbers of Little Egret. The reservoir is also one of the few inland sites for Purple Gallinule. It also attracts large numbers of wintering duck and Cormorant, and is used on passage by a range of waders including Avocet. The land immediately surrounding the reservoir is good for both birds of prey and steppe species, particularly Lesser Kestrel, Stone Curlew and Calandra Lark.

Timing

Throughout the year, although the main interest tends to be in spring.

Access

Immediately to the west of Toledo take the C4000 towards La Puebla de Montalbán where good views across the marshland can be obtained from the heights of Coto Alto, close to this road.

Access is restricted along the shores of the reservoir as most of this is private land. However, views can be obtained from the north shores from the area known as 'Las Barrancas'. Take a left turn onto a track at the 166 km marker post, this takes you up the cliffs with views down over the reservoir. This also passes through both cereal and uncultivated land with steppe birds such as Little Bustard, Stone Curlew and Black-bellied Sandgrouse.

Alternatively carry on a little further and take a left turn along a minor road (CM4050) to Polán which passes across the dam of the reservoir. Views can be gained here or from the jetty nearby.

Calendar

All year: Cattle Egret, Marsh Harrier, Water Rail, Purple Gallinule, Little Bustard, Stone Curlew, Black-bellied Sandgrouse, Eagle Owl, Calandra

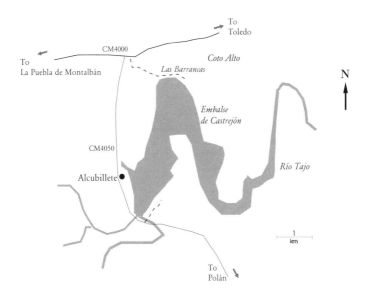

Lark, Crested Lark, Blue Rock Thrush, Cetti's Warbler, Fan-tailed Warbler, Penduline Tit, Great Grey Shrike, Raven, Spotless Starling, Spanish Sparrow.

Breeding season: Night Heron, Purple Heron, Little Egret, Montagu's Harrier, Short-toed Eagle, Booted Eagle, Lesser Kestrel, Great Spotted Cuckoo, Bee-eater, Roller, Short-toed Lark, Red-rumped Swallow, House Martin, Nightingale, Reed Warbler, Great Reed Warbler, Woodchat Shrike.

Winter: Cormorant, Grey Heron, Greylag Goose, Wigeon, Teal, Mallard, Pochard, Tufted Duck, Lesser Black-backed Gull, Short-eared Owl, Meadow Pipit.

Passage periods: Booted Eagle, Osprey, Black-winged Stilt, Avocet, Golden Plover, Lapwing, Little Stint, Sand Martin, Yellow Wagtail, Savi's Warbler, Moustached Warbler, Spotted Flycatcher.

CLM5   SIERRA DE AYLLÓN

Status: Parque Natural (87,807 ha), includes the beechwood at Hayedo de Tejera Negra.

Site description

The Sierra de Ayllón lies well south of the medieval walled city of Ayllón. This massif at the eastern end of the Sistema Central mountain range, lies in the far north of Castile-La Mancha and rises to 2262 m at its highest point, Pico Lobo, and is really an extension of the Sierra de Guadarrama. The mountains are very eroded in places and scrub is common with *Cistus* particularly abundant. There are also small woods of holm oak and beech, along with recent extensive pine plantations. The area is sparsely populated, with many abandoned small villages, and a limited amount of livestock grazing.

Spectacular waterfalls are common, especially around Valverde de los Arroyos. The area also has some of the southernmost beechwoods in Europe, the one at Tejera Negra being especially important, although there are others in the same range — the Hayedo de Puerto de la Quesera and the Hayedo de Montejo. There are also gorges, especially along the rivers Tiermes and Caracena.

Species

The Sierra de Ayllón is one of the best (dense population) areas for Golden Eagle in the whole of Spain, and they are relatively common in the sierra proper. The area immediately to the east of Ayllón is important for Griffon Vulture and Egyptian Vulture. Other birds of prey breeding in the sierra include Honey Buzzard, Short-toed Eagle, Booted Eagle, Bonelli's Eagle, Peregrine, and Eagle Owl. Capercaillie are also found in the woodland, and Golden Eagle, Red Kite and Goshawk are the most common birds of prey in the area of beech forest.

The lakes of Beleña, while they can sometimes be dry, are important because of their concentrations of wintering duck and Cranes, the latter sometimes numbering over 500.

Roe deer, wild boar, otter and Pyrenean desman are all relatively common.

Timing

Throughout the year but spring is best. The high tops can be among the coldest places in Spain during the winter, but lower slopes are relatively mild.

Access

The best part of the park is found at the junction of three regions, Castile-La Mancha, Castile-León and Madrid, although the eastern side is quite difficult to reach, and some parts have only forest tracks. Take the NI/E5 north out of Madrid, and around 65–75 km north of Madrid take a left turn to Lozoyuela or Buitrago de Lozoya, and head into the area as there a number of roads that lead to various villages in the foothills.

Other options include taking a left turn at the 104 km marker onto the N110 towards El Burgo and taking a left turn to Raiza and the SG114 to La Pinilla at the foot of the Pico del Lobo, where skiing takes place in the winter.

Cantalojas is the village nearest the Hayedo de Tejera Negra. The CM114 and CM110 roads lie immediately to the east, connecting the N110 to the north (at Ayllón) and the E90 to the south and Sigüenza. The turning west to Cantalojas is approximately 100 km north of Sigüenza.

Whether from north or south take the turning signed for Galve de Sorbe, and 6 km further west is Cantalojas. A forest road leads from

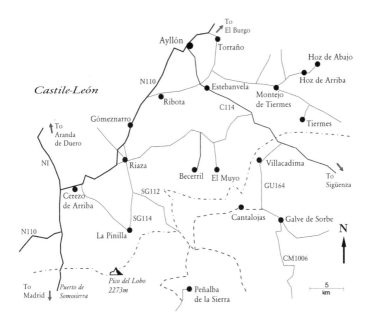

107

Cantalojas to the beechwood of Tejera Negra some 12 km from the village, which can be impassable after heavy rain and snow.

The river valleys and gorges of the River Tiermes should also be explored. Travelling north, still on the N110, drive past the turn to Ayllón and take the next main road left to Torraño, Cuevas, Liceras and Montejo de Tiermes. From here one can explore the gorges of the River Caracena, a tributary of the Duero, at Hoz de Arriba–Hoz de Abajo. Another option is 6 km east of Montejo de Tiermes, at a gorge on the River Tiermes, where at the ruins of the pre-Roman settlement of Teranica, is another Griffon Vulture colony close to the car park and easily viewed.

Calendar

All year: Red Kite, Griffon Vulture, Goshawk, Buzzard, Golden Eagle, Bonelli's Eagle, Peregrine, Eagle Owl, Long-eared Owl, Black Wheatear, Blue Rock Thrush, Crested Tit, Great Grey Shrike, Red-billed Chough, Rock Sparrow, Rock Bunting.

Breeding season: White Stork, Honey Buzzard, Black Kite, Egyptian Vulture, Short-toed Eagle, Booted Eagle, Hoopoe, Red-rumped Swallow, Water Pipit, Bluethroat, Redstart, Black-eared Wheatear, Rock Thrush, Melodious Warbler, Bonelli's Warbler, Woodchat Shrike, Ortolan Bunting.

Winter: Black Vulture, Spanish Imperial Eagle.

Passage periods: Honey Buzzard, Ring Ouzel.

CLM6   RÍO DULCE

Status: Parque Natural (6300 ha).

Site description

From its source in the Sierra Ministra, the River Dulce has cut its way through limestones rocks over the centuries to produce a series of spectacular ravines and gorges. The walls of the gorges vary considerably in height, and where the cliff and valley sides are less steep oak and juniper woodland has become established. From time to time the valley opens out into cultivated land, and occasional belts of riverine woodland on the banks. The river and its gorges, along with bankside woodland, mixed land use and vegetation cover provide a diverse habitat.

Species

The focus of interest is on the gorge areas, and Griffon Vulture, Egyptian Vulture, Bonelli's Eagle and Peregrine all breed here. However, there is also much to explore elsewhere along the river and its valley. The bankside woodlands have breeding Goshawk, Buzzard and Golden Oriole and the open valley bottoms and mosaic of cultivated areas are likely to produce birds such as Quail, Great Grey Shrike, Woodchat Shrike, Cuckoo and Black-eared Wheatear. Dipper and Grey Wagtail occur on the river itself.

Wild cat, otter and the rare Pyrennean desman are all known to occur here.

Timing
Late spring and early summer are the best times to visit.

Access
Take the NII–E90 from Madrid, past Guadalajara and after another 50 km turn left onto the CM 1101 towards Sigüenza. The gorge and river are to the right of this road and can be reached most easily by taking one of a number of right turns to one of the villages along the valley — Aragosa (after 6 km), La Cabrera or Pelegrina — where many of the tracks begin and end.

Calendar
All year: Griffon Vulture, Goshawk, Buzzard, Golden Eagle, Bonelli's Eagle, Peregrine, Red-legged Partridge, Barn Owl, Kingfisher, Green Woodpecker, Grey Wagtail, Dipper, Blue Rock Thrush, Great Grey Shrike, Red-billed Chough, Rock Sparrow, Cirl Bunting, Rock Bunting.

Breeding season: Egyptian Vulture, Quail, Cuckoo, Alpine Swift, Crag Martin, House Martin, Nightingale, Black-eared Wheatear, Melodious Warbler, Woodchat Shrike, Golden Oriole.

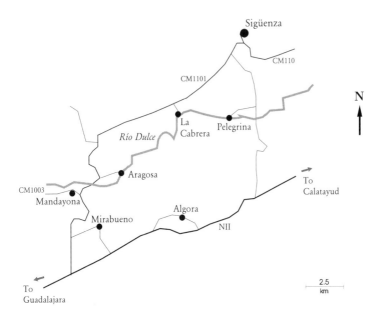

CLM7 ALTO TAJO

Status: Parque Natural (16,940 ha) and ZEPA (32,375 ha).

Site description

Unknown to many who visit Castile-La Mancha, Alto Tajo is a sparsely populated area with forestry and sheep rearing the main land use. The distance from most towns and limited access to the Upper Tajo has up until recently been the area's main protection. Today, its importance has also been recognised by its designation as a natural park, being named after the source of the Tajo, one of Spain's longest rivers. The River Tajo and its tributaries pass through a stunning landscape of gorges, pine forests and juniper woods. The deep gorges with their high cliffs, carved by the waters of the River Tajo are some 80 km long. Where the sides are less steep, then the slopes are covered by pine woods mixed in with stands of oak and some scrub maquis, but there is little true riverside woodland.

This was the ancient route of the 'gancheros' or loggers who until the 1950s rode their pine logs down the river, sometimes as far as Aranjuez. The loggers have now been replaced by canoeists, and this 'wild river of Iberia' as it is known in canoeing circles, is now famous throughout Europe for this sport.

Species

The gorges are very important for cliff-nesting birds, particularly Griffon Vulture (over 100 pairs), Egyptian Vulture, Bonelli's Eagle, and Eagle Owl and more widespread species such as Red-billed Chough, Raven, Jackdaw and Crag Martin.

Mammals include wild boar and otter.

Timing

Late spring and early summer are the best times to visit.

Access

Molina de Aragón is the largest town in the area and immediately to the north of the Alto Tajo Natural Park. Take the NII northeast from Madrid, continue well past Guadalajara, turning right after 135 km at Alcolea del Pinar along the N211 to Molina de Aragón. It is one of the most isolated areas in Spain to get to by public transport!

To the north of the natural park explore the gorge over the River Gallo at Barranco de la Virgen de la Hoz, 12 km from Molina. The monastery that gives its name to this particular gorge is perched at the summit, and there are superb views over the surrounding countryside.

Peralejos de las Truchas is a good place to start exploration of the southern part of the area. From Molina take the CM210 and CM211 south towards Terzaga and CM2106 to Peralejos de las Truchas. A track leads from here (negotiable by vehicle in the dry season) to Taravilla lagoon. The lagoon can also be reached along a surfaced road (CM210). This trail can then be followed parallel to the river Tajo to the bridge known as Puente De San Pedro along one of the most interesting and spectacular stretches of the river. The bridge can give good views along the cliffs. From here there are a number of possibilities — turn right

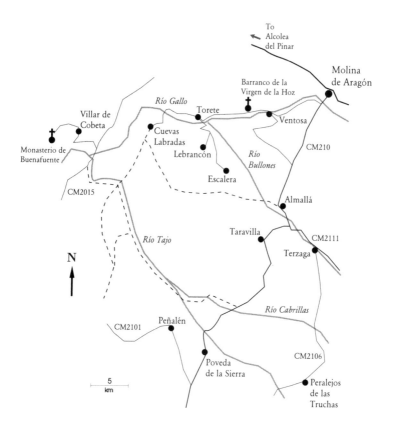

onto the CM2015 then left to Villar de Cobeta and the Monasterio de la Buenafuente del Sistal. Many minor roads and tracks lead into the area from these points.

Calendar

All year: Griffon Vulture, Goshawk, Sparrowhawk, Buzzard, Golden Eagle, Bonelli's Eagle, Peregrine, Eagle Owl, Tawny Owl, Hoopoe, Grey Wagtail, Dipper, Dartford Warbler, Chiffchaff, Crested Tit, Short-toed Treecreeper, Great Grey Shrike, Jay, Red-billed Chough, Jackdaw, Raven, Rock Sparrow, Cirl Bunting, Rock Bunting.

Breeding season: Black Kite, Booted Eagle, Short-toed Eagle, Egyptian Vulture, Bee-eater, Crag Martin, Wheatear, Reed Warbler, Subalpine Warbler, Ortolan Bunting.

CLM8 LA ALCARRIA

Status: Reserva Natural (26,400 ha).

Site description

La Alcarria rises up to around 1200 m and is crossed by the rivers Tajo and Guadiela. There are numerous limestone cliffs and dense areas of mixed oak scrub maquis and pine wood. Some of the plateau areas are now under cereal crops and there is also riverside woodland in the valley bottoms. The River Tajo has reed margins as well as poplar and elm riverine woodlands in the valley bottoms, and a number of reservoirs. The Alcocén pine woods, above the Entrepeñas reservoir, are the only remaining location of the Mediterranean pine in Guadalajara.

The rivers Tajo and Guadiela were exploited in the 1960s with the construction of a series of large dams which flooded large areas of river valley and countryside to create a number of reservoirs — the two largest being Entrepeñas and Buendia. Many other smaller reservoirs were also created further down the valley, including the one at Bolarque.

Buendia reservoir, created by the dam built on the river Guadiela just upstream of its confluence with the Tajo, flooded a large area of this part of La Alcarria. Although many rich riverine habitats were lost, fortunately thousands of wildfowl have found the wetland attractive and now winter here, and Cranes also use the site as a stopping off point on migration.

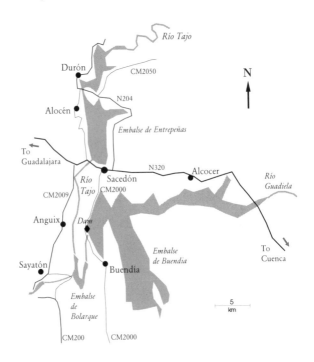

Species

The area is renowned for many breeding species of birds of prey, particularly cliff-nesting species such as Golden Eagle, Bonelli's Eagle, Peregrine and Eagle Owl, but also other passerine species such as Crag Martin and Red-billed Chough.

Buendía reservoir is an important feeding and roosting site for Cranes (used by thousands of birds on migration), and is strategically located between the Laguna de Gallocanta (AR15) in Aragón and the main wintering areas in Extremadura and Castile-La Mancha.

Timing

In spring for birds of prey and other species. November onwards for passage of Cranes and for wintering wildfowl.

Access

Take the N320 out of Guadalajara on the road towards Cuenca until you reach Sacedón which is in the heart of the area. Good views over Buendía reservoir can be obtained from the dam and the nearby Entrepeñas reservoir. The dam also gives good views over the surrounding countryside for birds of prey. Another reservoir, Bolarque, is close by and can be reached by taking the CM2009 turning off the N320, for Sayatón.

Calendar

All year: Mallard, Marsh Harrier, Buzzard, Golden Eagle, Bonelli's Eagle, Peregrine, Moorhen, Eagle Owl, Thekla Lark, Crag Martin, Blue Rock Thrush, Cetti's Warbler, Dartford Warbler, Red-billed Chough, Rock Sparrow, Serin, Linnet, Rock Bunting.

Breeding season: Little Ringed Plover, Alpine Swift, Bee-eater, Nightingale, Black-eared Wheatear, Subalpine Warbler, Orphean Warbler, Woodchat Shrike, Golden Oriole.

Winter: Cormorant, Grey Heron, Wigeon, Pintail, Pochard, Tufted Duck, Alpine Accentor, Wallcreeper.

Passage periods: Crane, Osprey, Avocet, Black-winged Stilt, Sand Martin.

CLM9 SERRANÍA DE CUENCA

Status: Reserva Nacional de Caza (25,000 ha), Reserva Nacional (89,200 ha) and Monumento Natural (*Ciudada Encantada*).

Site description

High above the headwaters of the Tajo rise the peaks of Serranía de Cuenca, a chain of mountains occupying the northeast corner of the province of Cuenca. The highest peak in the area is the Cerro de San Felipe (1839 m) near Tragacete. The hills and rocky cliffs are full of surprises with hot springs, caves, cliff-hanging villages and an 'enchanted city' the Ciudad Encantada, a strange limestone landscape where huge rocks have acquired strange mushroom-like forms through erosion.

The area is rich in orchids and butterflies and much of the ground is covered by pine forests and juniper woods, and it is one of the most important wooded limestone areas in Spain. The hills are crossed by three major rivers: the Cuervo and Escabas, which flow into the Tajo, and the Júcar, which flows into the Mediterranean and whose upper reaches go though one of the least spoiled parts of the Serranía de Cuenca.

Species

Very important for birds of prey including Egyptian Vulture, Griffon Vulture, Short-toed Eagle, Golden Eagle, Booted Eagle, Bonelli's Eagle, Peregrine and Eagle Owl.

Brown bear, mountain goat and wolf are kept in semi-freedom in the experimental game station in El Hosquillo which is one of the country's main deer-breeding stations.

Timing

Late spring and early summer. There can be heavy snowfall in the summer.

Access

Essentially this is a mountain range to the east of Madrid and can be approached from a number of directions including Guadalajara, Priego, Molina de Aragón and Cuenca. Many paths traversing the Serranía are not marked but access is relatively easy, particularly through the pine forests.

For views across the River Júcar and its gorges take the CM2105 out of Cuenca through Villalba de la Sierra, Uña and Huélamo to Tragacete. A popular but nonetheless spectacular viewpoint towering over the

100-m deep Júcar Gorge is the Ventano del Diablo about 23 km north of Cuenca. For the game station and less visited parts take a left turn at Villalba de la Sierra. In a triangle between Las Majadas, Fuertescusa and Vega del Codorno, the River Escabas crosses country of spectacular beauty, and this is one of the most productive areas for vultures and birds of prey. Numerous forest tracks cross the pine woods of these hills and they are generally in good condition except after heavy rains.

El Hosquillo, the experimental 'game station', is reached from the Las Majadas pass, although a permit is needed to visit the centre, and can be obtained in Cuenca at the Consejería de Agricultura, Calle Colón, 2 (tel: 966 28 80 22).

Other sites worth visiting, but not specifically for birds, are the *Ciudada Encantada* north of Cuenca, and to the east and south of Cuenca, geological formations known as *torcas*, natural depressions often containing water, found for example at Palancres and Cañada del Hoyo.

Calendar

All year: Griffon Vulture, Booted Eagle, Golden Eagle, Bonelli's Eagle, Peregrine, Red-legged Partridge, Great Spotted Woodpecker, Wren, Blue Rock Thrush, Crested Tit, Coal Tit, Nuthatch, Great Grey Shrike, Red-billed Chough, Jackdaw, Carrion Crow, Raven, Rock Sparrow, Serin, Citril Finch, Crossbill, Cirl Bunting.

Breeding season: Egyptian Vulture, Alpine Swift, Crag Martin, Swallow, Redstart, Wheatear, Rock Thrush, Bonelli's Warbler.

CLM10 LAS LAGUNAS DE RUIDERA

Status: Parque Natural (3780 ha).

Site description

An unusual series of interconnected lagoons that are mentioned by Cervantes in the novel *Don Quixote*. Ruidera comes from the Spanish for noise (*ruido*), and the village and lakes were named after the 'noise' made by the water running from lake to lake. They are separated from each other by natural barriers, but occasionally linked by spectacular waterfalls.

Occupying in total a surface area of some 3780 ha, the difference in altitude is some 25 m from the top lake to the bottom. The lakes comprise Cengosa, Coladilla, Cueva Morenilla, Laguna del Rey, Laguna Colgada, Laguna Batanas, Laguna Santo Amorcillo, Laguna Salvadora, Laguna Lengua (one of the deepest), Redondilla, San Pedro, Tinaja, Tomilla and Laguna Conceja. The Embalse de Peñarroya, whilst not a natural lake is sometimes regarded as part of the system. Not far from the sleepy village of Ruidera are the two largest natural lakes, the Laguna del Rey and La Gran Colgada. The protected area also includes the tributary valley of San Pedro and the cave of Montesinos.

The lagoons are permanent all year round and fed by underground water and springs. Reeds occur along the shore of many of the lakes and provide cover for duck, rails and herons. Woodland is generally absent other than the occasional poplar, holm oak and black pine, but scrub is abundant.

Species
While the main interest focuses on the lakes with Water Rail, Marsh Harrier, Red-crested Pochard, Kingfisher and passage herons and Osprey, the immediate surrounds are also rich in birdlife.

Timing
Spring, although there is some interest all year round.

Access
From Ciudad Real take the N430 via Daimiel and Manzanares to Ruidera (110 km). Most of the lagoons are to the south, although there some to the north including the Embalse de Peñarroya. To the south turn right along the AB650, while for the north turn left along the CM3115. The road from Ruidera (AB650) follows the lagoons and gradually ascends from one lake to the next. Several small lakes — Batana, Santo Amorcillo and Salvadora — are followed by La Lengua, which is very popular with fishermen. This lagoon is fed by small falls that pour into it from the next lake, Redondilla. This is turn receives water from San Pedro whose shores are partly developed with houses and plant

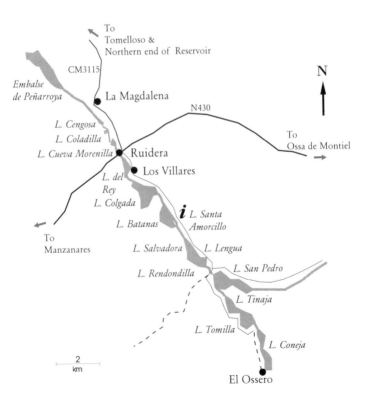

nurseries. The highest and least visited Laguna Conceja has a marshy shoreline and wooded surrounding hills, and is worth exploring.

An information centre is situated on the shores of Laguna Santas Morillo (tel: 926 528 116), and is normally open in the mornings and late afternoon onwards. There are various nature trails in the park.

Calendar

All year: Little Grebe, Great Crested Grebe, Mallard, Pochard, Red-crested Pochard, Shoveler, Marsh Harrier, Buzzard, Kestrel, Water Rail, Moorhen, Coot, Little Owl, Kingfisher, Grey Wagtail, Blackbird, Cetti's Warbler, Bearded Tit, Great Grey Shrike, Corn Bunting.

Breeding season: White Stork, Hobby, Little Ringed Plover, Lapwing, Turtle Dove, Cuckoo, Scops Owl, Bee-eater, Roller, Swallow, Nightingale, Reed Warbler, Great Reed Warbler, Melodious Warbler.

Winter: Grey Heron, Wigeon.

Passage periods: Purple Heron, Marbled Teal, Booted Eagle, Osprey, Spotted Crake, Common Tern, Whiskered Tern, Sand Martin.

CLM11   LAGUNAS DE LA MANCHA HÚMEDA

Status: Some but not all of the wetland areas are formally noted as being of importance by designation as ZEPA or Ramsar sites, and some sites are SEO ornithological reserves. ZEPA: Lagoons between Pedro Muñoz and Mota del Cuervo (600 ha). Ramsar sites: Laguna de la Vega o del Pueblo (34 ha), Lagunas de Alcazar de San Juan (240 ha), Laguna del Prado (52 ha), Laguna de Manjavacas (231 ha), SEO ornithological reserves: Laguna De Miguel Estaban.

The area is also part of a proposal for a larger reserva nacional.

Site description

In the very heart of the great plains of La Mancha is a complex of more than a 100 seasonal lagoons, temporary bodies of water of varying sizes, fed by a combination of rivers, springs and rainfall. Most have no outlet, and extreme evaporation as a result of high summer temperatures has left saline soils and muds, and many of these waterbodies become salt-encrusted early in the summer season. Most of these lagoons are very small but collectively they are a wetland of considerable stature and importance, which is recognised by their designations (see above). Another very famous site and national park, Las Tablas del Daimiel (CLM12), while geographically separated from these lagoons, also lies in 'La Mancha Húmeda', and has much in common with these lakes.

More details on individual sites are included below.

Like Las Tablas, the so-called 'La Mancha Húmeda' is but a ghost of its former self, losing much of the ornitholgical importance it had in the 1950s and 1960s. The lagoons are now isolated in a sea of cereals, vines and irrigated sunflowers in a huge area of intensive cultivation, where the continuing abstraction of large amounts of groundwater for irrigation poses a serious threat to the long-term survival of these lagoons. Some of the most important lagoons are between Pedro Muñoz and Mota del Cuervo, particularly Laguna de Manjavacas and Pedro Muñoz.

A reserve is planned for the area, the boundary of which is to include the entire length of the River Cigüela, from its source in the Sierra de Cabrejas in Cuenca to its entry into the Tablas de Daimiel. All the surviving or restorable lakes sprinkled across this vast area will be included. The administrative and information/visitor centre is planned to be located at Alcazar de San Juan.

Species

While still of immense importance, the whole area used to hold large populations of Bittern (now no longer present with few breeding sites left in Spain), Purple Heron and Collared Pratincole. Species have left or declined substantially through drainage and water abstraction.

The lagoons do still support internationally important populations of breeding Black-necked Grebe, with one of the largest breeding colonies in Europe. Other species with important numbers include Collared Pratincole, Gull-billed Tern, Shelduck, Red-crested Pochard, White-headed Duck, Marsh Harrier, Whiskered Tern, Savi's Warbler, Moustached Warbler and Bearded Tit. The list of breeding species also includes Little Bittern, Night Heron, Cattle Egret, Gadwall, Water Rail, Black-winged Stilt, Black Tern, Yellow Wagtail, Penduline Tit and Great Reed Warbler.

In winter, Grey Heron, Cormorant and various species of duck are present, while during the migration periods, particularly during the autumn passage, there are many waders on the salty and muddy shores such as those existing at Alcázar, Lillo, Manjavacas and Pedro Muñoz.

In some years migration can be especially good in late March and April with frequent records of 'rarities'. Lagoons that still hold water in summer, such as (usually) Manjavacas, can attract important concentrations of Black-necked Grebes and Gull-billed Terns in July.

Penduline Tit

118

The surrounding agricultural land is also important with Great Bustard, Little Bustard, Stone Curlew and many Pin-tailed Sandgrouse. The western part of this area is one of the best areas in Castile-La Mancha for Great Bustard.

Timing

Between late June and October there is little or no water, but outside these periods the area can be outstanding. The area can be very cold in winter and in spring there can be heat haze when the temperatures begin to pick up.

Access

The general area where most of the lagoons are located is in and around the town of Alcázar de San Juan, around 20 km east of the main NIV road between Madrid and Valdepeñas.

Many of the lagoons described in this section have hides, but a good proportion may be locked. They can be used, however, by prior arrangement. Contact the visitor centre at Cabañeros (CLM13).

Lagunas de Longar y Altillo From Tembleque on the NVI, take the C3000 to Lillo (17 km). In Lillo take the minor road, the CM3001 (12 km) to Villacañas and after 1.5 km turn right onto a track to the lagoon. The smaller seasonal lagoon of Altillo is to the left of the minor track almost opposite this turning. It is possible to get good views from the track and the area can be walked in a relatively short time.

These seasonal lagoons occur in a steppe habitat to the south of the village of Lillo, although Laguna de Longar now receives waste water from the village, and as a consequence it contains water all year round. The margins of the lake have a well-developed salt-influenced vegetation, and some areas also show signs of enrichment from the waste waters. As the site is near the village there is a certain amount of disturbance.

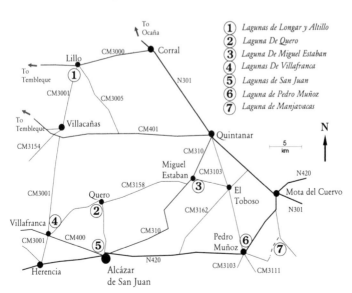

1. Lagunas de Longar y Altillo
2. Laguna De Quero
3. Laguna De Miguel Esteban
4. Lagunas De Villafranca
5. Lagunas de San Juan
6. Laguna de Pedro Muñoz
7. Laguna de Manjavacas

Steppe and scrub occur around the lakes, and the vegetation is dominated by albardine *Lygeum spartum*. Although the main focus of interest is the lakes, the steppe area can produce many species typical of this habitat, and including some species that have a restricted distribution, notably Great Bustard and Dupont's Lark.

Laguna De Quero Take the NIV from Madrid to Madridejos, turn left along the CM400 to Villafranca de los Caballeros (16 km). At Villafranca, take the minor road CM3158) to Quero (14 km), the site of the lagoon. The lagoon is visible from the roadside.

A medium-sized brackish lagoon with water levels that vary considerably, with little marsh vegetation. The lagoon has a number of small islands and associated ditches.

Laguna De Miguel Estaban Take the NIV form Madrid and turn left at Ocaña on the N301 to Quintanar de la Orden, then take the CM 310 road to Miguel Estaban. Take a left here (CM3162) towards El Toboso and after a couple of kilometres the lagoon is on the right, away from the road near a church, where a track leads to the shore. It is an SEO reserve.

A natural lagoon which like other lagoons now receives waste water from the local village, this time the village of Miguel Estaban. Next to these lagoons is an area which remains flooded in winter.

The lagoon has many of the key species of the area including Black-necked Grebe, Avocet, Black-winged Stilt, Whiskered Tern and Gull-billed Tern, and is also important for White-headed Duck. Steppe birds such as sandgrouse, Little Bustard and Short-toed Lark occur on the adjoining land with Yellow Wagtail and waders on the wetter ground.

Lagunas De Villafranca Take the NIV from Madrid to Madridejos, and turn right onto the CM400 to Villafranca de los Caballeros (16 km), and then northeast on the CM3158 minor road to Quero. Outside Quero towards Miguel Estaban a left turn for the lagoons is signed after 2–3 km.

Two lakes, Laguna Grande and Laguna Chico are fed by a river, and therefore water levels here are more constant than at many of the other lakes in La Mancha Húmeda. As a consequence they have a much more well-developed fringe of emergent vegetation. Tracks lead to and surround the wetlands and the area suffers from disturbance and development. Typical key species include Gull-billed Tern, but the area is favoured by other species that prefer cover, including Purple Heron. Surrounding land has Little Bustard and Pin-tailed Sandgrouse. There is a hide at Laguna Grande.

Lagunas de San Juan Take the NIV from Madrid to Madridejos, then a left on the CM400 towards Alcázar de San Juan. A track to the left off this road, 4–5 km before you reach Alcázar de San Juan and near two white buildings, leads to two lagoons.

There are two hides at the larger and shallower Camino de Villafranca lagoon. The second lagoon, Las Yeguas, is also saline, shallow and subject to dramatic changes in water level. The shores of Las Yeguas are muddy and devoid of marsh vegetation, and it is linked to the adjoining lagoon by a channel. The water can be heavily polluted, but despite this, the lagoon does have some typical species such as Black-necked Grebe, Black-winged Stilt, Avocet and Gull-billed Tern, and can also be good for waders and other species on passage such as Black Tern.

Laguna de Pedro Muñoz Take the NIV from Madrid to Ocaña, then onto the N301 to Quintanar de la Orden. Then take a left along the minor road (CM3103) to El Toboso and Pedro Muñoz . The lagoon is located next to Pedro Muñoz on the road leading to El Toboso. This site is about 25 km east of Alcazar on the N420.

This is one of the most important lagoons in the complex of wetland sites and like others receives waste water from a village, making the lagoon at the very least semi-permanent. There is a hide which is open to the public and a track that follows the lagoon's shoreline. There are some problems with disturbance given its proximity to the village, and substantial rubbish dumping has reduced the size of the lagoon to under 40 ha, but a restoration programme is underway.

Key species include Black-necked Grebe, Red-crested Pochard, White-headed Duck and Whiskered Tern. Very good for passage migrants notably Ferruginous Duck, Osprey and occasionally Red-throated Pipit.

Laguna de Manjavacas Take the NIV from Madrid to Ocaña, then the N301 to Mota del Cuervo. Take the N420 towards Alcázar de San Juan, and just outside the centre of Mota, turn left onto the minor road for Las Mesas. The lagoon is near the chapel of Manjavacas, around 3 km along this road. Take the track from the chapel to the lagoon, although there are many other tracks to other parts of the lagoon.

Another very important and large lagoon of around 200 ha but subject to considerable fluctuations in water levels. It does, however, have well-developed marsh vegetation and areas of shallow water that are attractive to waders on passage. It has most of the key species including Black-necked Grebe, Red-crested Pochard, Whiskered Tern and Gull-billed Tern. Good for passage waders with Temminck's Stint, Ruff and Spotted Redshank.

Calendar

All year: Black-necked Grebe, Little Grebe, Great Crested Grebe, Little Egret, Cattle Egret, Shelduck, Gadwall, Mallard, Red-crested Pochard, White-headed Duck, Marsh Harrier, Water Rail, Coot, Kentish Plover, Little Bustard, Great Bustard, Stone Curlew, Black-bellied Sandgrouse, Pin-tailed Sandgrouse, Black-headed Gull, Little Owl, Hoopoe, Dupont's Lark, Calandra Lark, Thekla Lark, Bearded Tit, Cetti's Warbler, Rock Sparrow, Corn Bunting.

Breeding season: Night Heron, Little Bittern, Purple Heron, Teal, Shoveler, Pochard, Black Kite, Spotted Crake, Black-winged Stilt, Avocet, Little Ringed Plover, Lapwing, Redshank, Common Sandpiper, Collared Pratincole, Gull-billed Tern, Little Tern, Whiskered Tern, Black Tern, Bee-eater, Great Spotted Cuckoo, Short-toed Lark, Tawny Pipit, Yellow Wagtail, Black-eared Wheatear, Savi's Warbler, Fan-tailed Warbler, Reed Warbler, Great Reed Warbler.

Winter: Wigeon, Teal, Shoveler, Pochard, Ferruginous Duck, Hen Harrier, Merlin, Peregrine, Common Sandpiper, Curlew, Lesser Short-toed Lark, Penduline Tit.

Passage periods: Black-necked Grebe, Pintail, Garganey, Osprey, Crane, Ringed Plover, Grey Plover, Knot, Little Stint, Dunlin, Ruff, Temminck's Stint, Black-tailed Godwit, Spotted Redshank, Redshank, Greenshank, Whiskered Tern, Black Tern, Red-throated Pipit.

CLM12   LAS TABLAS DE DAIMIEL

Status: Parque Nacional, Biosphere Reserve, Ramsar site and ZEPA (1928 ha).

Site description

In the province of Ciudada Real is the national park of Las Tablas de Daimiel, the smallest of all Spain's national parks and situated at the heart of what is known as La Mancha Húmeda or 'wet' La Mancha — an extensive area peppered with inland lagoons, flooded areas and crossed by Castilian rivers. Las Tablas is only one of a small number of wetlands found in this zone, others occur, and some of best of these areas are described elsewhere (CLM11).

Las Tablas became a national park in 1973 and is located at the confluence of the rivers Guadiana and Cigüela. In La Mancha, *tablas* is the word used for the flooded areas that occur along stretches of some rivers and which can remain waterlogged for lengthy periods of time during the year. Las Tablas de Daimiel is primarily fed by the brackish water from the Cigüela river and freshwater from the Guadiana. Unfortunately, and rather sadly, just under 2000 ha only of the 30,000 ha of wetland that formerly occurred along these two rivers now remains and this is protected by the park's status. Unregulated and substantial irrigation through the pumping of ground water over many years has led to the loss of huge areas and much of the former wetland is now dry and farmed.

Remedial measures have since been put into practice to try to save Las Tablas, and additional water is now provided for the park by diverting water from the River Tagus through a wetland restoration plan. The site, however, is still of considerable importance as is obvious from the many designations bestowed on it.

The area is a maze of islands, channels, loops and flooded land, and has been called on many occasions 'the Venice of La Mancha'.

Species

In spite of the long history of irrigation and the huge reduction in the extent of the wetland in the heart of Spain, Tablas de Daimiel is still a

Red-crested Pochard and Teal

122

very important inland wetland, and one of the most important in Spain, with plenty of interest all year round. It is especially rich in breeding herons with Little Bittern, Night Heron, Purple Heron and Little Egret, small numbers of Red-crested Pochard and a large variety of other key wetland species such as Bearded and Penduline Tits, and Great Reed and Savi's Warblers. In the winter it is home to thousands of wildfowl (up to 50,000) including Wigeon, Pochard and Shoveler and, most importantly, Red-crested Pochard whose numbers are normally somewhere between 500 and 1,000.

Set amongst cereals and in an arid landscape, a remnant steppe bird population hangs on with Little Bustard, Stone Curlew, Pin-tailed Sandgrouse, Montagu's Harrier and Lesser Kestrel.

Timing

There is much to see at Las Tablas at any time of year, with its considerable breeding, wintering and passage interest. However, the summer months are the least rewarding because of the intense drought, when there is little if any open water. It can also be very cold in the winter and weekends can be busy.

Access

The national park is around 140 km from Madrid and about 40 km from Ciudad Real. From Ciudad Real take the N430 to Daimiel (28 km). The park and its information centre are signed from the road, and there is no need to go into Daimiel. The park is around another 11 km from the main road, and the visitor centre (tel: 926 85 20 58) is at the entrance to the park. The park and centre are normally closed on Mondays.

Paths take you to most of the interesting parts of Las Tablas, including the 'Itenario Isla del Pan' and the 'Itenario de la Torre'. A number of hides, including multi-storey, are situated throughout the reserve.

Calendar

All year: Black-necked Grebe, Gadwall, Mallard, Red-crested Pochard, Marsh Harrier, Coot, Moorhen, Little Bustard, Stone Curlew, Pin-tailed

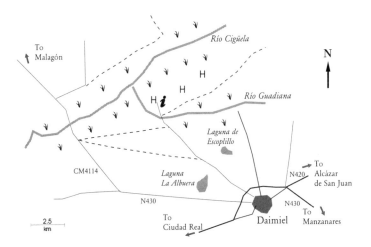

Sandgrouse, Hoopoe, Stonechat, Cetti's Warbler, Fan-tailed Warbler, Bearded Tit, Penduline Tit.

Breeding season: Little Bittern, Night Heron, Purple Heron, Little Egret, White Stork, Garganey, Black Kite, Montagu's Harrier, Short-toed Eagle, Booted Eagle, Lesser Kestrel, Hobby, Water Rail, Black-winged Stilt, Collared Pratincole, Whiskered Tern, Great Spotted Cuckoo, Bee-eater, Roller, Red-rumped Swallow, Savi's Warbler, Reed Warbler, Great Reed Warbler, Melodious Warbler.

Winter: Cormorant, Grey Heron, Pintail, Wigeon, Teal, Shoveler, Spanish Imperial Eagle, Merlin, Hen Harrier, Lapwing, Short-eared Owl, Bluethroat, Reed Bunting.

Passage periods: Ferruginous Duck, Garganey, Black-tailed Godwit, Snipe, Gull-billed Tern, Whiskered Tern, Black Tern, Wryneck, Sand Martin, Ortolan Bunting.

CLM13   CABAÑEROS

Status: Parque Natural (40,000 ha) and ZEPA (25,615 ha).

Site description

Cabañeros belongs to the area known as the Montes de Toledo, *montes* being huge estates used for extensive livestock rearing, forestry and hunting. Situated in the northwest part of Ciudad Real, the rivers Bullaque and Estena mark the eastern and western boundaries of the site, the Macizo de Rocigalgo the north, and the Sierra de Miraflores the south. Cabañeros was until recent times the largest estate in Europe, and was known by hunters as 'The Cathedral' because of the high concentrations of red deer.

The Ministry of Defence originally had plans to use the area for an army firing and bombing range, but following a public outcry and a campaign of opposition Cabañeros was declared a natural park in 1988.

Much of the area is densely vegetated and virtually unihabitated with extensive *dehesa* of evergreen oak, dense areas of *Cistus* scrub, strawberry tree, mastic tree, turpentine tree, honeysuckle, myrtle and olive. Cabañeros is the best and largest example of this Mediterranean-type forest, and the Sierra de Chrito, Valdefuentes and the Cordal del Rostro areas are covered in this thick Mediterranean woodland. Between these hills is the large plain or Rana de Cabañeros, which is dotted with very old evergreen oaks, and where each evening large concentrations of deer gather to graze. Because of its dimensions and the richness of its fauna, Cabañeros is frequently called the 'Spanish Serengeti'.

The banks of the River Bullanque have riverine woodland, a rare habitat in Europe, and the Torre Abraham reservoir holds reasonable numbers of wildfowl at certain times of year.

Species

Around 200 species of bird have been recorded, and Cabañeros also boasts the second largest population of Black Vultures in Spain, with over 120 pairs. In addition it has a diverse and important population of birds of prey, notably Spanish Imperial Eagle, Short-toed Eagle, Golden Eagle and Booted Eagle. Black Stork also breeds in the park.

A population of Great Bustard remains on the *rana* or central plain, along with Little Bustard, Stone Curlew and Black-eared Wheatear.

Its red deer are famous, but there are also roe deer, wild boar, *meloncillo* or European mongoose and lynx.

Timing

Imperial Eagle are very noticeable when they display, during February and March. Late April to June is the best time for most of the breeding birds, while winter is good for Cranes and the resident raptors.

Access

The best starting point for a visit to the park is from the visitor centre at Pueblo Nuevo del Bullaque. From Ciudad Real take the CM412/403 northwest towards Porzuna and then Pueblo Nuevo del Bullaque, where the visitor centre is situated. Alternatively from the north and Toledo take the CM401 until it joins the CM403 where you turn left to Las Ventas con Peña Aguilera and further south to El Bullaque.

The park entrance itself is halfway along a local road in between the information centre and Santa Quiteria. Guided walks can be booked by prior arrangement: normally two trips are offered which cover the best areas of the park with guaranteed sightings of most key species. For more information contact Cabañeros National Park, Pueblo Nuevo del Bullaque 13194, Ciudad Real (tel: 926 78 32 97).

Independent birdwatching is also possible along the roads within the park, for example the road from Navas de Estrena to Retuerta del Bul-

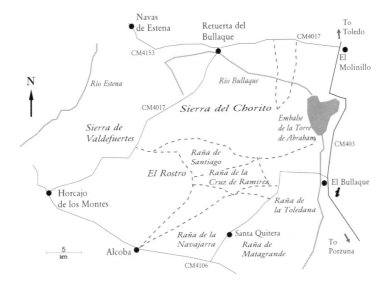

laque, the old sheep trail used for transhumance, and the CM4017 from Retuerta del Bullaque to Cabañeros and Horcajo de los Montes. The roads around the margins of the park can also be very good for birds.

Calendar

All year: Black Stork, Black-shouldered Kite, Red Kite, Griffon Vulture, Black Vulture, Goshawk, Sparrowhawk, Buzzard, Golden Eagle, Spanish Imperial Eagle, Kestrel, Little Bustard, Great Bustard, Eagle Owl, Long-eared Owl, Hoopoe, Woodlark, Blue Rock Thrush, Dartford Warbler, Sardinian Warbler, Firecrest, Crested Tit, Great Grey Shrike, Azure-winged Magpie, Cirl Bunting.

Breeding season: White Stork, Honey Buzzard, Black Kite, Egyptian Vulture, Montagu's Harrier, Short-toed Eagle, Booted Eagle, Hobby, Great Spotted Cuckoo, Scops Owl, Bee-eater, Roller, Black-eared Wheatear, Melodious Warbler, Spectacled Warbler, Bonelli's Warbler, Golden Oriole, Woodchat Shrike.

Winter: Great Crested Grebe, Cormorant, Grey Heron, Shoveler, Ferruginous Duck, Coot, Hen Harrier, Peregrine, Merlin, Crane.

CLM14   SIERRA DE LA CANALIZAS

Status: ZEPA (18,000 ha).

Site description

This area occupies a wide *dehesa* plain to the south of the Montes de Toledo and immediately north of the Valle de Alcudia, with small isolated hill ranges rising to just short of 900 m. Mediterranean-type scrub oak woodland covers the hills, with scattered oak on the *dehesas*, and extensive grasslands on the plain. The area is sparsely populated, with sheep and cattle grazing.

Tree Sparrow

Species

The site now has one of the largest concentrations of Black Vulture in Spain (the population has increased to around 65 pairs). It is also important for Spanish Imperial Eagle and Golden Eagle (a few pairs breed at this site), Black Stork and White Stork. An excellent area for *dehesa* and open country-species, with Black Kite, Quail, Turtle Dove, Red-rumped Swallow, Azure-winged Magpie and Tree Sparrow.

Mongoose and wild boar occur, and as the sierra is sparsely populated, the area still holds a few lynx.

Timing

Late winter and early spring for displaying eagles, but spring for most of the other species.

Access

Take the N430 west out of Ciudad Real through Piedrabuena and Luciana which is at the northeast corner of the Sierra de Canalizos. The area is delimited by the roads that link Luciana to Puebla de Don Rodrigo (on the N430 — the north boundary) and from Pedro de Don Rodrigo to Agudo (CM4103) and Almadén (N502), marking the western boundary, and from Almadén to Abenójar (C424) and back to Luciana, marking the south and eastern boundaries.

Small estate roads and tracks penetrate the area from these encircling roads, with Saeruela at the centre of the area, and excellent views of the area can be obtained from a variety of these roads.

Calendar

All year: Black Stork, Black-shouldered Kite, Red Kite, Black Vulture, Buzzard, Spanish Imperial Eagle, Golden Eagle, Bonelli's Eagle, Red-legged Partridge, Stock Dove, Eagle Owl, Little Owl, Little Bustard, Black-bellied Sandgrouse, Green Woodpecker, Hoopoe, Crested Lark, Woodlark, Skylark, Azure-winged Magpie, Goldfinch, Tree Sparrow, Serin, Corn Bunting,

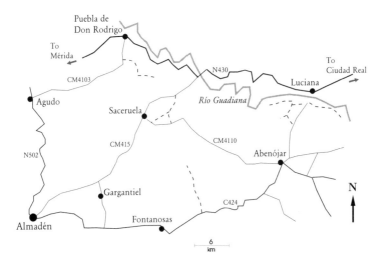

Breeding season: White Stork, Black Kite, Egyptian Vulture, Short-toed Eagle, Lesser Kestrel, Quail, Turtle Dove, Great Spotted Cuckoo, Bee-eater, Short-toed Lark, Red-rumped Swallow, Spotted Flycatcher, Woodchat Shrike.

CLM15 VALLE Y SIERRA DE ALCUDIA

Status: ZEPA (26,000 ha).

Site description

This is a broad valley occupied by sheep pasture and holm oak *dehesa* in a large depression and surrounded by hills to the north of the main mountain ranges of the Sierra Madrona. The area is a traditional wintering ground for sheep flocks and is mostly treeless apart from those areas of *dehesa*. There are many abandoned lead mines and the area is sparsely populated.

Species

The valley has over ten pairs of Montagu's Harrier, 100 pairs of Little Bustard, over 100 pairs of Stone Curlew, and with over 50 pairs each of Black-bellied Sandgrouse, Pin-tailed Sandgrouse and White Stork, although these population figures now need reassessing.

Black Stork, Black-shouldered Kite, Spanish Imperial Eagle, Black Vulture and Golden Eagle are all possible, and all of which breed in the adjoining countryside and mountains.

The area supports winter flocks, not just of sheep, but also of Little Bustard, Crane and Golden Plover.

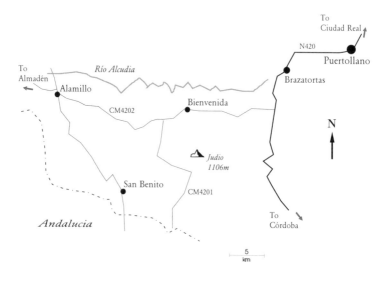

128

Timing

Spring and winter.

Access

Take the N420 south from Ciudad Real to Puertollano, and then travel for a further 30 km south turning right off the N420 onto a minor road (CM4202) to Bienvenida and Alamillo. This road can be particularly good for scanning the steppe and takes you west along the valley into the broad plains which have good populations of Little Bustard and Stone Curlew. There are many abandoned mines in the valley, some of which are now in ruins but are used by a number of species including White Stork, Kestrel, and Red-billed Chough as nesting sites.

Calendar

All year: Black-shouldered Kite, Red Kite, Goshawk, Eagle Owl, Little Bustard, Stone Curlew, Great Spotted Woodpecker, Calandra Lark, Thekla Lark, Woodlark, Black Wheatear, Mistle Thrush, Dartford Warbler, Sardinian Warbler, Blackcap, Great Grey Shrike, Azure-winged Magpie, Hawfinch.

Breeding season: White Stork, Black Stork, Short-toed Eagle, Booted Eagle, Red-necked Nightjar, Bee-eater, Roller, Short-toed Lark, Red-rumped Swallow, Redstart, Melodious Warbler, Subalpine Warbler, Orphean Warbler, Golden Oriole, Woodchat Shrike.

Winter: Merlin, Crane, Golden Plover, Lapwing, Redwing, Fieldfare.

CLM16   SIERRA MADRONA

Status: Planned Reserva Natural (217,000 ha).

Site description

The Sierra Madrona is an extensive mountain range, some 75 km long, that forms part of the Sierra Morena system, and is the mountain chain that separates the southern part of Castile-La Mancha from Andalucia. The site includes foothill areas to the south, with steep river gorges and cliffs. A large natural reserve is planned which will cover an area of more than 217,000 ha.

The Sierra Madrona still supports important extensive Mediterranean ecosystems, especially ancient oak woodland, in which are found the last remaining wolves (around 30) in Castile-La Mancha, and which roam this part of the mountains, but also travel extensively into the neighbouring provinces of Jaén and Córdoba. It is also one of the most important areas for the Spanish lynx.

The woodland is particularly tall and dense in some places on the northern slopes, and patches of low mountain vegetation of strawberry tree and heather also occur as well as areas of scrub and some pine plantations.

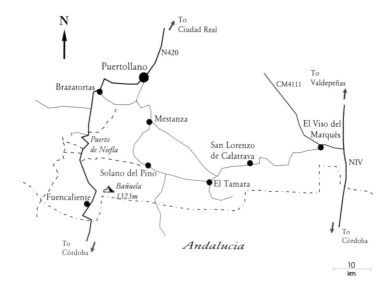

Species

A very important area for birds of prey with Black Vulture, Spanish Imperial Eagle, a large population of both Golden Eagle and Bonelli's Eagle — both into double figures — with Eagle Owl in the rocky gorges. Small numbers of Black Stork also breed.

Timing

Early spring for displaying birds of prey; spring and early summer for other interesting species.

Access

Take the N420 south out of Ciudad Real through Puertollano and carrying on towards Fuencaliente and the border. Various forest tracks and minor roads penetrate the woods either side of Puerto de Niefla. There are cave paintings at Peña Escrita near Fuencaliente. A good way to get to know the area is to take the picturesque road from Puertollano to Andújar, through Mestanza and Solano del Pino, San Lorenzo de Calatrava and El Viso del Marqués.

Calendar

All year: Griffon Vulture, Black Vulture, Goshawk, Spanish Imperial Eagle, Golden Eagle, Bonelli's Eagle, Peregrine, Eagle Owl, Crag Martin, Blue Rock Thrush, Nuthatch, Jay, Red-billed Chough, Raven, Rock Sparrow, Rock Bunting.

Breeding season: Black Stork, Egytpian Vulture, Short-toed Eagle, Booted Eagle, Redstart, Bonelli's Warbler.

OTHER SITES WORTH VISITING

CLM17 Montes de Toledo
A range of mountains to the southwest of Toledo, in which Cabañeros Natural Park (CLM13) is found. The highest peak is 1447 m, and this is a huge area, part of which is a proposed 'natural area' of some 250,000 ha. Stonghold of the lynx in Spain. Excellent for birds of prey including Spanish Imperial Eagle, Golden Eagle and Black Vulture; also Black Stork. From Toledo take the CM401 or the N401 south.

CLM18 Laguna de Pozuela de Calatrava
Small shallow seasonal lagoon with three hides. Has Black-winged Stilt, Avocet and Kentish Plover and is one the few sites with breeding Little Tern. Isolated from the main concentration of lakes in La Mancha Húmeda (CLM11) and near Ciudad Real. From Ciudad Real, take the CM412 towards Valdepeñas until you reach the town of Pozuela de Calatrava (12 km). A track leads left beside a garage in the town.

CLM19 La Guardia–Tembleque–Romeral
Good example of steppe with Great Bustard, Little Bustard and Pin-tailed Sandgrouse. A small marshy area at the Dehesa de Monreal alongside the River Cedrón has breeding Gull-billed Tern and Marsh Harrier with wintering Red-crested Pochard. Area is around 20 km south of Aranjuez in a triangle to the east of the NIV.

CLM20 Embalse de Almoguera
A small long thin reservoir situated to the south of the village of Almoguera. Extensive reedbed. Breeding Red-crested Pochard, Purple Heron and Osprey and Cranes on passage. From Guadalajara take the N320 towards Sacedón, and after 18 km turn left onto the CM2006 to Pastrama then the CM200/CM219 south towards the village of Almoguera. The reservoir is off to the left before you reach the village.

CLM21 Paramera de Maranchón, Embid y Molina
A highland 'páramo' or plateau between 1000–1200m (very cold in the winter). Located in the far northeast of the region between Guadalajara and Zaragoza (in Aragón). The N211 forms its southern boundary. Mainly grassland, cereal cultivation and some scrub. Important for its steppe bird community including Montagu's Harrier, Great Bustard, Stone Curlew, Black-bellied Sandgrouse and Dupont's Lark. Take the C211 left at Alcolea del Pinar (NII) for 22 km to Maranchón, the plateau is between Maranchón and Mazarete. Similar areas also occur around Embid and Molina further to the east.

CLM22 Laguna de El Hito
A seasonal lagoon situated near the village of Montalbo just south of the NIII, around 115 km southeast of Madrid. Important site for Cranes with hundreds using the site on passage in late autumn and early spring. The general area around is also very important for Great Bustard.

CLM23 Llanos de Valdelobos
Upland plateau steppe area between the towns of Villarobledo and San Clemente, with Great Bustard, Little Bustard, Stone Curlew and sandgrouse. North of Albacete (71 km) on either side of the N301.

CLM24 Valeria, Guadazaón and Moya

These three separate areas in the province of Cuenca comprise plateau land around 1000 m, totalling some 6000 ha and particularly important for Dupont's Lark. All three areas are devoted to cereals, although there are areas of genista, lavender and thyme scrub. The first area is south of Cuenca along the CM2100 to Valeria, the second around 40 km to the east of Cuenca, south of the N420 around Carboneras de Guadazaón, and the third in the far east on the borders with Aragón and Valencia. Take the N420 east from Cuenca to Torrebaja (113 km), then south on the CM9221 towards Santa Cruz de Moya.

CLM25 Río de Cabriel

Gorges found upstream of the Embalse de Contreras, but also other river habitats with meanders, and surounding pine woods. Excellent for Egyptian Vulture and other birds of prey such as Golden Eagle and Eagle Owl. East of Cuenca along the N420 and left at Carboneras de Guadazaón along the CM2109 towards the reservoir and headwaters.

CLM26 Llanos de Montiel

Succession of stony plains dotted with evergreen oak and juniper. Steppe birds including Montagu's Harrier, Lesser Kestrel, Great Bustard, Stone Curlew and Dupont's Lark. Around 50 km east of Valdepeñas south of the C412. Turn right at Villahermosa.

CLM27 Sierra de Alcázar y Alto Segura

Landscape of impressive gorges and steep-sided mountains with some of the highest peaks in Castile-La Mancha. Extensive forests and riverside woodland with Griffon Vulture, Egyptian Vulture, Goshawk, Short-toed Eagle and Bonelli's Eagle. Also otter and lynx. Take the N322 southwest of Albacete to Alcaraz and then the CM3216 into the Sierra towards and beyond Tortas.

CLM28 Hoces del Río Mundo y Río Segura

Limestones gorges along these two rivers with pine woods and scrub. Golden Eagle, Bonelli's Eagle, Eagle Owl and Red-billed Chough. Around 60 km south of Albacete along the C3203 towards Ayna.

CLM29 Salinas de Cordovilla

Important saline habitat south of the main body of lagoons and south of Albacete. Includes the small lake Laguna de Alboraj with concentrations of wintering and passage birds. Area immediately to the east of Tobarra, 51 km south of Albacete off the N301.

CLM30 Llanos de Chincilla–Almansa

Upland plain with extensive cereal and vine cultivation. Great Bustard, Little Bustard, Stone Curlew and Black-bellied Sandgrouse. Also includes a number of seasonal lagoons (Laguna de Pétrola and Laguna Salobralejo) with Little Bittern, Red-crested Pochard, Kentish Plover and Whiskered Tern, and good for passage. Extensive area that extends east of Albacete to Almansa along the N430 and to the borders with Valencia and Murcia. For Pétrola lagoon take the CM3211 right off the N430 to the village of the same name. For Salobralejo continue a little further on the N430 and turn left on the CM3209 signed for Higueruela. The lagoon is on the right after the railway line.

CASTILE-LEÓN

A huge area, so huge that it is the largest single region in the European Union. Castile-León is full of history from the Christian reconquest, with a landscape that is dominated by castles, and romantic legends that spawned the Christian hero El Cid. There is much to occupy the bird-watcher here, along with plenty of distractions in the architecture, bars, impressive squares and history of the region's towns and cities — Ávila, Segovia, Salamanca, Palencia and León itself.

The great plain — a flat, semi-arid table top, 700–1000 m above sea level and known as the Meseta Norte — is vast, with cereals as far as the eye can see, broken up by vines, extensive sheep rearing, and now more commonly encountered, a whole series of irrigated crops such as sunflowers. Covering over two-thirds of the region and still extremely important for its steppe birds, the north Meseta is the one of the best areas to see Great Bustard in Spain, with one of the most rewarding sites being Lagunas de Villafáfila (CAS2). Here, it is also possible to see Little Bustard, Black-bellied Sandgrouse, Stone Curlew, Montagu's Harrier, Lesser Kestrel, Short-toed Lark, Calandra Lark, Tawny Pipit and Spectacled Warbler. You would be lucky to see Pin-tailed Sandgrouse here, but it is found further southeast, for example in the Estepas de Madrigal (CAS13), along with the other species already mentioned. Dupont's Lark does not occur in the west of Castile-León, but does occur further east on the Meseta, in the steppe areas above some of the gorges such as Hoces del Río Duratón (CAS8).

Wetlands are at a premium in Castile-León, and more so these days given the continuing loss of wetland areas through extensive water abstraction for irrigation. There are some seasonal lagoons still on the plains, and good examples are found at Laguna de Villafáfila (CAS2) which is an important site for wintering and roosting wildfowl and a breeding site for Black Tern and the Shelduck (the latter a very rare breeding species in Spain). The nearby reservoir, the Embalse de Ricobaya, contributes substantially to the interest of the area as this is the only regular wintering site for Bean Goose in Spain. Other steppe wetlands are few and far between, but La Nava de Fuentes (CAS14) deserves special mention. This is the former site of a substantial wetland and is now part of a restoration programme which is already reaping rewards by attracting many passage waders, and serving as a post-breeding site for White Stork.

Riverine habitats are the major other wetland of note, and the best examples occur on the banks of the River Duero with important Night Heron colonies at Río Carrión y Canal de Castilla (CAS15) and Riberas de Castronuño (CAS3), which also has good numbers of Grey Heron, the site being its centre of population here in this region. Duero Valley is also a core area for Penduline Tit, and Cattle Egret has recently colonised the valley.

To the south of Zamora and between Salamanca and the western border the predominant landscape is *dehesa,* with extensively grazed land mixed with scattered holm oaks — an extension of the habitat found in neighbouring Extremadura. Here are White Stork, Black Stork,

Black-shouldered Kite, Black Kite, Great Spotted Cuckoo, Roller, Azure-winged Mapie, Red-rumped Swallow and Spanish Sparrow. All of these species can be found at the Arribes del Duero site (CAS4) but this landscape is widespread and extends well beyond the river valley.

The Río Duero (Arribes del Duero — CAS4) that forms the western boundary with Portugal is quite spectacular. A breathtaking landscape of high river cliffs towering over the river with Alpine Swift, Red-billed Chough, Golden Eagle, Bonelli's Eagle, Crag Martin, Peregrine and both Griffon and Egyptian Vulture all vying for places on the rock faces. Indeed Castile-León is well represented by its gorges, and in addition to the cliffs above the Duero, other good examples include Cañón del Rio Lobos (CAS10), Hoces del Río Duratón (CAS8), Hoces del Ría Riaza (CAS9) and Hoces del Ría Ebro y Rudrón (CAS17). These have similar species to the above but can also have Eagle Owl, Blue Rock Thrush, Rock Sparrow and Rock Dove.

The north Meseta plain and basically the whole of Castile-León is surrounded by mountain chains apart from at its western boundary. To the north is the Cordillera Cantabrica, with a very important high mountain bird community comprising Capercaillie, Black Woodpecker, Middle Spotted Woodpecker, Wallcreeper, Alpine Chough, Ring Ouzel and Snow Finch — also well represented in the adjoining regions of Asturias and Cantabria, but which spill over into Castile-León — and is most famous for the Picos de Europa (AS6). Less well known but also of note is Fuente Carrionas (CAS16) which has all the species above plus brown bear and wolf. The Sistemo Ibérico mountain range to the east on the borders with La Rioja, misses out on most of the high mountain species, but the two mountain blocks do share Grey Partridge, Woodcock, Hen Harrier, Yellowhammer, Treecreeper and Bullfinch. These latter species have a mainly northern distribution and are not found in central or southern Spain; Sierra de Urbion (CAS11) is a good site for these species, for example.

To the south is the Sistema Central — dominated by the high mountain ranges of the Sierra de Gredos (CAS6) and the Sierra de Guadarrama which rises to 2592 m at the Pico Almanzo. What it lacks in the presence of certain northern high-altitude species, it makes up for in its scenery and the presence of Spanish Imperial Eagle and Black Vulture (the Sistemo Central has one of the largest concentrations of Black Vulture in Spain with up to 130 pairs). You are also likely to come across Alpine Accentor and Citril Finch here, and this is one of the easiest sites at which to see Bluethroat in Spain, occurring in the summer above 1600 m in scrub heath habitats.

Finally, there are a number of additional species that deserve mention, including some that do not fit neatly into habitat parcels and are more widespread. Castile-León is important for a number of these, being a stronghold for both Red and Black Kite, along with owls. Eagle Owl is particularly numerous along the Duero Valley, while Long-eared Owl is relatively abundant in the eastern part of the region. An owl not normally encountered on a trip to Spain is Short-eared Owl, and almost the whole of the Spanish population is confined to the Meseta Norte in Castile-León.

The Rook may seem a strange bird on which to end this brief introduction to the region, but while it winters widely in Spain, its breeding distribution is restricted to cultivated land along river valleys only in the León province of Castile-León.

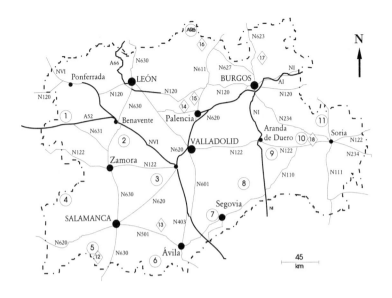

Main sites

1   CAS1   Lago de Sanabria
2   CAS2   Lagunas de Villafáfila y Embalse de Ricobaya
3   CAS3   Riberas de Castronuño
4   CAS4   Arribes del Duero
5   CAS5   Las Batuecas y Sierra de Peña de Francia
6   CAS6   Sierra de Gredos
7   CAS7   Caserio de Allas
8   CAS8   Hoces del Río Duratón
9   CAS9   Hoces del Ría Riaza
10 CAS10 Cañón del Río Lobos
11 CAS11 Sierra de Urbión

Other sites worth visiting

12 CAS12 Arca y Buitera
13 CAS13 Estepas de Madrigal
14 CAS14 La Nava de Fuentes
15 CAS15 Río Carrión y Canal de Castilla
16 CAS16 Fuente Carrionas
17 CAS17 Hoces del Ría Ebro y Rudrón
18 CAS18 Sabinar de Calatañozar

CAS1 LAGO DE SANABRIA

Status: Parque Natural (22,365 ha).

Site description

While the main attraction for most visitors is Sanabria lake, it is the mountains of Montes de León rising up from the lake that are the attraction for birdwatchers. This natural park covers the lake and a large expanse of mountain encompassing the Sierra Segundera and the Sierra de la Cabrera Baja, plus a large number of smaller glacial lakes, valleys and rivers. The rivers that flow down to the lake occupy deep ravines, while the mountain slopes are a mosaic of woods of Pyrenean oak, chestnut, holly and yew, together with scrub and meadows.

Sanabria lake covers an area of 5027 ha, and sits at around 1000 m, while the highest peak in the sierras to the north reaches 2127 m (Peña Trevinca).

Species

Nothing of note is associated with the lake apart from the odd Mallard and Common Sandpiper. It is the mountains that hold the interest with 17 species of birds of prey and a chance of Golden Eagle, Short-toed Eagle and Goshawk in the woodlands. Grey Partridge (Spanish race), Crag Martin, Rock Thrush and Bluethroat all breed in the sierras surrounding the lake, and lower down Red-backed Shrike and Montagu's Harrier occur.

Timing

Spring and summer.

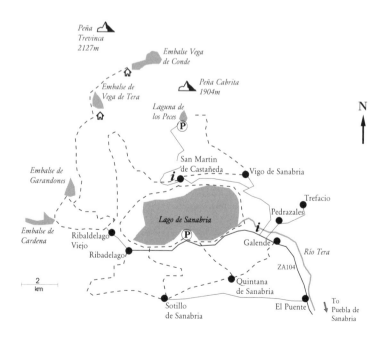

Access

Located in the far west of Castile-León, close to the border with Galicia. Take the N630 north out of Zamora, and bear left after 23 km on the N631 until it joins the main A52. Turn left and head west along the A52 as far as Puebla de Sanabria, then take the ZA104 to Puente de Sanabria and the lake. Roads take you along both south and north shores. A road also goes up to the Laguna de los Peces to the north, where there is parking. There is also a well-marked track that goes up to this lake from the village of Vigo de Sanabria, and another route to another lake (Embalse de Cárdena) at the western end of Sanabria, from the village of Ribadelago. Other possibilites include a link between the two villages of San Martin de Castañeda and Ribadelago, a long and a shorter route. There are many parking areas and an information centre at San Martin.

Calendar

All year: Mallard, Hen Harrier, Goshawk, Sparrowhawk, Buzzard, Golden Eagle, Red-legged Partridge, Grey Partridge, Moorhen, Wood-pigeon, Eagle Owl, Tawny Owl, Kingfisher, Woodlark, Crag Martin, Water Pipit, Grey Wagtail, Dipper, Dunnock, Black Redstart, Blue Rock Thrush, Dartford Warbler, Blackcap, Coal Tit, Short-toed Treecreeper, Jay, Bullfinch, Serin, Cirl Bunting.

Breeding season: Short-toed Eagle, Montagu's Harrier, Booted Eagle, Hobby, Common Sandpiper, Wryneck, Swallow, Nightingale, Blue-throat, Redstart, Rock Thrush, Melodious Warbler, Bonelli's Warbler, Spotted Flycatcher, Red-backed Shrike, Ortolan Bunting.

CAS2 LAGUNAS DE VILLAFÁFILA Y EMBALSE DE RICOBAYA

Status: Espacio Nacional, Reserva Nacional de Caza and ZEPA (32,682 ha); Ramsar site (2854 ha).

Site description

Brackish lagoons set in a open steppe landscape of plains with few trees, farmed and famous for its cereals, being on the edge of the so-called Tierra del Pan or 'Bread Basket', in the province of Zamora. The lagoons are seasonal and sometimes locally referred to as saltmarshes, and the three largest lagoons, Laguna de Barrillos, Salina Grande and Salina de Villarín, are all that remain of a much larger wetland complex comprising over 20 separate lagoons. Despite the intensive farming all around, the lagoons are still an important wintering and roosting site for thousands of migrating waterfowl, and the farmland itself is extremely important for steppe birds. Although outside the main area of interest the Embalse de Ricobayo is noteworthy as a wintering site for wildfowl, particularly Bean Geese. It is a relatively narrow reservoir, covering a stretch of the River Esla.

Great Bustards

Species

During some winters, up to 15,000 Greylag Geese congregate here, and it is also the only regular wintering site in Spain for Bean Goose. However, the population has been dramatically reduced in recent years, and numbers have dwindled to fewer than 50 birds (30 in 1996). This fall in numbers is inconsistent with an increase in the breeding population in northern Europe, but a reduction in the southern wintering grounds is affecting much of the Mediterranean. The geese that roost on Ricobayo reservoir usually graze in the grain fields surrounding the dam, and are often seen together with flocks of Greylag Goose and even Great Bustard. Flocks of Greylag Goose should always be checked for Bean Goose and individuals of other species that occasionally turn up including Bar-headed Goose and Barnacle Goose.

The lagoons are also a breeding site for Shoveler, a very rare breeding bird in Spain with fewer than 50 pairs in total.

The neighbouring fields of grain also provide shelter for a large community of steppe birds: Black-bellied Sandgrouse, Stone Curlew, Little Bustard and especially Great Bustard, which here has one of the largest breeding concentrations in Spain. Of the suite of steppe birds, Pin-tailed Sandgrouse does not breed in the area but is found further south and east in Castile-León.

Timing

Throughout the year. Winter has wildfowl and waders, particularly geese and duck. Spring and autumn passage can bring a variety of waders, and other species such as Black Stork and Common Crane. Spring and early summer have considerable breeding bird interest associated with the farmland.

Access

The Villafáfila area is located to the east of the main León–Zamora road (N630). At Benavente take the NVI southeast towards Tordesillas, but at San Esteban del Molar (around 13 km from Benavente) turn left and under the main road along the ZA704 to Villafáfila. The lagoons (normally dry in summer) all lie next to the road that runs from Tapioles to

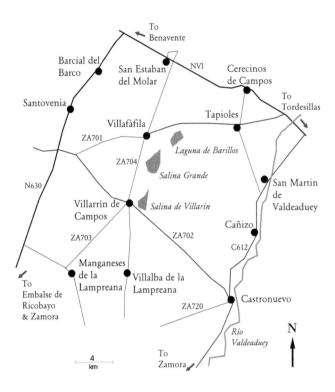

Villafáfila to Villarrín. The general area is criss-crossed by roads and tracks, and one can get good views across all the lagoons. The areas under cereal are worth searching all around the area, but especially to the immediate east of the lagoons towards the River Valdeaduey.

Calendar

All year: Shoveler, Marsh Harrier, Buzzard, Little Bustard, Great Bustard, Stone Curlew, Black-bellied Sandgrouse, Little Owl, Fan-tailed Warbler, Calandra Lark.

Breeding season: White Stork, Black Stork, Black Kite, Montagu's Harrier, Lesser Kestrel, Black-winged Stilt, Red-necked Nightjar, Bee-eater, Roller, Hoopoe, Short-toed Lark, Tawny Pipit, Spectacled Warbler.

Winter: Bean Goose, Greylag Goose, Wigeon, Mallard, Teal, Pintail, Pochard, Red Kite, Hen Harrier, Peregrine, Merlin, Crane, Golden Plover, Lapwing.

Passage periods: Spoonbill, Crane, Snipe, Avocet, Dunlin, Ruff, Redshank.

CAS3 RIBERAS DE CASTRONUÑO

Status: Unprotected.

Site description
This site comprises riverine woodland alongside the banks of the River Duero and a small artificial lake. There are also well-established reedbeds, extensive poplar plantations and, in the immediate surrounds, holm oak woodland. The River Duero has been dammed to produce the relatively shallow and small Embalse de San José which has extensive reedbeds and alluvial woods of willow, poplar and elm.

Species
The riverine woods support one of the largest heronries in Castile-León made up of Grey Heron (around 150 pairs) and betwen 70–80 pairs of Night Heron. While the main feature of this site is the river and its marginal habitats, the adjacent countryside is not without interest with a number of steppe and open-country birds including Pin-tailed Sandgrouse and Roller.

Timing
All year, although the main interest is in spring and early summer.

Access
Situated almost equidistantly between Salamanca and Valladolid. From Salamanca take the N620 north towards Tordesillas and Valladolid. At around 56 km turn left at Alaejos on the C112 to Castronuño and the River Duero. From Tordesillas take the main N620 south for around 9 km before taking a right on the VA600. From Zamora take the N122 to Tordesillas, and after 32 km take the C112 to Castronuño. Head for the dam just north of Castronuño and explore the area on the inner bend of the river. It is also worth exploring the countryside around the minor road to San Román de Hornija.

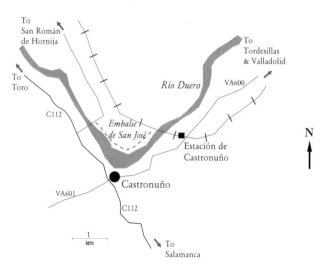

Calendar

All year: Little Grebe, Great Crested Grebe, Grey Heron, Marsh Harrier, Peregrine, Moorhen, Stone Curlew, Tawny Owl, Long-eared Owl, Kingfisher, Azure-winged Magpie, Cetti's Warbler, Fan-tailed Warbler.

Breeding season: Night Heron, Purple Heron, White Stork, Black Kite, Hobby, Little Bustard, Black-bellied Sandgrouse, Pin-tailed Sandgrouse, Great Spotted Cuckoo, Roller, Bee-eater, Great Reed Warbler, Reed Warbler, Savi's Warbler, Melodious Warbler, Penduline Tit, Golden Oriole.

Winter: Cormorant, Greylag Goose, Pochard, Shoveler, Wigeon, Avocet, Golden Plover.

CAS4 ARRIBES DEL DUERO

Status: ZEPA (86,000 ha).

Site description

A huge area with corresponding interest. This site encompasses the upper reaches of the River Duero and its catchment. From south to north this includes, in addition to the Duero, its main tributaries — the rivers Agueda, Huebra, and Tormes — and the reservoirs — Embalse de Saucelle, Almendra, Villalcampo and Castro. The Duero itself forms the border between Portugal and Spain and the southern part of this large site is very remote.

Spectacular river cliffs, rock faces and gorges are the main features of interest for this site but the extensive areas of scrub, holm oak woodland, extensive pasture and areas of cereal should not be ignored. The rivers have been modifed through the construction of dams to form reservoirs.

Red Kite

Species

The Duero river and its tributaries have a varied bird fauna and the area was designated a ZEPA because of its populations of Griffon Vulture, Black Stork, Peregrine, Egyptian Vulture, Red-billed Chough, Eagle Owl, Golden Eagle and Bonelli's Eagle. These species and others such as Alpine Swift, Rock Dove and Crag Martin are all associated with the river cliffs.

The scrub and open countryside is good for Spectacled Warbler and other scrub warblers, plus Red-necked Nightjar, Great Spotted Cuckoo, Hoopoe and Azure-winged Magpie.

A few wolves hang on in the more remote parts.

Timing

April onwards into summer.

Access

There are endless alternatives to explore the River Duero, its tributaries and its cliffs depending on your itinerary and where you are based.

From Ciudad Rodrigo take the SA324 north to Lumbrales from where one can head out in a number of directions, towards the Portuguese border and the villages of Vega de Terron, Salto Saucelle and Saucelle, and possibly Vilvestre. The road between Lumbrales and Vitigudino is also good, especially where it crosses the River Huebra between the villages of Cerralbo and Picones.

The central part of the area is best visted from Vitigudino, the key area being around the Embalse de Aldeadávila.

The area between the Embalse de Almendra/Río Tormes and the Portuguese border can be very good and the roads ZA334 and C525 that cross the river and its cliffs are good, similarly the road from Fermoselle to the Portuguese border (C527), which is also very scenic.

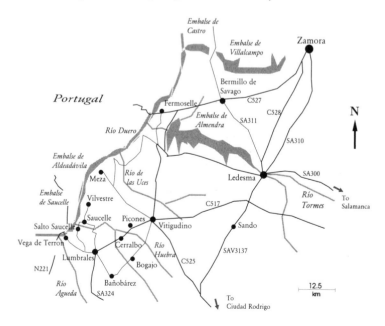

Calendar

All year: Grey Heron, Red Kite, Griffon Vulture, Goshawk, Sparrowhawk, Buzzard, Golden Eagle, Bonelli's Eagle, Kestrel, Peregrine, Rock Dove, Eagle Owl, Hoopoe, Kingfisher, Thekla Lark, Woodlark, Crag Martin, Dipper, Black Redstart, Black Wheatear, Blue Rock Thrush, Dartford Warbler, Great Grey Shrike, Azure-winged Magpie, Red-billed Chough, Raven, Rock Sparrow, Rock Bunting.

Breeding season: White Stork, Black Stork, Black Kite, Egyptian Vulture, Short-toed Eagle, Booted Eagle, Lesser Kestrel, Great Spotted Cuckoo, Cuckoo, Red-necked Nightjar, Alpine Swift, Bee-eater, Red-rumped Swallow, Wheatear, Black-eared Wheatear, Spectacled Warbler, Sub-alpine Warbler, Sardinian Warbler, Orphean Warbler, Golden Oriole.

CAS5 LAS BATUECAS Y SIERRA DE PEÑA DE FRANCIA

Status: Espacio Natural, Reserva Nacional de Caza and ZEPA (21,500 ha).

Site description

This site is the isolated part of the central Cordillera, called the 'French mountains', having been populated with settlers from France in the 11th century after the Christian reconquest. It is still a very isolated part of Spain with vast areas covered in forest, mountain pastures and scrub. At 1732 m, Peña de Francia is the highest peak in the sierra. Much of the woodland in this area is natural with a variety of oak species and sweet chestnut. The southern-facing slopes have more of a Mediterranean influence with strawberry tree, holly, mastic tree, yew, and heaths and *Cistus*. Some areas have been forested with pine.

Species

A very important area for birds of prey with Black Vulture, Griffon Vulture, Peregrine, Egyptian Vulture and Golden Eagle. Also designated as a ZEPA for its Black Stork. This is the northwestern limit of Black Wheatear and southern edge of Dunnock distribution in Spain. Interesting for its population of Lesser Spotted Woodpecker and its Ortolan Bunting which are at the southern end of their main distribution here.

Wolf and lynx.

Timing

Best in spring and early summer.

Access

Situated about halfway between Plasencia to the south and Salamanca to the north. From the north take the N620 out of Salamanca towards Ciudad Rodrigo, and take a left turn around 46 km onto the C525 towards Tamames. Alternatively, take the C512/SA210 direct from Sala-

manca to Tamames. From the south and Plasencia take the N630 to Béjar and then a left turn on the SA515 to Santibañez de la Sierra. Various options to explore the mountains are then possible from these two entry points to the sierra.

One of the main sites to aim for is the monastery at the peak of Peña de Francia, along the SA204 from Tamames, but a much more circuitous route from the eastern approach. Another possibility is to explore the area around the other monastery at Las Batuecas south of Alberca, along an extremely interesting and winding road towards Las Mestas, just over the border in Extremadura.

Calendar

All year: Griffon Vulture, Black Vulture, Goshawk, Buzzard, Golden Eagle, Peregrine, Lesser Spotted Woodpecker, Red-legged Partridge, Thekla Lark, Grey Wagtail, Dipper, Dunnock, Black Wheatear, Blue Rock Thrush, Dartford Warbler, Crested Tit, Nuthatch, Short-toed Treecreeper, Red-billed Chough.

Breeding season: White Stork, Black Stork, Black Kite, Egyptian Vulture, Short-toed Eagle, Montagu's Harrier, Lesser Kestrel, Hobby, Quail, Great Spotted Cuckoo, Alpine Swift, Bee-eater, Crag Martin, Red-rumped Swallow, Black-eared Wheatear, Rock Thrush, Ortolan Bunting.

CAS6 SIERRA DE GREDOS

Status: Reserva Nacional.

Site description

Part of the Sistema Central, the area of mountainous ground in the centre of Spain, the Sierra de Gredos continues westwards the mountain chain started by the Sierra de Guadarrama. This major mountain range lies immediately to the southwest of Ávila and west of Madrid. The northern and southern slopes of the Sierra de Gredos are very different, the northern gradually rising in a series of hills, while the southern side is much more abrupt, plunging or rising very steeply. The eastern massif lies between the Peña del Cadalso and the pass, Puerto del Pico, the central portion includes Almanzor (the highest peak at 2593 m), while the western section is to the west of the pass, the Puerto de Tornavacas.

The slopes of the Sierra Gredos are clothed in Pyrenean oak and pine, while the higher parts have alpine meadows and scrub.

The central part was once a royal hunting reserve, the Coto Real de Gredos, which was established by Alfonso XIII in 1905 to save the Spanish ibex from extinction. He also established Spain's first ever parador nearby, the Parador de Gredos!

The Circo de Laguna Grande is the centrepiece of the Gredos range and is dominated by the highest peak, Almanzor (2593 m), towering above it.

Species

The most famous inhabitant of the Sierra de Gredos is not a bird, it is Spanish ibex, *Capra hircus pyrenaica,* which would have become extinct around the turn of the last century had it not been for the efforts of Alfonso XIII. The present population is now into five figures and reintroduction programmes are under way to establish the ibex in other mountain areas in Spain.

The Sierra de Gredos is a superb mountain habitat for birds, especially when combined with birdwatching trips to the northern and southern valleys, with their riverine habitats, reservoirs and steppe and *dehesa.* The sierra itself is one of the best places to see Bluethroat in Spain, and provides one of the few opportunities outside the Pyrenees and Cordillera Cantabrica for seeing Alpine Accentor. Other key upland species are also possible with Bonelli's Eagle, Rock Thrush, Water Pipit and Citril Finch. Lower slopes and surrounding areas should be checked for Spanish Imperial Eagle and Black Vulture.

Timing

Spring and summer. The weather in the mountains can still be very cold in late spring. Avoid weekends and the summer when visiting some of the more accessible areas and villages, including the Hoyoas del Espino road. But during the week and off season, the whole area can still be very quiet.

Access

For many of the routes described below take the N110 out of Ávila towards Plasencia, but soon afterwards (4 or 5 km), take the N502 south which takes you into the heart of the Gredos, and Ramacastañas.

There are many high-level routes throughout the range, and more casual paths around the villages and from some of the roads. There are published walks of the area in a number of leaflets and books; if you have not purchased them already then they are for sale in the some of the major towns and also at Arenas de San Pedro in the heart of the Gredos. There are also a good number of mountain refuges if you are a keen walker.

Northern slopes and the Tormes valley Around 45 km later there is a right turn along the C500, following the Tormes valley, this takes you to the Hoyos del Espino and the road (AV931) up to *La Plataforma,* and to the western end of the Gredos.

From Hoyos del Espino you can actually drive well into the mountains along the AV931 to the start of path up to the Circo de Laguna Grande, which can take around 2 hours' walking. This road up is scenic and very good for birds, and at certain times of year you can get interesting birds in the car park, *La Plataforma,* at the top including Rock Bunting, Blue Rock Thrush and Rock Thrush. Exploring the mountains in the immediate vicinity of the car park should also get you Bluethroat, but you may well need to walk up to the lake for the chance of Spanish ibex and Alpine Accentor.

Southern slopes and the Tiétar Valley If you stay on the N502 this climbs up to the pass, Puerto del Pica and from here there is the journey down the south side. Off this road is the turning (on the right) for Arenas de San Pedro (AV923) and villages above. Before this turning there is a road (AV913) that takes you into the eastern portion to San Esteban and beyond. It is also possible to reach these points from Burgohondo in Alberche Valley at the foot of the northern slopes.

Walks are possible from the higher villages of El Arenal — from where it is possible to walk over the top of Gredos via the Puerto de

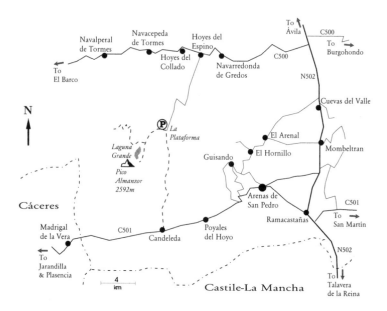

146

Cabrilla — and El Hornillo, the recognised start of the *Circo de Gredos*. Other options are possible from the villages, or one can just explore the general area, both of which choices can be very productive for birds.

It is also possible to make further exploration of the Gredos from the southern side. Carry on through Arenas which will take you to Candeleda, Madrigal de la Vera and Jarandilla along the C501. For the eastern side, stay on the N502 to Ramacastañas and do not go to Arenas. From Ramacastañas take a left turn onto the C501 which follows the foothills east towards Madrid. Various minor roads lead off to the left which take you higher into the mountains.

There are many other routes through the Gredos from the south, possibilities which include trails starting from the village of Madrigal de la Vera, and Guijo de Santa Barbara, which is situated above Jarandilla de la Vera on the C501.

Calendar

All year: Red Kite, Griffon Vulture, Black Vulture, Goshawk, Sparrowhawk, Buzzard, Spanish Imperial Eagle, Golden Eagle, Bonelli's Eagle, Peregrine, Kestrel, Rock Dove, Eagle Owl, Long-eared Owl, Dipper, Alpine Accentor, Black Redstart, Blue Rock Thrush, Dartford Warbler, Goldcrest, Crested Tit, Great Grey Shrike, Azure-winged Magpie, Red-billed Chough, Raven, Rock Sparrow, Citril Finch, Crossbill, Hawfinch, Rock Bunting.

Breeding season: White Stork, Black Stork, Black Kite, Honey Buzzard, Egyptian Vulture, Short-toed Eagle, Booted Eagle, Great Spotted Cuckoo, Hoopoe, Red-rumped Swallow, Water Pipit, Bluethroat, Redstart, Black-eared Wheatear, Rock Thrush, Melodious Warbler, Orphean Warbler, Bonelli's Warbler, Pied Flycatcher, Woodchat Shrike, Ortolan Bunting.

CAS7 CASERIO DE ALLAS

Status: SEO Reserva Ornitológica (600 ha).

Site description

Situated in the River Moros valley in the province of Segovia, this is a bird reserve that SEO has established with a private owner. Mixed habitats include riverine woodland, stands of stone pine, cereals, meadows and a small reservoir.

Species

The major importance of this reserve is the presence of 120 breeding pairs of White Stork, that use the stone pines for their nests — the largest breeding site in Castile-León. The site also has a colony of Grey Herons that also use the pines, and for its size the reserve has a rich avifauna including a number of breeding species of raptor and owl. In addition, three species of vulture — Black, Griffon and Egyptian plus Black Stork all visit the reserve from time to time to feed.

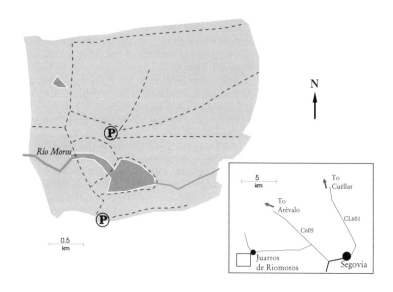

Timing

Spring and summer.

Access

From Segovia take the N110 to Ávila, but after about 3 km turn right onto the C605 towards Arévalo. After approximately another 5 km turn to Valverde del Majano, Martin Miguel and Juarros de Riomoros. The reserve is just outside the last of these villages.

Permission is normally required and access is restricted to certain areas of the reserve. For more information and for permission to visit, contact SEO/Birdlife, Ctra. de Húmera, 63-1, 28224 Pozuela de Alarcón, Madrid. Parking areas are provided at the site.

Calendar

All year: Grey Heron, Red Kite, Griffon Vulture, Black Vulture, Buzzard, Kestrel, Stone Curlew, Tawny Owl, Scops Owl, Little Owl, Barn Owl, Red-legged Partridge, Kingfisher, Hoopoe, Crested Lark, Skylark, Corn Bunting.

Breeding season: White Stork, Black Stork, Black Kite, Egyptian Vulture, Short-toed Eagle, Booted Eagle, Quail, Swallow, Tawny Pipit, Yellow Wagtail, Nightingale.

CAS8 HOCES DEL RÍO DURATÓN

Status: Parque Natural and ZEPA (5037 ha).

Site description

Situated in the province of Segovia just to the north of the Sierra de Guadarrama, the Hoces del Río Duratón was declared a natural park in 1989. The river and gorge run for 25 km from the town of Sepúlveda in the east to the Burgomillodo reservoir and there are cliffs up to 100 m high along the gorge's most spectacular sections. In addition, the gorge also has caves and riverine woodland of willow and poplar, which contrasts sharply with that of the surrounding 'barren' plain. The park protects a greater area than the gorge itself and the surrounding land is important for steppe birds. There are some areas of pine wood within the park's boundaries and the sides of the gorge have scrub vegetation. Within the whole area of the natural park there are three reserve areas, *Zonas de Reserva*, where access is restricted or controlled.

Species

Over 130 species of bird have been recorded with considerable variety, of species, not surprising given the presence of a mixture of habitats. The main interest, however, rightly focuses on the river and the gorge itself which has a large colony of Griffon Vulture (over 250 pairs), Egpytian Vulture, Eagle Owl, Blue Rock Thrush, Black Redstart and Red-billed Chough.

The other feature of interest is species associated with the rocky steppe habitats above the gorge, and most especially the presence of Dupont's Lark. The whole area is, however, well worth exploring with birds such as Bee-eater and Golden Oriole, Little Owl and Azure-winged Magpie in the valley. The park is also excellent for other species of raptor including Goshawk, Booted Eagle and Short-toed Eagle.

Timing

Spring and early summer. It can get very hot here in the summer.

Blue Rock Thrush

149

Access

There is an interpretative centre in Sepúlveda, in the La Iglesia de Santiago (Santiago church), Conde de Sepúlveda, 30 403000 Sepúlveda, (Segovia) (tel: 921 54 05 86).

From Segovia take the CL601 north for around 10 km then turn right onto the C603, and then the SG231 to Sepúlveda.

In Sepúlveda take the paths that lead to the bridges (Talcano and Picazos) over the rivers Duratón and Caslilla (ask at the visitor centre) where there are good views down into the gorge. One of the other main vantage points down into the gorge is at the Ermita de San Frutos. Take the road out of Sepúlveda to Villar de Sobrepeña and across the river to Villaseca. From Villaseca a track leads to the ruined monastery, and you can park about 1 km from here — look out for steppe birds on the journey.

Calendar

All year: Great Crested Grebe, Cormorant, Grey Heron, Red Kite, Griffon Vulture, Goshawk, Sparrowhawk, Buzzard, Golden Eagle, Bonelli's Eagle, Peregrine, Stone Curlew, Eagle Owl, Tawny Owl, Long-eared Owl, Hoopoe, Green Woodpecker, Dupont's Lark, Calandra Lark, Thekla Lark, Grey Wagtail, Black Redstart, Dartford Warbler, Long-tailed Tit, Crested Tit, Great Grey Shrike, Azure-winged Magpie, Red-billed Chough, Rock Sparrow, Rock Bunting,

Breeding season: White Stork, Black Kite, Egyptian Vulture, Short-toed Eagle, Montagu's Harrier, Booted Eagle, Hobby, Lesser Kestrel, Common Sandpiper, Great Spotted Cuckoo, Bee-eater, Roller, Short-toed Lark, Crag Martin, Tawny Pipit, Nightingale, Wheatear, Black-eared Wheatear, Blue Rock Thrush, Spectacled Warbler, Golden Oriole.

CAS9 HOCES DEL RÍA RIAZA

Status: Espacio Natural, Refugio Nacional de Caza and ZEPA (2100 ha).

Site description
This is a deep limestone ravine along the River Riaza, that holds large numbers of vultures. The area has some protected status and forms part of a larger area, Montejo de la Vega, identified as a ZEPA. Holm oak, scrub and cereals are found on surrounding land.

Species
Interest is centred around cliff-nesting species, especially Griffon Vulture, Egyptian Vulture and Eagle Owl, although Golden Eagle and Peregrine also breed here along with Red-billed Chough and Crag Martin. Again, while the gorge holds the main interest, the surrounding land that forms part of the Montejo de la Vega is good for many more widespread species in Spain and is also a site for the rarer and more localised Dupont's Lark.

Timing
April and May, through into June.

Access
Immediately east of the main NI/E5 between Aranda del Duero and Madrid. Instead of taking the NI/E5 out of Aranda, take the C114 to Fuentelcésped, and here take a minor road to Montejo de la Vega de la Serrezuela. A trail can be followed from Montejo along the gorge.

To explore the other end of the gorge, continue along the C114 at Fuentelcésped, and instead of going to Montejo proceed towards

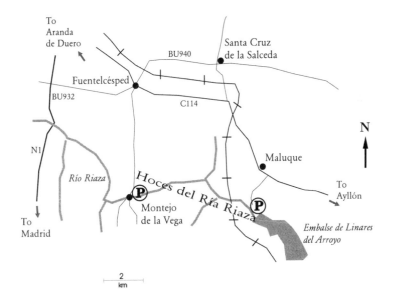

151

Ayllón. After a further 10 km take a right turn signed to Embalse de Linares, a reservoir. The road ends at a quarry next to the reservoir, and it is possible to get down into the gorge from here.

For more information contact ADENA/WWF at Santa Engracia 6, 28010 Madrid (tel: 91 308 23 10).

Calendar

All year: Griffon Vulture, Golden Eagle, Kestrel, Peregrine, Rock Dove, Barn Owl, Eagle Owl, Little Owl, Kingfisher, Green Woodpecker, Great Spotted Woodpecker, Hoopoe, Dupont's Lark, Thekla Lark, Black Wheatear, Azure-winged Magpie, Red-billed Chough, Great Grey Shrike, Spotless Starling, Rock Sparrow.

Breeding season: Egyptian Vulture, Hobby, Scops Owl, Alpine Swift, Bee-eater, Wryneck, Crag Martin, House Martin, Tawny Pipit, Black-eared Wheatear, Rock Thrush, Spectacled Warbler, Subalpine Warbler, Whitethroat, Bonelli's Warbler, Woodchat Shrike, Golden Oriole.

CAS10   CAÑÓN DEL RÍO LOBOS

Status: Parque Natural and ZEPA (9580 ha).

Site description

On its journey through the province of Soria, the River Lobos (river of wolves) has carved a deep gorge with sheer limestone walls, set in a landscape dominated by plains. Cañón Gorge is one of a number in this area and, given the opportunity and the time, these should also be visited. Despite the towering size of the cliffs some riverine woodland exists and other woodland covers slopes that are less steep, where trees can get a foothold. The area was designated a natural park in 1985.

Species

The gorge supports a typical cliff-nesting community including colonies of Griffon Vultures; also Egpytian Vulture, Golden Eagle, Bonelli's Eagle, Peregrine, Eagle Owl, Red-billed Chough, Rock Sparrow, Alpine Swift, Rock Bunting.

Timing

Spring and early summer. It can get crowded in certain parts of the gorge at weekends and during the summer months. Most visitors enter the park from the south, so if you want the park to yourself come in the morning — and from the north end.

Access

You can approach either end of this gorge, although it is a little ambitious to walk the whole length, unless you have two vehicles and can leave one at each end. For the northern end, take the N234 from Soria westwards towards Burgos, and turn left at San Leonardo de Yagüe (42 km) onto the minor road (SO960) towards Santa Maria de las

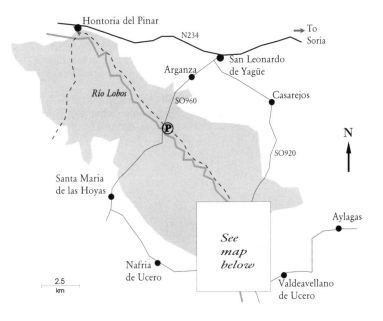

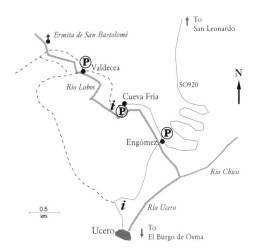

Hoyas. This road goes over the river and there is parking here at the bridge.

For the southern end take the N122 out of Soria as far as El Burgo de Osma where you turn right onto the SO920 to Ucero. From here a forestry road takes you to the southern entrance to the gorge where there is parking and an information centre at the entrance. Other information is at Cueva Fría. Parking is possible at Engómez, Cueva Fría or Valdecea. Parking is restricted on certain days in the month, especially in high summer.

Calendar

All year: Griffon Vulture, Goshawk, Golden Eagle, Peregrine, Rock Dove, Eagle Owl, Kingfisher, Woodlark, Dipper, Black Redstart, Black Wheatear, Azure-winged Magpie, Red-billed Chough, Jackdaw, Rock Sparrow, Chaffinch, Citril Finch, Serin, Cirl Bunting, Rock Bunting.

Breeding season: Egyptian Vulture, Short-toed Eagle, Scops Owl, Alpine Swift, Crag Martin, House Martin, Black-eared Wheatear, Subalpine Warbler, Whitethroat, Golden Oriole, Ortolan Bunting.

Winter: Wallcreeper.

CAS11   SIERRA DE URBIÓN

Status: Espacio Natural, and part of Reserva Nacional de Caza (Picos de Urbión — 100,023 ha).

Site description

A mountainous area close to the border with La Rioja, and an area that is clothed with extensive pine forests, with smaller amounts of beech and Pyrenean oak. The ground that is not covered by pine is a mixture of steep rocky slopes, high meadows and heath. The Sierra de Urbión is part of the much larger game reserve, Picos de Urbión, which, with an area of 100,023 ha, is the second largest in Spain after the Saja reserve in Cantabria. The area froms part of the watershed between the Ebro and Duero basins. The highest peak, Urbión (2229 m), sits on the border with La Rioja.

The sierra has a number of mountain lakes, the most famous being Laguna Negra de Urbión, sitting at 1700 m in the heart of the Sierra de Urbión. Even higher up at 2100 m the River Duero starts on its journey westwards through Castile-León and then Portugal to the Atlantic Ocean.

Species

An area that has a number of species typical of the northern mountain ranges of the Pyrenees and the Cordillera Cantabrica. This includes birds such as Alpine Accentor, Grey Partridge, Woodcock, Marsh Tit, Bullfinch, Yellowhammer and Citril Finch. For some of these species this is their southern limit in Spain.

Timing

Spring and summer. It may be difficult to reach the lake and the pass during cold springs when snow lies deep.

Access

The focus for most visitors to the sierra is the Laguna Negra, and while the lake has little of interest to the birdwatcher it does allow you access to climb quite high into the mountains, with a chance of Citril Finch, Water Pipit and, higher still, Alpine Accentor.

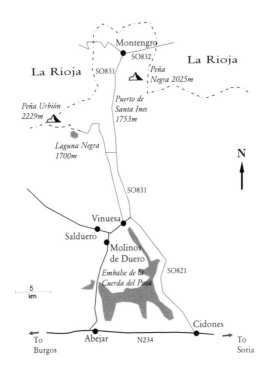

From Soria take the N234 westwards to Cidones. Turn right here onto the SO821 to Vinuesa, and onwards on the SO830 to the Laguna Negra. The SO830 also goes up through the Santa Ines pass and down into Rioja, and this would also be a target for a visit for Alpine Accentor.

Calendar

All year: Griffon Vulture, Goshawk, Buzzard, Golden Eagle, Grey Partridge, Woodcock, Great Spotted Woodpecker, Tawny Owl, Long-eared Owl, Water Pipit, Tree Pipit, Meadow Pipit, Woodlark, Skylark, Dipper, Alpine Accentor, Blackcap, Goldcrest, Crested Tit, Marsh Tit, Citril Finch, Crossbill, Bullfinch, Yellowhammer.

Breeding season: White Stork, Honey Buzzard, Egyptian Vulture, Short-toed Eagle, Booted Eagle, Hobby, Cuckoo, Bee-eater, Wheatear, Whitethroat, Garden Warbler, Bonelli's Warbler, Pied Flycatcher.

OTHER SITES WORTH VISITING

CAS12 Arca y Buitera

Located in the southwest part of Castile-León on the border with Cáceres, immediately to the south of Las Batuecas y Sierra de Peña de Francia (CAS5), and comprises the area between the Embalse de Gabriel y Galán and the village of Valdelageve to the northeast. Black Vulture, Spanish Imperial Eagle, Egyptian Vulture, Black Stork.

CAS13 Estepas de Madrigal

Former steppe now used for cereal production, important for Great and Little Bustard and Black-bellied and Pin-tailed Sandgrouse; also Montagu's Harrier and Lesser Kestrel. Unfortunately more pressure is now being put on the habitat and birds with increasing irrigation schemes. Main interest between Madrigal de las Atlas Torres and Peñaranda de Bracamonte on the C610 and farmland to the east of this which is crossed by many minor roads. Take the N501 east out of Salamanca towards Ávila. At Peñaranda turn left towards Madrigal on the C610 and explore the general area taking a right turn along this road into the cereal lands.

CAS14 La Nava de Fuentes

Site of a substantial former wetland area that was lost over the years but is now part of an exciting restoration programme. Shoveler, Marsh Harrier, Water Rail, a post-breeding site for hundreds of White Stork, and many passage waders. Take the N610 west out of Palencia towards Benavente. At Mazariegos (17 km) turn right onto the P940 to Fuentes de Nava. Before you reach Fuentes de Nava the wetland is signed to the right of this road.

CAS15 Río Carrión y Canal de Castilla

Riverine woodland of poplar, alder, willow and elm. Large Night Heron colony, with Little Bittern, Purple Heron, Penduline Tit, Great Reed Warbler and Golden Oriole. Take N611 north out of Palencia and after 15 km take a left turn along a minor road (P984) to Ribas de Campos. Continue through the village for another few kilometres until you reach the canal. The river is on your left.

CAS16 Fuente Carrionas

Mountainous area with peaks up to 2500 m and much oak and beech forest. Black Woodpecker, Alpine Accentor, Wallcreeper and Snow Finch. Also brown bear and wolf. On border with Cantabrica. Take the N611 north out of Palencia as far as Aguilar de Campoo, then left, westwards along the P212 to Cervera de Pisuerga. Various routes from this town, both north and west.

CAS17 Hoces del Ría Ebro y Rudrón

Gorges along the River Rudrón and where it joins the Ebro in the far north of Castile-León. Cliff-nesters including Griffon Vulture, Bonelli's Eagle, Peregrine, Alpine Swift and Alpine Chough. Take the N623 north from Burgos towards Santander. Turn right after around 60 km into the village of Valdelateja to explore Rudrón Gorge, and the next village of Quitanilla Escalada a few kilometres further on for the Ebro.

CAS18 Sabinar de Calatañozar

Woodland, juniper scrub and small river gorges. Egyptian Vulture, Short-toed Lark, Dupont's Lark, Subalpine Warbler and Ortolan Bunting. Take the N122 southwest out of Soria towards El Burgo and after about 30 km turn right for Calatañozar. Tracks along River Avión to next village of Aldehuela de Calatañozar.

CATALUNYA

In terms of diversity, Catalunya is probably the richest region in Spain for birds; and its diversity does not stop there. Catalunya (or *Catalonia* in English, *Cataluña* in Castilian Spanish) also has its own language, its own history, and its own customs and culture — and suffered the consequences of this independence during Franco's reign. Since his demise, Catalunya has blossomed — Barcelona has for many become the top Spanish city, a lively energetic metropolis famous for Las Ramblas and its Modernista buildings — that sums up the vibrancy of this dynamic region in the northeast corner of Spain.

This semi-autonomous region can feel like a different country, especially so when the road signs are in a different language — from Spanish that is! The diversity that is present in Catalunya extends to its landscape, habitats and birds — all of which are immensely varied. In a relatively compact area we have the high mountains of the Pyrenees, the rocky coast of the north (Costa Brava) and sandy to the south (Costa Dorada) with the remarkable Ebro Delta — one of the most important wetlands in Europe, and inland to the steppes in the Ebro valley around Lleida, and the wooded volcanic plugs of Garrotxa.

Catalunya's coast was one of the first stretches of the Spanish littoral to be developed for mass tourism — and for the main part any excesses have been confined to the south. The Costa Brava has been saved by its rocky coast, Cabo de Creus (CAT3) (with Bonelli's Eagle, Blue Rock Thrush and Pallid Swift) and the conservation measures centred around Aiguamolls de L'Empordà (CAT4), and these two gems of Catalunya sit side by side, and are an excellent base for a holiday. The wetland of Aiguamolls is one of the finest wetlands to visit in the country, the best place for Lesser Grey Shrike in Spain, and has over 300 species of bird recorded, with breeding Purple Gallinule (a reintroduction), Bittern, Whiskered Tern and Moustached Warbler. You will not be satisified by a single visit to this site nor will you be able to do it justice at any one time of year.

The Llobregat delta (CAT6) is a must if you are staying in or visiting Barcelona. Not such a pleasant backdrop as Aiguamolls, but this site, as well as being handy for the city is another important coastal wetland with Little Bittern, Spotted Crake and huge numbers of wintering Mediterranean Gull, and which also seems to picks up quite a number rarities on passage.

The Ebro Delta (CAT9) overshadows everything in comparison and is unlike any other site in Spain (apart form the nearby Albufera de Valencia, perhaps). What it lacks in the compactness and ease of observation that Aiguamolls has, it makes up for in scale — not merely in the size of the delta but also of the number of species likely to be encountered and the size of the breeding and wintering populations. It would be impossible to the delta justice in a few lines or even adequately describe its interest, but with 90% of the world's Auduoin's Gull population (>90,000 pairs), over 10,000 pairs of breeding terns spread amongst seven species, 1,500 pairs of Red-crested Pochard, 70 pairs of Collared Pratincole, 500 pairs of Slender-billed Gull, and the odd Bittern and Purple Gallinule, its importance is easy to grasp. Come in the winter and there could be approaching 100,000 wildfowl around and many thousands of herons and egrets! The main thing to bear in mind is that it can be easy to get lost in this huge area and you will need to focus your visit, if time is short.

From one superlative to the next — the Pyrenees. Catalunya has one of the most beautiful parts of the mountain chain, especially the Parc Nacional d'Aigüestortes (CAT1), sometimes described as the the Spanish equivalent of the Swiss Alps with a landscape dotted with lakes, and surrounded by huge peaks, pastures and forest. Cadí-Moixeró (CAT2) is another excellent area, and there are many others waiting to be discovered. This, the most eastern part of the Pyrenees, has all the high-altitude specialities, Lammergeier, Ptarmigan, Wallcreeper, Alpine Accentor, Alpine Chough, Snow Finch and Ring Ouzel. Move into the forested parts and given luck and patience you should see Capercaillie, Black Woodpecker, Citril Finch and Siskin. But perhaps the species most typical of the high altitude forests, is Tengmalm's Owl, and Catalunya has the bulk of the Spanish population of around 100 pairs.

The lower altitudes, valleys, woods and pastures are not often given the time they deserve on the way up to the peaks; one good example is the Sierra de Boumort (CAT10). Griffon and Egyptian Vultures, Honey Buzzard, Grey Partridge, Woodcock, Red-backed Shrike, Tree Pipit, Whinchat, Marsh Tit, Bullfinch and Yellowhammer all make time here well spent — and while some of the species are also relatively widespread in the UK, they are at their southern limits in Europe here.

Finally there is that forgotten part of Catalunya — its steppes around Lleida (CAT7) — where the eastern part of the Ebro Valley and Los Monegros sneak into the region, with White Stork, Black Kite, Montagu's Harrier, Little Bustard, Stone Curlew, Pin-tailed Sandgrouse, Dupont's Lark and Calandra Lark, Roller and the other stronghold of Lesser Grey Shrike in Spain. And if you do have a day or two left at the end of your holidays, then why not travel the short distance to la Zona Volcanica de la Garrotxa (CAT12) with its 30 extinct volcanoes, or there again there is the Ebro Delta!

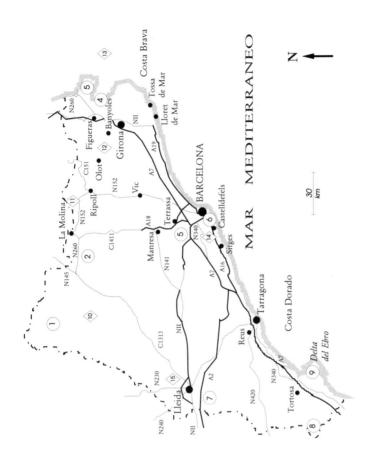

Main sites

1 CAT1 Parc Nacional d'Aigüestortes i Estany de Estany de Sant
Maurici
2 CAT2 Cadí–Moixeró
3 CAT3 Cabo de Creus
4 CAT4 Aiguamolls de L'Empordà
5 CAT5 Muntanya de Montserrat
6 CAT6 Delta de Llobregat
7 CAT7 Las Estepas de Lleida y Embalse de Utxesa
8 CAT8 El Ports de Beceite (Puertos de Beseit)
9 CAT9 Delta del Ebro

Other sites worth visiting

10 CAT10 Sierra de Boumont
11 CAT11 La Vall de Núria
12 CAT12 Parc Natural de la Zona Volcanica de la Garrotxa
13 CAT13 Illes Medes
14 CAT14 Estepas de Algerri
15 CAT15 Parc Natural de Garraf

CAT1 PARC NACIONAL D'AIGÜESTORTES I ESTANY DE SANT MAURICI

Status: Parc Nacional (14,119 ha) and ZEPA (10,230 ha).

Site description

The National Park of D'Aigüestortes i Estany de Sant Maurici was established in 1955, formally designated in 1988, and extended to its current size in July 1997. It is one of only nine national parks in Spain and the only one in Catalunya. There is one other national park in the Pyrenees — Ordesa and Monte Perdido (AR4) — in the adjoining region of Aragón.

Found in the high Pyrenees in the province of Lleida, it comprises two distinct halves — Aigüstortes (Catalan for 'winding or twisted waters') in the west near Boi Valley, and the lake of Sant Maurici in the eastern half.

With over 100 lakes, along with many streams, waterfalls and marshes, the park has some of the most beautiful scenery in the whole of the Pyrenees. With forests, meadows, and jagged snow-capped peaks to complement its wetland features it is often referred to as the 'jewel of the Catalan Pyrenees'. Few places in Europe can match the beauty of Lake of Sant Maurici in particular, which is completely encircled by trees and mountains. Comoloformo, at 3030 m, is the highest peak in the park.

The valleys are a mixture of pasture lands with woodlands of mountain pine, silver fir, beech and silver birch, and at Caldes de Boi there are 37 hot springs and a spa.

Species

Like many parts of the Pyrenees this area is especially important for birds of prey, particularly Lammergeier, Golden Eagle and Short-toed Eagle; key forest species including Black Woodpecker and Capercaillie

Wallcreeper

are scattered throughout, and Tengmalm's Owl is found further up the mountain slopes in the high-altitude woods around the lakes. Overall it has a very rich woodland bird fauna.

The other group of birds contains those that breed at the highest altitudes including Ptarmigan, Wallcreeper, Alpine Accentor, Ring Ouzel, Snow Finch, Rock Thrush and Water Pipit. Citril Finch is relatively widespread within the park, around the margins of forests in open glades (and car parks and picnic sites!). Other species occurring at lower altitudes in the valleys are Whinchat, Red-backed Shrike and Yellowhammer.

Otters are found in some of the lakes, and chamois breed in the park but are seen more easily in the winter when they come down for shelter.

Timing

May through to early July. Weekends can be very busy and some of the roads are blocked in the winter by snow.

Access

There are two main access points to the park, but generally vehicles are not allowed into most areas. It is possible to arrange transport in official four-wheel-drive vehicles to certain parts of the park. Take care in map reading as some lakes have the same name, e.g. Negre!

Aigüestortes This is the western part of the national park. Take the N230 north out of Lleida towards the French border and soon after Pont de Suert, turn right on a minor road (L500) to Caldes de Boí. The turning into the national park, some 2 km before reaching the spa, is well signposted and there is car parking. The track is in good condition, and becomes a road on reaching the lake of Llebrera and ends at the famous winding waters of Sant Nicolau Valley. The track continues as far as the Llong lake but private vehicles are not permitted to use this road.

A track leads from here to the Estany Llong refuge. Just after the springs at Planell Gran, on the other side of the river, a track begins which zig-zags up to the lake of Dellui. This track climbs smoothly until you reach Prats d'Aiguadassi and then crosses to the other side of the river via a series of footbridges across the watercourses and leads up to the refuge, located in a spectacular position above a ravine. A short distance later a track takes you to Rodó lake, from where there are superb views of both parts of the national park. It is quite feasible given the right conditions, but you must be a relatively experienced walker, to link with Sant Maurici, across the Portarró d'Espot pass.

Another possibility is from Caldes de Boí. A road continues past the spa as far as the dam at Cavalles lake, where there is a car park. A track follows the right-hand side of the lake as far as the other end, the Pleta del Ríu Malo.

Estany de Sant Maurici Access to the eastern side of the national park is again from Lleida. Take the C1313 towards Balaguer, after the turning to Balaguer, and around 25 km from Lleida, take another left onto the C147 which takes you towards the park. At around 125 km, after passing through Tremp, La Pobla de Segur and Collegats Gorge (CAT10), turn left on a minor road to Espot.

To reach Sant Maurici lake continue through Espot along a tarmac road which stops at the lake, where there is another information office.

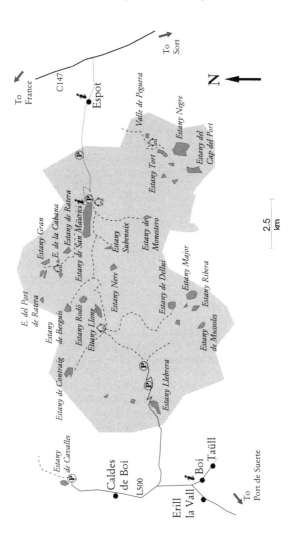

From the Estany de Sant Maurici, paths lead up to Ratera lake, and the Amitges lakes (Gran, Mitjá and Petit) and there is a refuge beside the lakes at 2400 m.

Again, there are many possibilities within the park for birdwatching, for example, take the road to the ski slopes, cross the bridge and follow the forest track along the river Peguera. Once past the Peguera meadows the track disappears and the path up to the Peguera lakes begins, taking you to Tort de Peguera and Negre de Peguera.

In summer there are information offices in Espot and Boi where you can buy maps and guides, and ask after transport, if needed. There are several well-marked trails of varying difficulty and more information can be obtained at the information offices. If you wish to contact the park offices, the address is Parc Nacional d' Aiguestortes i Estany de Sant Maurici, Camp de Mart, 35, 25004 Lleida.

Calendar

All year: Lammergeier, Griffon Vulture, Goshawk, Golden Eagle, Kestrel, Peregrine, Ptarmigan, Capercaillie, Grey Partridge, Eagle Owl, Tengmalm's Owl, Black Woodpecker, Dipper, Black Redstart, Blue Rock Thrush, Mistle Thrush, Marsh Tit, Crested Tit, Goldcrest, Firecrest, Redbilled Chough, Alpine Chough, Raven, Rock Sparrow, Snow Finch, Citril Finch, Siskin, Bullfinch, Crossbill, Yellowhammer.

Breeding season: Honey Buzzard, Red Kite, Short-toed Eagle, Woodcock, Crag Martin, Water Pipit, Grey Wagtail, Alpine Accentor, Whinchat, Rock Thrush, Ring Ouzel, Nuthatch, Wallcreeper, Garden Warbler, Bonelli's Warbler, Chiffchaff, Golden Oriole, Red-backed Shrike, Rock Bunting.

CAT2   CADÍ–MOIXERÓ

Status: Parc Natural and ZEPA (41,342 ha).

Site description

A high mountain range in the eastern part of the Pyrenees, south of Andorra, with peaks covered by snow for most of the year. The area has been protected by natural park designation since 1983. It comprises the ranges of Cadí and Moixeró, the mount of Pedraforca and much of the La Tosa d'Alp and Puigllançada mountains and covers an area of over 41,000 ha. A very wild area with peaks, valleys, meadows, pastures and forests (altitudes ranging from the 900 m in the valley floors to the 2647-m Puig de la Canal Baridana). Above 2000 m are, typically, alpine meadows, and the lower slopes are covered with pine forests, silver fir, beech and oak woods. Although very close to the Mediterranean, this has little influence on the vegetation or bird species.

Species

There is considerable bird interest, in particular Lammergeier, Capercaillie, Wallcreeper, Alpine Accentor, Tengmalm's Owl and Black Woodpecker. The higher pastures have Citril Finch, Water Pipit and Rock Thrush.

In addition to the species listed above the forests and woodlands have Goshawk, Short-toed Eagle, Honey Buzzard, Grey Partridge and both species of treecreeper. The component species present in the park differ according to the dominant tree species, woodland composition and altitude.

Meadows and valleys have Skylark, Yellowhammer, Red-backed Shrike and Wryneck.

Timing

Spring and summer are the best months, and as the park is not so high as some other Pyrenean areas snow is less of a problem in early spring.

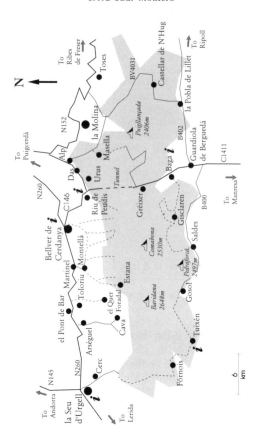

Access

The park is best approached northwards along the C1411, directly north of Barcelona and, more specifically, Manresa. The first stop should be at Baga where there is an information centre for the park. There is a route that starts from Baga that takes you up to the Coll de Pal, but there are many roads, forest tracks and walks that can be tackled throughout the park that will enable you to spend time in all the main habitats including forest, pastures, cliffs and mountain peaks.

The southern areas of the park can be explored by taking roads west or east of the main C1411. Westwards take the B400 left before reaching Baga and before Guardiola de Berguedá. This road takes you right along the southern margins and then northwards to join the main road (N260) that follows the northern boundary of the park. A number of forest tracks and walks can be taken off this road.

For the eastern route take the right turn at Guardiola de Berguedá on the B402, another stunning drive to La Pobla de Lillet, then a return along a minor road to La Molina. Various options to follow tracks that lead off the main northern road (N260) are also possible.

Calendar

All year: Lammergeier, Griffon Vulture, Goshawk, Golden Eagle, Bonelli's Eagle, Peregrine, Ptarmigan, Capercaillie, Grey Partridge, Rock Dove,

Eagle Owl, Tengmalm's Owl, Black Woodpecker, Great Spotted Wood-pecker, Crag Martin, Skylark, Water Pipit, Dipper, Alpine Accentor, Stonechat, Black Redstart, Blue Rock Thrush, Goldcrest, Firecrest, Crested Tit, Nuthatch, Wallcreeper, Short-toed Treecreeper, Treecreeper, Red-billed Chough, Alpine Chough, Raven, Rock Sparrow, Snow Finch, Citril Finch, Crossbill, Yellowhammer, Rock Bunting.

Breeding season: Honey Buzzard, Black Kite, Short-toed Eagle, Alpine Swift, Hoopoe, Wryneck, Subalpine Warbler, Melodious Warbler, Bonelli's Warbler, Rock Thrush, Red-backed Shrike.

CAT3 CABO DE CREUS

Status: Unprotected.

Site description

This rocky headland at the eastern end of the Pyrenees is also the easternmost point of the Spanish mainland. Lying just south of the French border it is part of the Costa Brava but because is has a rocky coastline it remains relatively unspoilt by tourist developments. This is an important seawatching location made up of many headlands, bays, small islets and low coastal mountains found between the small towns of Llançà and Roses (Rosas). Inland this rises to around 670 m above sea level at its highest point Sant Salvador, and the windswept penin-sula supports a mixture of land uses on its poor thin soils, including maquis shrub, small pine plantations, holm and cork oak trees, vines and olive groves.

Species

A range of seabirds such as gulls, shearwaters and occasionally skuas are visible offshore at certain times of year.

It is also an important area during migration with scrub and trees important for spring and autumn falls of migrants, and the coastline for waders. The olive groves and the scrub support breeding Red-legged Partridge, Thekla Lark, scrub warblers including Sardinian Warbler, Subalpine Warbler and Spectacled Warbler, and Ortolan Bunting. Lesser Grey Shrike may also be possible, and this is one of the few areas in Spain in which it breeds. In Catalunya it also occurs at the nearby Aiguamolls de L'Empordà (CAT4) and Las Estepas de Lleida (CAT7).

More open ground has Black-eared Wheatear, whilst the cliffs are home to Bonelli's Eagle, Blue Rock Thrush and Black Wheatear. The monastery, Sant Pere de Rodes, also has breeding Blue Rock Thrush. Unfortunately, Lesser Kestrel disappeared from the area but a reintro-duction programme is in progress.

The high-altitude species occur on the headland from early winter onwards with Alpine Accentor on San Salvador and also around the monastery on rocks and boulders, and with Wallcreeper recorded reg-ularly at Cabo de Creus.

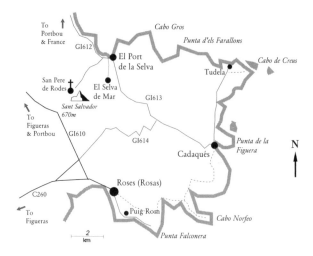

Timing

Particularly rewarding during the migration period (March and April), although it has a good range of breeding species so early summer can also be very productive. Early winter for high-altitude species such as Alpine Accentor and Wallcreeper.

Access

Cabo de Creus is east of Figueras, which is 24 km south of the French border and 32 km north of Girona. The whole peninsula is worth exploring.

Two roads run parallel north–south, the A7 motorway or the N11. Take the Figueras exit and the C260 towards Roses. About 2 km before Roses turn left on the G614 for Cadaqués. A minor road takes you to the Cabo de Creus from Cadaqués. A track from the lighthouse goes to the headland. Many tracks off the minor road can be worth exploring particularly during migration. There are other headlands on the peninsula, such as Cabo Norfeo which is reached from Roses via a partly surfaced road. Tracks lead you round the headland.

El Port de la Selva can be reached from Cadaqués along the Gl613. The streamside at Port de la Selva is also worth checking during migration time for waders and herons, as are the sheltered parts of the coastline. From here take a minor road to San Pere de Rodes monastery, where there is a car park. There is a short walk to the monastery and a path up to the peak of Sant Salvador.

Calendar

All year: Cory's Shearwater, Yelkouan Shearwater, Buzzard, Bonelli's Eagle, Kestrel, Peregrine, Red-legged Partridge, Barn Owl, Little Owl, Crested Lark, Thekla Lark, Crag Martin, White Wagtail, Stonechat, Black Wheatear, Blue Rock Thrush, Fan-tailed Warbler, Dartford Warbler, Sardinian Warbler, Firecrest, Raven, Rock Sparrow, Serin, Goldfinch, Cirl Bunting, Rock Bunting, Corn Bunting.

Breeding season: Lesser Kestrel (re-introduction), Hobby, Turtle Dove, Short-toed Lark, Alpine Swift, Pallid Swift, Red-rumped Swallow, Tawny Pipit, Nightingale, Black-eared Wheatear, Rock Thrush, Spectacled

Warbler, Subalpine Warbler, Orphean Warbler, Lesser Grey Shrike, Woodchat Shrike, Ortolan Bunting.

Winter: Shag, Gannet, Golden Eagle, Great Skua, Razorbill, Guillemot, Alpine Accentor, Wallcreeper.

Passage periods: Gannet, Purple Heron, Arctic Skua, Little Gull, Kittiwake, Sandwich Tern, Whiskered Tern, Black Tern, Great Spotted Cuckoo, Short-eared Owl, Redstart, Wood Warbler.

CAT4 AIGUAMOLLS DE L'EMPORDÀ

Status: Parc Natural and Ramsar site (4824 ha) and ZEPA (867 ha).

Site description

One of the best coastal wetland sites for birds in the whole of Spain, with an excellent infrastructure, making it easy to get round and get good views of a range of species. Second only in importance in Catalunya to the Ebro Delta (CAT9). Since its designation as a natural park in 1983 there has been much activity to maintain and enhance the interest of this very important site, including water level controls to flood certain areas, and the construction of pathways and hides to enable visitors to make the most of their visit. Over 300 species have been recorded, and over 100 species breed. The management has resulted in increases in some breeding birds, some former breeders have returned, and White Stork and Purple Gallinule have been reintroduced.

Aiguamolls is what remains of what was once a much more extensive coastal wetland system found in the bay of Roses and most if not all interest is focused on the area between the rivers Fluvià and Muga. There is a huge variety of habitats in what is a relatively compact space, including coastal brackish lagoons, freshwater lagoons, reedbed, sand dunes, periodic flooded meadows (*closes*), riverine woodland and rice fields. Some of the areas of former rice fields are now reverting to meadows and are grazed by cattle and Camargue horses.

The reserve is made up of three main areas — from north to south:

Estany de Mornau and Estany de Vilaüt Freshwater marshes and two freshwater lagoons (Estany de Mornau and Estany de Vilaüt) and surrounding pastures and scrub. The main focus of attention for this site is the hide overlooking Estany de Vilaüt.

El Cortalet Freshwater and saltwater lagoons at El Cortalet. This is the main focus for visitors to the site, with a visitor centre, many paths and hides and probably the greatest variety of species. This site holds the areas of brackish lagoons, although a freshwater lagoon has now been created next to the visitor centre.

River Fluvià The River Fluvià and its riverine woodland of willows, white and black poplar, alder, elm, ash and tamarisk, near Sant Pere Pescador.

Lesser Grey Shrike

Species

The range of species is great and the whole area is worth exploring for species such as Bittern, Purple Gallinule (reintroduction), Lesser Grey Shrike, Penduline Tit and Moustached Warbler, all of which occur at both the north and main reserve areas. Bittern is now very rare in Spain (fewer than 35 calling birds), and Lesser Grey Shrike is at its western-most outpost in Europe here.

The flooded meadows and old rice paddies can be excellent for waders such as Black-winged Stilt, and duck such as Garganey (with around 10 pairs — 10% of the Spanish population) and Shoveler. It is also good for Glossy Ibis, Purple Gallinule (where numbers are now around 30 pairs), Whiskered Tern and Gull-billed Tern.

The lagoons with reedbeds have Purple Heron, Bittern (a few pairs), Little Bittern, Moustached Warbler and Bearded Tit (3–4 pairs). Marshy areas can have Lesser Grey Shrike (the most important site for this species in Spain with up to 30 pairs), and Marsh Harrier breed and can be seen regularly quartering the wetland.

Saline lagoons are important throughout the year with duck and Greater Flamingo in winter, and waders (e.g. Dotterel) and terns during the passage periods. (Restricted access — see below.)

The coast can be good for seawatching in the winter, and also in spring and summer when you get breeding waders and passage migrants. (Restricted access — see below.)

Non-avian species include painted frog, stripe-necked terrapin and otter.

Timing

A site that can be visited all year round and which has much interest at any time of year, although quietest at the peak of the summer in July and August. Heat haze can be a problem for viewing during the hottest parts of the day.

In spring during periods when strong northerly winds (*tramuntana*) blow down from the Pyrenees, migration can be difficult, and as a consequence the park can be a refuge for many species, some in large numbers.

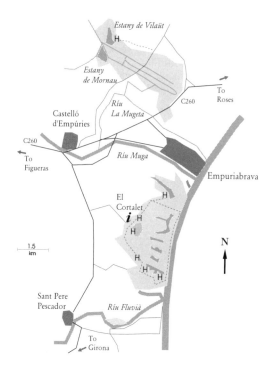

Access

Take the A7 or NII north of Barcelona towards Figueras, or south from France and Perpignan (A9/E15 or N9). At Figueras take the C260 towards Castelló d'Empúries. Take a right turn towards Sant Pere Pescador before you cross the river, and a left turn about 3 km along this road for the main part of the reserve and the visitor centre. It is probably better to start in this central portion to get your bearings and make use of the information at the centre. Well-signed trails guide you through the reserve, and there are paths and hides scattered throughout the site — it is possible to do a circuit, although some sections may be closed off in the breeding season — check at the visitor centre before starting. The information centre, El Cortalet, is open all year round in the mornings and late afternoon, although the exact times vary with the seasons.

For the northern part of the site (which is physically separated from the central part), retrace your steps to Castelló and turn right back onto the C260, crossing the River Muga towards Roses, and then taking a left turn on the outskirts of Castelló along a minor road towards the village of Palau-Saverdera and following the Ría La Mugeta on your right. After around 4 km the road will cross three channels and after the third channel around 0.5 km further on, a track leads off left to the Estany de Vilaüt and the hide. Good views can be had along this road, and across other minor roads which cross the area to the east and west.

The third area of interest is focused along the Ría Fluvià to the south. From the main part of the reserve, turn left onto the main road to Sant Pere Pescador. Go through Sant Pere across the river and then immediately left towards the coast and a campsite. Again various tracks lead along the coast and back to the river.

Calendar

All year: Little Grebe, Great Crested Grebe, Coot, Bittern, Cattle Egret, Little Egret, Grey Heron, Shoveler, Red-legged Partridge, Water Rail, Marsh Harrier, Purple Gallinule (reintroduction), Stone Curlew, Collared Dove, Monk Parakeet, Kingfisher, Hoopoe, Cetti's Warbler, Moustached Warbler, Fan-tailed Warbler, Sardinian Warbler, Bearded Tit, Penduline Tit.

Breeding season: Little Bittern, Night Heron, Purple Heron, White Stork (reintroduction), Garganey, Black Kite, Short-toed Eagle, Little Crake, Baillon's Crake, Black-winged Stilt, Kentish Plover, Whiskered Tern, Great Spotted Cuckoo, Bee-eater, Roller, Short-toed Lark, Yellow Wagtail, Nightingale, Savi's Warbler, Reed Warbler, Great Reed Warbler, Melodious Warbler, Subalpine Warbler, Golden Oriole, Lesser Grey Shrike, Woodchat Shrike.

Winter: Black-throated Diver, Great Crested Grebe, Gannet, Cormorant, Greylag Goose, Wigeon, Gadwall, Teal, Mallard, Pintail, Pochard, Tufted Duck, Hen Harrier, Golden Plover, Lapwing, Curlew, Razorbill, Short-eared Owl, Chiffchaff.

Passage periods: Squacco Heron, Black Stork, Glossy Ibis, Spoonbill, Greater Flamingo, Marsh Harrier, Red-footed Falcon, Eleanora's Falcon, Hobby, Spotted Crake, Crane, Collared Pratincole, Dotterel, Knot, Little Stint, Curlew Sandpiper, Dunlin, Ruff, Snipe, Wood Sandpiper, Marsh Sandpiper, Redshank, Auduoin's Gull, Gull-billed Tern, Black Tern, Bluethroat, Wheatear, Wood Warbler.

CAT5   MUNTANYA DE MONTSERRAT

Status: Parc Natural (*c* 5000 ha).

Site description

This site is only 50 km from Barcelona and as famous for its 9th-century monastery and shrine of the Black Madonna as it is for spectacular jagged peaks (the highest is San Jerónimo at 1238 m) and pinnacles and its natural history. It offers a good opportunity to mix culture with birdwatching.

The slopes of the massif are clothed in forest of pine and oak, although the southern slopes have a more Mediterranean influence with fewer trees, more scrub oak and aromatic shrubs and herbs. Designated as a natural park in 1989, the massif is around 10 km long and 5 km wide, and from a scenic viewpoint is best viewed from the north when the origin of its name Montserrat, 'sawn-off mountain', is plain to see. It has been compared by many visitors to a cathedral.

The site was badly affected by a widespread fire in 1986 and the effects of this are still clearly obvious, although there some areas of woodland and scrub that managed to avoid the fires, and these are mainly found around the southern area below the monastery. The area is, however, slowly recovering.

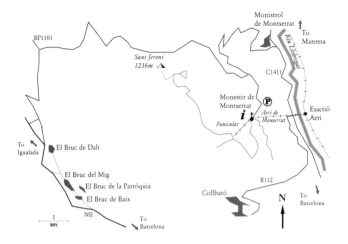

Species

The site is especially good for a mixture of species that favour mid-altitude rocky ground, and for cliff-nesters, including in particular Bonelli's Eagle, Eagle Owl, Alpine Swift, Crag Martin and Blue Rock Thrush.

Scrub warblers including Sardinian, Dartford and Subalpine also breed as does Rock Bunting and Rock Sparrow.

Timing

Spring and early summer, but the park can be extremely busy at weekends and during holiday periods. The mountains are also very popular with climbers.

Access

Out of Barcelona take the A2 and then the A7 motorways toward Tarragona as far as the Martorel exit (no. 25). This brings you initially onto the NII towards Lleida but take a right turn shortly afterwards onto the C1411 towards Manresa. Carry on this road as far as Monistrol, and then take a left turn onto a minor road that is signed to the monastery.

It is also possible to reach the monastery by train to the Aeri Montserrat station then on the funicular railway up to the monastery.

Once on top there are numerous tracks that take you across the massif, but care should be taken walking across the mountain. Many of the routes are marked.

Calendar

All year: Sparrowhawk, Buzzard, Bonelli's Eagle, Peregrine, Red-legged Partridge, Rock Dove, Collared Dove, Barn Owl, Eagle Owl, Crested Lark, Woodlark, Crag Martin, Black Redstart, Blue Rock Thrush, Sardinian Warbler, Dartford Warbler, Crested Tit, Raven, Starling, Rock Sparrow, Serin, Cirl Bunting, Rock Bunting.

Breeding season: Turtle Dove, Cuckoo, Scops Owl, Alpine Swift, Bee-eater, Wryneck, Rock Thrush, Melodious Warbler, Subalpine Warbler, Bonelli's Warbler, Golden Oriole, Woodchat Shrike, Ortolan Bunting.

Winter: Alpine Accentor, Wallcreeper.

CAT6 DELTA DE LLOBREGAT

Status: Reserva Natural and ZEPA (573 ha).

Site description

Sandwiched in between industrial areas and Barcelona airport, this wetland is made up of two nature reserves separated by the city's main airport, although they are still linked by the beach. Their formal designation has saved the area from further developments, at least for the time being, but the whole area is still under extreme pressure. Despite their position and the closeness to the bustling city of Barcelona, the reserves protect a coastal wetland of considerable importance and are well worth a visit if you are visiting Barcelona and do not mind the surrounding backdrop of urban and industrial land use.

The reserve is focused around the Llobregat river as it enters the Mediteranean Sea immediately south of the city of Barcelona. The park is a coastal floodplain with small lagoons and fields that flood at certain times of year, reedbeds, pine woods and the coast itself with beaches.

Species

A good selection of wetland species. The reedbeds are especially important for Little Bittern, with small numbers of Water Rail, Spotted Crake, Baillon's Crake, Purple Heron and Night Heron with Great Reed Warbler and Cetti's Warbler. Shoveler are also known to breed along with a small number of Sandwich Tern.

The flooded fields have Yellow Wagtail, Black-winged Stilt, Gull-billed Tern and Cattle Egret.

The area comes into its own during the spring when passage can be important, especially for Black Tern. Large numbers of Mediteranean Gull use the site in winter, sometimes exceeding 10,000 birds in total.

Timing

Spring and winter. Weekends can be very busy.

Access

There are two main access roads to the coast but both involve taking the C246 south out of the city towards the airport and El Prat de Llobregat.

The first is closest to the city but involves driving through industrial areas once off the main road. Cross over the Llobregat river and take a left turn to the beach *Platja* and the golf course *Campo de Golf-Playa*. The road takes you down to the beach and campsite. Before reaching the coast another road turns off to the left and leads to the northern part of the site. Alternatively carry on to the beach and then to the right which leads to the second reserve past the golf course. Various paths lead you through the reserve, although during the breeding season some paths are blocked, primarily in the beach area.

For an alternative and slightly easier access continue on the C246 to the 11 km marker and turn left towards the coast signed *Camping Toro Bravo*. It is worth stopping when you can after you have turned off the

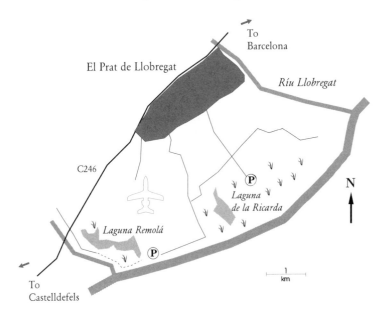

main road as there are good habitats for birds right down the road to the campsite, where the road stops. At the campsite one can then walk to the beach.

Back in El Prat de Llobregat there is a museum which has displays about the area.

Calendar

All year: Little Grebe, Marsh Harrier, Buzzard, Water Rail, Kentish Plover, Sandwich Tern, Monk Parakeet, Cetti's Warbler, Fan-tailed Warbler, Sardinian Warbler, Short-toed Treecreeper, Penduline Tit.

Breeding season: Little Bittern, Night Heron, Purple Heron, Spotted Crake, Black-winged Stilt, Little Ringed Plover, Whiskered Tern, Gull-billed Tern, Great Spotted Cuckoo, Scops Owl, Short-toed Lark, Yellow Wagtail, Great Reed Warbler, Reed Warbler.

Winter: Yelkouan Shearwater, Gannet, Cormorant, Cattle Egret, Little Egret, Ferruginous Duck, Golden Plover, Little Gull, Mediterranean Gull, Razorbill, Kingfisher, Water Pipit, Moustached Warbler.

Passage periods: Hen Harrier, Little Crake, Sanderling, Spotted Redshank, Audouin's Gull, Black Tern.

CAT7 LAS ESTEPAS DE LLEIDA Y EMBALSE DE UTXESA

Status: Unprotected.

Site description

These are the best areas of grassland and steppe in Catalunya. Utexsa reservoir is situated to the west within the steppe area and, although relatively small, is also important with an impressive reedbed.

This is an area of marginal farmland, with a mixture of some pasture and low intensity cereal production, along with some areas that are occasionally left fallow; an extension of the Los Monegros steppe area of Aragón (AR13), and situated at the eastern extremity of the steppe. The main areas of interest are found to the south and west of Lleida, and some areas have unfortunately been lost through the planting of conifers and industrial developments.

The whole area whilst not being the most scenic, has a very rich and varied bird fauna and it is easily possible to get a very respectable list from a day's birdwatching here.

Species

The best site in Catalunya for steppe birds with good numbers of Little Bustard and Pin-tailed Sandgrouse, and with smaller numbers of other key species such as Montagu's Harrier, Stone Curlew and Black-bellied Sandgrouse. A range of species of lark occur, most notably Dupont's Lark.

While the steppe area is worth visiting in its own right, the reservoir is an unexpected bonus and makes an excellent day's birding with Purple Heron, Little Bittern, Water Rail, Cetti's Warbler and Great Reed Warbler.

The open country south of Lleida can also be productive for birds of open country, with Lesser Kestrel, White Stork, Hobby, Roller, Great Spotted Cuckoo, Scops Owl, Red-necked Nightjar and, perhaps of greatest interest, Lesser Grey Shrike. The latter is a very rare bird in Spain, on the western edge of its limit in Europe, and one which has suffered from the intensification of agriculture and the increasing use of pesticides. It also suffers badly from nest predation, particularly by corvids.

Timing

Mainly spring although interest at Uxtesa reservoir in the autumn and winter also.

Access

Much of the steppe interest is found directly south of Lleida, and in the area delimited by the C230 to the west, the A2 to the north and the C242 to the south, although there are scattered remnants further west and north. Take the C230 south out of Lleida and explore the countryside by taking one of the left turns off the C230, for example the L700 to Alcaño and then into the hinterland eastwards.

For Uxtesa reservoir take the N230 south and then soon after take a right (exit no. 4 for Albàtarrec and Sudanell and Torres de Segre). A track leads to the reservoir immediately outside of Torres de Segre, and follows the western margins of the reservoir.

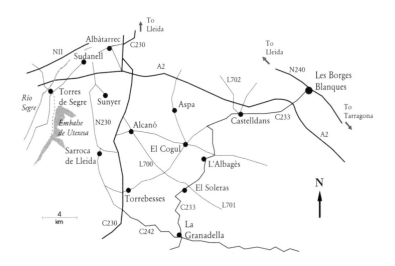

Calendar

All year: Marsh Harrier, Buzzard, Peregrine, Water Rail, Red-legged Partridge, Little Bustard, Black-bellied Sandgrouse, Pin-tailed Sandgrouse, Little Owl, Long-eared Owl, Green Woodpecker, Dupont's Lark, Calandra Lark, Lesser Short-toed Lark, Thekla Lark, Black Wheatear, Blue Rock Thrush, Cetti's Warbler, Sardinian Warbler, Penduline Tit, Great Grey Shrike, Raven, Starling, Rock Sparrow, Cirl Bunting.

Breeding season: Purple Heron, Little Bittern, White Stork, Egyptian Vulture, Montagu's Harrier, Short-toed Eagle, Hobby, Lesser Kestrel, Quail, Stone Curlew, Great Spotted Cuckoo, Scops Owl, Red-necked Nightjar, Bee-eater, Roller, Tawny Pipit, Short-toed Lark, Black-eared Wheatear, Great Reed Warbler, Reed Warbler, Spectacled Warbler, Subalpine Warbler, Savi's Warbler, Lesser Grey Shrike, Woodchat Shrike, Golden Oriole.

CAT8   EL PORTS DE BECEITE (PUERTOS DE BESEIT)

Status: Reserva Nacional de Caza (30,000 ha).

Site description

A little visited part of Spain and a forgotten range of mountains that runs parallel to the popular coasts of Catalunya and Valencia. Situated immediately behind Tortosa and the Ebro Delta, El Ports de Beceite is a national game reserve, taking its name from the fruit-growing village of Beceite.

The limestone mountains have many cliffs and are deeply dissected by gullies, but there are also extensive areas of pine and oak. The southern portion of the reserve near La Seina contains impressive beech woods that climb high up the mountain slopes and are of considerable age and size. The highest peak in the range is Mont Caro (1447 m).

Species
The limestone cliffs are excellent for Griffon Vulture, Golden Eagle, Bonelli's Eagle and Red-billed Chough, with Black Redstart, Blue Rock Thrush and Rock Sparrow all relatively common.

The woodlands are also very rich and should not be overlooked, with breeding Short-toed Eagle, Goshawk, Crossbill and Bonelli's Warbler.

The lower slopes of the mountain are also worth exploring, with the lower valleys, orchards and olive groves good for Orphean Warbler, Hoopoe, Wryneck and Melodious Warbler.

Timing
Spring and summer months.

Access
For the northern part of the site take the C237 off the main coastal road (N340) opposite the Ebro Delta towards Tortosa. From here there are a number of options. At Tortosa you can take the road to Roquetes and

176

from Roquetes the T342 to Alfara de Carles. Alternatively, take a left turn off the T342 before you reach Els Reguers up to the peak of Mont Caro and beyond by another 15 km to Xerta, where you take a left turn to Pauls on a minor road.

The southern part can be explored by taking the TV3421 out of Tortosa towards La Sénia, through Mas de Barberáns.

Views across the whole area are excellent from these roads and there are numerous tracks and paths that lead off from here into woodland or along gullies. Some of these are driveable at least for part of the way.

Calendar

All year: Griffon Vulture, Goshawk, Golden Eagle, Bonelli's Eagle, Kestrel, Peregrine, Red-legged Partridge, Rock Dove, Barn Owl, Little Owl, Green Woodpecker, Woodlark, Crag Martin, Dipper, Black Redstart, Blue Rock Thrush, Sardinian Warbler, Dartford Warbler, Jay, Red-billed Chough, Raven, Spotless Starling, Cetti's Warbler, Rock Sparrow, Crossbill, Cirl Bunting.

Breeding season: Short-toed Eagle, Booted Eagle, Turtle Dove, Cuckoo, Alpine Swift, Swift, Bee-eater, Hoopoe, Wryneck, Nightingale, Swallow, House Martin, Orphean Warbler, Melodious Warbler, Bonelli's Warbler.

Winter: Alpine Accentor, Wallcreeper.

Passage periods: White Stork, Honey Buzzard, Black Kite, Marsh Harrier, Ring Ouzel.

CAT9 DELTA DEL EBRO

Status: Parc Natural and Ramsar (7736 ha). Whole delta (32,000 ha).

Site description

Delta del Ebro is the largest wetland in Catalunya and the second largest in Spain after the Coto Doñana, covering an area of 320 sq km, and is arguably the most important wetland in the western Mediterranean after the Camargue. This internationally important area for birds was recognised formally by its designation as a natural park in 1986, with a total area of 7736 ha.

The Ebro Delta extends into the Mediterranean Sea for around 20 km, attracting birds by the tens of thousands, and includes a huge area of rice fields in one of the most extensive rice-growing areas in Spain. While much of the natural vegetation has disappeared under rice — over half of the delta — paddies are fortunately very attractive to a range of birds, including herons, ducks, terns and waders, providing large areas of open water on the site for the greater part of the year.

The management of the rice paddies through manipulation of water levels, and the movement of water between areas through the myriad of canals and channels is crucial to maintaining the interest of the area. Waterlilies grow in some of the small freshwater ponds, *ullals*, and can cause problems by spreading into the rice paddies and the numerous canals that cross the area.

One should not, however, disregard the value and importance of the natural features including the lagoons, reedbeds, woods, sand dunes and saline steppes. In addition to the rice paddies, fruit and vegetables are grown on the inland side of the delta, but nearer to the coast, there are large lagoons bordered by reed and other emergent plants, wide expanses of sandy ground with a saltmarsh vegetation, and long sandy beaches with sand dunes with marram grass. The salty zones often include sand dunes and are known locally as *tores*. Reedbeds are common, and in areas of deeper water, sedges and reed mace are found. Riverside woods are found on the banks of the Ebro with poplar, willow, alder, eucalyptus and plane trees. Where the influence of the sea is strongest the wood becomes thinner and oleander and tamarisk become dominant.

The site has two information centres, one in Deltebre and one next to the largest lagoon L'Encanyissada, and there are many hides scattered throughout the site.

Species

The size of the bird population is most obvious in the autumn months of October and November when the rice has been harvested and the paddies remain waterlogged and consequently attract thousands of passage and wintering birds. Duck numbers can reach over 75,000, and along with over 15,000 Coot, this represents over 90% of the waterfowl wintering in Catalunya, and 10% of the whole of Spain's wintering population. Although the majority of duck are Mallard, around 6,000 Red-crested Pochard winter here and a range of other species including Shoveler, Wigeon, Shelduck, Gadwall, Teal and Pochard stay in smaller numbers.

Over 30,000 waders also use the delta with 600 Avocet and a similar number of Kentish Plover. The delta is also important for many other wintering species with over 150 Black-necked Grebe, up to 2,500 Cattle Egret, up to 1,400 Little Egret, and a staggering 150 Marsh Harrier.

The breeding season is similarly impressive, again for a wide range of species. The site is especially important for terns and gulls, and in some years seven species of tern breed here: Common Tern, up to 5,500 pairs, Sandwich Tern, increasing with around 1,800 pairs, 1,500 Whiskered Tern and increasing, 650 pairs of Little Tern, 300 pairs of Gull-billed Tern (lagoon islands), one to two pairs of Lesser Crested Tern and the odd pair of Caspian Tern from time to time.

Over 500 pairs of Slender-billed Gull breed, and the Ebro Delta now has the world's largest colony of breeding Audouin's Gull, which has been steadily increasing in size here and now supports over 9,000 pairs and around 90% of the world's population.

Herons and egrets are also well represented, with a few pairs of a very rare bird in Spain, the Bittern, hundreds of Little Bittern, around 500 pairs of Purple Heron, 350 pairs of Squacco Heron, 2,500 Cattle Egret and 1,000 Little Egret.

If this is not enough, there are over 1,500 pairs of breeding Red-crested Pochard, most of the small Spanish population of Shelduck, ten pairs of Purple Gallinule, 350 pairs of Water Rail, around 2,000 pairs of

Gull-billed Tern

Black-winged Stilt (but sometimes twice this number, or more), 70 pairs of Collared Pratincole, the same number of Redshank, and 30 pairs of Oystercatcher (about half of the Spanish population). Up to 2,000 Greater Flamingo are present all year round in good years and during the 1990s they have started breeding at the Ebro. Around 50 pairs of Bearded Tit are found in the reedbeds.

The following is a summary of the main areas of interest at the Ebro Delta.

Rice fields and canals Purple Heron, Little Bittern, Cattle Egret, Little Egret, terns, especially Whiskered Tern, Black-winged Stilt, Avocet and many other waders on passage, including Temminck's Stint.

Bassa de les Olles Small lagoon with good variety of duck and herons, offering some good views.

Punta del Fangar Sandspit and dunes. Large tern colony, mainly Sandwich and Little, but Gull-billed Tern and Slender-billed Gull recently established. Also Kentish Plover. Coastal waders on passage including Grey Plover and Curlew. Bay itself has Great Crested Grebe, Black-necked Grebe and Red-breasted Merganser, and in winter Common Scoter, Velvet Scoter and Eider. Gulls on passage and wader roosts.

Canal Vell Large lagoon with hide at southern shore. Marsh Harrier, Greater Flamingo, Little Bittern, Whiskered Tern.

El Garxal Important shallow sea lagoon at the mouth of the Ebro, important for wildfowl, terns and Little Egret. Red-crested Pochard gather here, and Audouin's Gull and Slender-billed Gull are relatively easy to see. Best place to head for at times of passage and can be brilliant for waders, ducks, gulls and terns.

L'Encanyissada Largest lagoon on the delta with ducks, cormorants, grebes and gulls. Marsh Harrier in autumn and winter. Whiskered Tern, Purple Heron, Little Bittern, Red-crested Pochard. Reedbed with warblers. Excellent for views of herons. Little Crake. Favoured roosting area.

La Noria Small lagoon with reedbeds, impressive mixed heronry of Little Bittern, Purple Heron, Night Heron, Cattle Egret and Little Egret, also small numbers of Squacco Heron. Also Savi's Warbler, Great Reed Warbler, Reed Warbler, Moustached Warbler, Bearded Tit and Marsh Harrier.

Illa de Buda/El Calaixos Specially protected with restricted access. Lagoon and coastal sands and scrub. Breeding Little Bittern, Squacco Heron, Bittern, Little Tern, Whiskered Tern. Excellent wintering and passage area also.

La Tancada Lagoon next to the adjacent Sant Antoni saltplains which are excellent for waders including Kentish Plover, Little ringed Plover, Avocet and Black-winged Stilt, all relatively common. Short-toed and Lesser Short-toed Lark also breed, and good for passage waders such as Grey Plover, Ruff, Spotted Redshank, Little Stint. One of the best areas for breeding Collared Pratincole. Also good for terns with the chance of Caspian and Slender-billed Gull. Good roosting site.

Punta de la Banya Sandy spit with saltpans. Good for Slender-billed Gull, Audouin's Gull, Sandwich Tern and Gull-billed Tern. Avocet and Flamingo at northern edge of saltpans where a hide allows viewing. Duck such as Gadwall and Shoveler in autumn.

Timing

At weekends, and particularly in the summer, the beaches can be busy. The rice fields are at their driest in the first part of the year between January and March, when most of the interest is focused on the natural lagoons and the saltpans. Brilliant throughout the year, but birdwatching affected by heat haze in summer.

Access

The Ebro Delta is to the east of the coastal roads, the A7/E15 and N340, between Tarragona to the north and Peníscola in Valencia region to the south. There are a number of exits off the N340 towards Deltebre on the northern part of the delta. Car ferries link the northern and southern halves.

The road network on the delta is very complex and many areas and places of interest are not signed. It is a good bet to start at the information centre (tel: 977 48 96 79) and *Ecomuseu* next door (situated in an old farmhouse) at Deltebre (north side) where there is detailed information on species present and areas to visit, and maps are available. The area is large and criss-crossed with many tracks so it can be quite easy to lose your way. There is another visitor centre, *Casa de Fusta Information Centre*, on the southern part of the delta on the northern side of L'Encanyissada lagoon.

See map for location of main areas of interest.

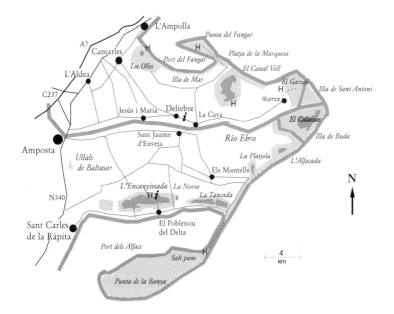

Calendar

All year: Black-necked Grebe, Bittern, Cattle Egret, Little Egret, Greater Flamingo, Shelduck, Gadwall, Teal, Red-crested Pochard, Marsh Harrier, Water Rail, Purple Gallinule, Avocet, Kentish Plover, Slender-billed Gull, Sandwich Tern, Whiskered Tern, Hoopoe, Lesser Short-toed Lark, Crested Lark, Cetti's Warbler, Moustached Warbler, Fan-tailed Warbler, Bearded Tit, Penduline Tit, Reed Bunting.

Breeding season: Little Bittern, Night Heron, Squacco Heron, Purple Heron, Garganey, Spotted Crake, Baillon's Crake, Oystercatcher, Black-winged Stilt, Collared Pratincole, Little Ringed Plover, Redshank, Audouin's Gull, Gull-billed Tern, Lesser Crested Tern, Caspian Tern, Common Tern, Little Tern, Black Tern, Bee-eater, Short-toed Lark, Savi's Warbler, Reed Warbler, Great Reed Warbler, Woodchat Shrike.

Winter: Great Northern Diver, Cory's Shearwater, large numbers of mixed species of heron and egrets, Spoonbill, huge numbers of duck (up to 75,000), sea-duck including Scaup, Eider, Common Scoter and Velvet Scoter; Marsh Harrier (over 150), Hen Harrier, Merlin, Peregrine, Mediterranean Gull, Short-eared Owl, Meadow Pipit, Water Pipit, Bluethroat.

Passage periods: Manx Shearwater, Gannet, Great White Egret, Glossy Ibis, Hobby, Eleonora's Falcon, Osprey, Little Crake, Grey Plover, Lapwing, Knot, Sanderling, Little Stint, Temminck's Stint, Pectoral Sandpiper, Curlew Sandpiper, Dunlin, Ruff, Snipe, Black-tailed Godwit, Bar-tailed Godwit, Whimbrel, Curlew, Spotted Redshank, Marsh Sandpiper, Greenshank, Green Sandpiper, Wood Sandpiper, Common Sandpiper, Turnstone, Great Skua, Long-tailed Skua, Lesser Black-backed Gull, Kittiwake, Caspian Tern, White-winged Black Tern, Razorbill, Red-throated Pipit, Brambling.

OTHER SITES WORTH VISITING

CAT10 Sierra de Boumont

Large Griffon Vulture colony and other cliff-nesting birds including Alpine Swift on limestone massif; also Lammergeier. C147 north from Balaguer to La Pobla de Segur, then right onto a minor road to El Pont de Claverols, and follow signs to St Martí and Pessonada. Track leads from this last village. Also try Collegats Gorge on the main N260 north of La Pobla where there is car parking — good for views of vultures and birds of prey.

CAT11 La Vall de Núria

Part of the Reserva Nacional de Freser i Setcases. High mountain area with Ptarmigan, Alpine Accentor, Ring Ouzel, Citril Finch and chamois. N152 north from Barcelona and Ripoll to Ribes de Frase. Minor road to village of Queralbs, then a 'rack' railway up to sanctuary and ski resort at Núria. Marked paths from here.

CAT12 Parc Natural de la Zona Volcanica de la Garrotxa

Best volcanic landscape in Spain, and one of the finest in Europe with some 30 volcanic cones now mostly covered in woodland, but with some scrub and meadows. Mixed bird communities. Goshawk, Short-toed Eagle, Hobby, Dartford Warbler and Red-backed Shrike. Much of the area of interest is to the east of the town of Olot towards Banyoles.

CAT13 Illes Medes

Small islands close to coast off L'Estartit in the north of Catalunya. Large colony of Yellow-legged Gulls, Shag, Storm Petrel, Cory's Shearwater, Peregrine, Pallid Swift — and a coral reef! NII north from Girona, take a right turn on the Gl633 to Torroella and L'Estartit. Boat cruises to the islands from L'Estartit, some with glass bottoms for viewing reef and coral fish.

CAT14 Estepas de Algerri

Fragments of steppe north of Lleida with Montagu's Harrier, Little Bustard, Red-necked Nightjar, Quail, Calandra Lark, Roller and Tree Sparrow. C1313 northeast out of Llieda for 28 km, then take a left turn to Balaguer on C148 to Algerri and the plains.

CAT15 Parc Natural de Garraf

Stony and rocky limestone massif to the south of Barcelona with ravines and coastal cliffs. Open scrub landscape with Black Wheatear, Tawny Pipit, Black-eared Wheatear, Spectacled Warbler, Ortolan Bunting and Great Grey Shrike. Coastal cliffs between La Ginesta and Sitges along C246, and hinterland via Begues on the BV2441 to the viewpoint, *Mirador de les Solius*, on the eastern side of the area. Information centre at Vallgrassa on minor road in massif reached off main C246 coast road. Turning to right once out of built up area of Castelldefels.

EUSKADI (PAÍS VASCO)

The Basque Country is known in the Basque language as Euskadi, literally 'collection of Basques', which in reality includes people and land in the neighboring regions as well as the Basque Country proper. At the other end of the Pyrenees from Catalunya it has much in common despite a separate language, history and customs. However, if you have come to Spain to enjoy a relaxed and slower pace of life for a week or two, then perhaps the Basque country is not for you. Take care if you dare to chance your arm at pelota — a game invented by the Basques and thought to be the 'fastest game on earth'!

For its relatively small size Euskadi has a long coastline, the Costa Vasca, stretching from the border with France, passing through the elegant and smart resort of Donastia (San Sebastián), along an extremely wild but attractive rocky coastline that is battered by some impressive storms in the winter. A number of small inlets and harbours pass until you reach the highest point on the Basque coast, Cabo Ogoño (280 m) with breeding Storm Petrel, Peregrine, Raven and Blue Rock Thrush and part of the large Urdaibai reserve (E1). The road then has to come 12 km inland to cross this beautiful and important coastal wetland before rejoining the coast proper at Bermeo, a dynamic fishing port, then continuing to the far west of the region and the industrial port of Bilbo (Bilbao), the first port of call for many visitors on their way to the Pyrenees or the Picos de Europa.

While there is much to interest the visiting birdwatcher all through the year on the coast, it is in migration periods and winter that the year really hits the high spots. Anything can turn up on passage but during the winter months you are likely to pick up an excellent range of seabirds such as Great and Sooty Shearwaters, Black-throated and Red-throated Divers, Great Skua and Long-tailed Skua, auks — especially Razorbill — and ducks such as Common and Velvet Scoter.

The coast during the breeding season is not without interest, being important for Storm Petrel, Shag, Savi's Warbler, Moustached Warbler and Grasshopper Warbler. While Grasshopper Warbler is not restricted to the coast in Euskadi, the region is a key area for this bird in Spain, and where a good proportion of the total 250–300 breeding pairs reside.

Although there is much more to the coast of the Basque Country than Urdaibai (E1), it is this site more than any other that dominates the region, not only through its bird and natural history interest, but also the sad part it played in Spain's civil war. On the 26th April 1937 General Franco's German allies attacked the town of Gernika from the air in Europe's first mass air attack on a civilian target, killing thousands of local people. Sixty years on memories are still strong, but the town is now not just a focus for the strength of the region's people, but also the core of the Biosphere reserve of Urdaibai. Around 250 species are recorded annually at this reserve, which extends well beyond the shores of the estuary and is well placed for passage migrants given its geographical position between the Bay of Biscay and the Pyrenees. However, with 100 breeding pairs of Water

Rail and even the possibility of Wallcreeper in the winter, it has much more than a wader interest.

While the southern influence is missing from the coast, one does not have to travel too far inland before encountering more unfamiliar species such as Black Kite, Golden Oriole and Spotless Starling (Starling is only present along the coastal fringe), and further south towards its borders with Rioja, when White Stork, Bee-eater, Black-eared Wheatear and Sardinian Warbler appear. Eagle Owl also occurs in the far south of the region.

The hinterland of Euskadi is fairly intensively cultivated but it is also well wooded in parts, especially as you begin to increase in altitude, and Euskadi has especially strong populations of Honey Buzzard. It also does remarkably well with woodpeckers with the chance of four species. Lesser Spotted Woodpecker has its core area here in Spain with at least 10% (150 pairs) of the Spanish population, but possibly more. There is also the possibility of Middle Spotted Woodpecker in the far east of the region, and Black Woodpecker also occurs here.

The gorges of the Ebro such as the Hoz de Sobrón (E3) are the place to head for vultures and this site has the largest population of Griffon Vultures in Euskadi, in addition to Egyptian Vulture and Golden Eagle. Wetlands, however, are thin on the ground away from the coastal marshes and rivers, although the reservoirs to the north of Gasteiz (Vitoria) — Embalse de Urrunga and Embalse de Ullívarri have breeding Shoveler.

The main mountain ranges to the east of the region, in which the sites Aitzgorri (E2) and Sierra de Aralar (E5) are located, are the link between the Pyrenees to the east and the Cordillera Cantabrica to the west, and the cliffs, meadows, forests and peaks have Alpine Accentor, Alpine Chough, Rock Thrush, Black Woodpecker and Citril Finch; and there is a good chance that a Lammergeier may even drift over the border into the region — the furthest west in Spain for this species.

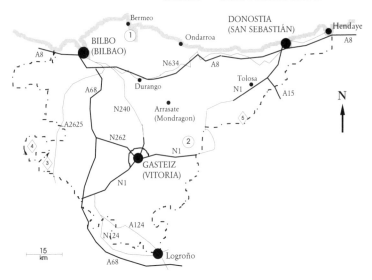

Main sites

1 E1   Urdaibai
2 E2   Aitzgorri

Other sites worth visiting

3 E3   Hoz de Sobrón
4 E4   Valderejo
5 E5   Sierra de Aralar

E1 URDAIBAI

Status: Biosphere reserve (22,041 ha), Ramsar site (945 ha) and ZEPA (23,000 ha).

Site description

Urdaibai comprises a deep estuary and rocky stretch of coastline with one of the most important saltmarshes on the whole of the north coast, and is found in the Basque province of Bizkaia. This is a typical north Spanish estuary with a marshy intertidal zone, with extensive saltmarsh and sandbanks which are uncovered at low tide.

Urdaibai, also known as Riá de Guernica, is situated around 30 km northeast from Bilbo (Bilbao) between the Matxitxako and Ogoño headlands, extending eastwards to Arbolitx point and including the small island of Izaro at the mouth of the estuary. It was declared a Biosphere reserve in 1984, and while the estuary is the focus of bird interest, the reserve extends well away from the estuary both east and west, and also inland well beyond the town of Gernika-Lumo (Guernica) to include 12 towns and villages, and part of another ten! The prime reason for this is that the Urdaibai reserve boundaries are fixed by the river catchments, so it includes the immediate areas around the rivers Oka and the smaller Golako, Mape, Artike and Laga.

The Oka river, which forms the axis of the valley has its source in the slopes of Mount Oiz, and it is from the town of Gernika seawards that it opens out to form the estuary, extending for about 12 km from the town to the coast. The reserve is a complex mosaic of sandy and mudflats, saltmarsh, reedbeds, rocky coast and cliff faces, wet pasture, arable land, holm oak woodland (the northernmost in Spain), and deciduous and coniferous woodland.

Species

Over 250 species are recorded at the reserve annually, which demonstrates the value of the site to birds. The reserve is a good site for species that may be difficult to get elsewhere in Spain: Barnacle Goose, Brent Goose, Long-tailed Duck, Velvet Scoter, Eider, Red-breasted Merganser and Reed Bunting.

It is very good for wintering and passage shearwaters, divers, skuas and sea-duck. Equally so for passage waders which, while not occurring in huge numbers, more than make up for this in terms of diversity of species with rarities regularly turning up. Other notable passage includes Spoonbill, with around 280 records annually, and similar records for Greylag Goose.

Breeding records of Storm Petrel, Shag (30 pairs), Water Rail (100 pairs), Little Ringed Plover, Grasshopper Warbler, Reed Warbler, Great Warbler and Cetti's Warbler all add to the interest throughout the seasons. When one takes in the adjoining habitats that are part of the reserve, then Short-toed Eagle, Peregrine, Hobby, Barn Owl, Lesser Spotted Woodpecker, Red-rumped Swallow and Red-backed Shrike make for an enjoyable and interesting day or two's birding.

Timing

The area is very popular in the summer months, and the beaches on the eastern side, Laiga and Laga can get crowded occasionally. Huge interest throughout the year.

Access

From Bilbo (Bilbao) east along the N634 to the BI635 which travels the length of the reserve from north to south between Amorebieta–Echano and Bermeo. In the west the BI631 connects Mungia to Bermeo. There are many smaller roads crossing the reserve.

Cabo Matxitxako The most northerly point of the Basque Country and an ideal site for seawatching and good for Shearwaters, Shag, Gannet, Peregrine, Skuas, terns, Guillemot and Blue Rock Thrush. Around 5 km north of Bermeo along a minor road.

The island of Txatxarramendi A special area to observe birds in the afternoon in autumn and winter as many species roost here in and around the island at the mouth of the estuary (Izaro). Species can include Great Northern Diver, Sandwich Tern, Arctic Tern, Lesser Black-backed Gull, Great Black-backed Gull, Avocet. Off the Gernika–Bermeo road (BI635, around 7 km from Gernika).

Saltmarshes of San Cristobal
This is the most important site for birdwatching in the saltmarshes and intertidal areas, and good for waders in particular including Curlew, but also Osprey, Spoonbill, Fantailed Warbler, Little Egret and Cormorant. Off the Gernika–Bermeo road (BI635, around 5 km from Gernika).

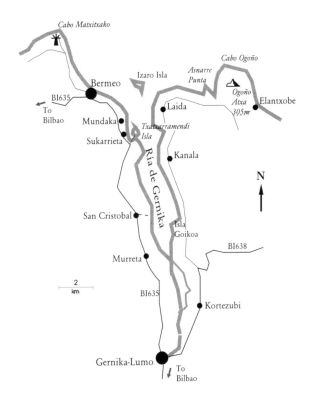

Reedbeds and wet meadows Marsh Harrier, Water Rail and Great Reed Warbler. Roosts in the winter.

Isla Goikoa Elevated ground with views across the estuary. On the road from Gernika to Laida beach on the eastern side of the estuary.

Asnarre point and Cabo Ogoño This is a good place to see the cliffs of Urdaibai and the highest point on the Basque coast at 280 m. Here it is easy to see Peregrine, Crag Martin, Shag, Kingfisher and Yellow-legged Gull. Less easy for Storm Petrel; occasionally Wallcreeper in the winter. Situated around 12 km from Gernika.

For those interested in contacting a company that runs birdwatching tours, then a local contact is: Aixerreku, Apdo. de correos 234, 48300 Gernika (tel: 6870244).

Calendar

All year: Shag, Little Egret, Grey Heron, Peregrine, Water Rail, Common Sandpiper, Yellow-legged Gull, Barn Owl, Little Owl, Tawny Owl, Great Spotted Woodpecker, Lesser Spotted Woodpecker, White Wagtail, Grey Wagtail, Blue Rock Thrush, Cetti's Warbler, Fan-tailed Warbler, Black-cap, Crested Tit, Serin, Yellowhammer, Reed Bunting, Corn Bunting.

Breeding season: Short-toed Eagle, Hobby, Little Ringed Plover, Crag Martin, Red-rumped Swallow, Tawny Pipit, Yellow Wagtail, Wheatear, Grasshopper Warbler, Reed Warbler, Great Reed Warbler, Melodious Warbler, Spotted Flycatcher, Red-backed Shrike.

Winter: Red-throated Diver, Black-throated Diver, Great Northern Diver, Slavonian Grebe, Manx Shearwater, Cormorant, Common Scoter, Ringed Plover, Sanderling, Dunlin, Black-tailed Godwit, Bar-tailed Godwit, Curlew, Redshank, Greenshank, Turnstone, Great Skua, Arctic Skua, Long-tailed Skua, Great Black-backed Gull, Razorbill, Guillemot, Great Grey Shrike.

Passage periods: Sooty Shearwater, Great Shearwater, Gannet, Purple Heron, Spoonbill, Red Kite, Osprey, Whimbrel, Little Stint, Spotted Redshank, Sandwich Tern, Common Tern, Arctic Tern, Wryneck, Sand Martin, Moustached Warbler, Willow Warbler, Pied Flycatcher.

E2   AITZGORRI

Status: Parque Natural (18,000 ha).

Site description

A limsestone massif, the highest in the Basque Country reaching an altitude of just over 1500 m. This mountainous area is made up of the sierras of Aitzgorri, Elgea, Urkilla and the mountains of Altzania, and comprising undulating rocky outcrops with rounded peaks, deep gullies and the limestone gorges of Arantzazu and Jaturbe-Araotz.

The mountain slopes are covered in large areas of beech forest, particularly on the slopes of Gipuzkoa, while there are also some oak woodlands and a rarity for Spain, peat bogs. The grazing pastures in the mountains are home to the traditional 'latxa' sheep.

Species

The three main habitats in this upland area include high-altitude species such as Alpine Accentor, Water Pipit, Citril Finch and Alpine Chough; species of gorges and rock faces such as Griffon Vulture and Egyptian Vulture, and woodland species including Booted Eagle, Goshawk and Black Woodpecker (the latter at the western end of its Pyrenean range).

Timing

Spring and summer.

Access

From Gasteiz (Vitoria) take the Gl627 north and go past the town of Arrasate (Mondragon) and take a right turn at San Prudencia on the Gl2630 to Oñati. At Oñati it is signed to the Sanctuary of Arantzazu, from

Wryneck

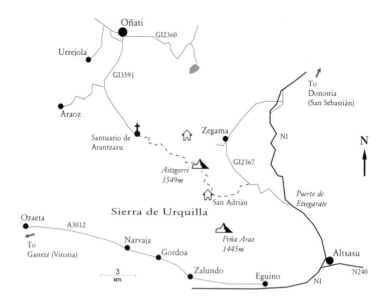

where tracks lead up into the mountains, meadows and woodland. Access is also possible from the eastern end but it is not so easy. Take the NI out of Gasteiz towards Donostia (San Sebastián), and go past Altsasu towards the Etxegárate pass (Puerto de Etxegárate). Before reaching the pass take a left on the GI2637 towards Zegama. At the Otsuarte pass on ths road (about 8 km before reaching Zegama) take a left along a forestry road to the mountain refuge of San Adrián, from where there is a mountain route to the top of Aitzgorri. Alternatively, there is much to explore lower down, including the cave of Saint Adrian.

Calendar

All year: Griffon Vulture, Sparrowhawk, Buzzard, Tawny Owl, Black Woodpecker, Crag Martin, Stonechat, Black Redstart, Mistle Thrush, Chiffchaff, Firecrest, Spotted Flycatcher, Nuthatch, Short-toed Tree-creeper, Treecreeper, Jay, Red-billed Chough, Alpine Chough, Starling, Tree Sparrow, Rock Sparrow, Citril Finch, Bullfinch, Yellowhammer, Cirl Bunting, Rock Bunting.

Breeding season: Egyptian Vulture, Booted Eagle, Wryneck, Water Pipit, Alpine Accentor, Wheatear, Rock Thrush, Whitethroat, Garden Warbler, Bonelli's Warbler, Pied Flycatcher, Red-backed Shrike.

OTHER SITES WORTH VISITING

E3 Hoz de Sobrón
Thickly wooded gorge along the River Ebro, on the border with Castile-León. A very large Griffon Vulture colony, also Egyptian Vulture, Bonelli's Eagle and Red-billed Chough. A road off the main N625 from Pancorbo in the south to Laudio (Llodio). After crossing the Ebro and going through the village of Puentelarra take the next left towards Sobrón. Continue past the turning for Sobrón for the gorge.

E4 Valderejo
Sparsely populated beautiful valley with limestone crags, pine forest and beech woods. Largest Griffon Vulture colony in the Basque Country at Vallegrull. Golden Eagle, Peregrine, Crossbill, Crested Tit. Occasional wolf sightings. Take N625 south out of Bilbo (Bilbao), past Orduña, turning right onto A2622 towards Valdegovia and Bóveda. Turn left at San Millán which takes you into the heart of the area. There is an interpretative centre at Lalastra.

E5 Sierra de Aralar
Set right in the heart of Goierri — which in Basque means 'high lands'. High massif with huge limestone outcrops, upland pastures and beech, holm oak and mixed oak woods. Booted Eagle, Black Woodpecker, Citril Finch and Alpine Chough. Take the NI south out of Donostia (San Sebastián) towards Gasteiz (Vitoria). Come off at Ordizia for Zaldibia and the sierra along the GI 133, or off at Beasain for Ataun and beyond along the GI120.

GALICIA

Galicia is a region that contrasts sharply with the image typically held of the Spanish countryside and its plains, and has more in common with the landscape and climate of Ireland than it has with Andalucia or Castile-La Mancha. In the nortwesternmost corner of Spain, it is very Atlantic in character: greener and wetter than anywhere else in the peninsula. Its people are Celtic in origin, the language spoken by a large percentage of the population being *Gallego*. It has more than the weather in common with Ireland (or Brittany come to that matter) with the national musical intrument being the *gaita,* very similar to Irish bagpipes. While not so intense as with the Basques and the Catalans, there is a strong nationalist movement here which has championed the revival of Gallego, and road signs and maps these days tend to be in Gallego, so take care!

Apart from the countryside and its rightly famous coast, the main reason for most tourists visiting the region is Santiago de Compostela, the greatest goal for pilgrims in medieval Europe and still as popular to this day. Countless people have gone to Compostela on pilgrimage since Saint James's tomb was discovered in the early 9th century, and even if you have come to Galicia on a coastal or birdwatching holiday it would be tragic not to spend one day in this splendid city.

Galicia's coast is spectacular, receiving the full force of the Atlantic winter storms which drive in from the west and north across the Atlantic itself or the equally stormy Bay of Biscay. Indented with many estuaries — fjord-like rías — the northern coast is especially wild, and the Sierra Capelada plunges straight into the sea at the cliffs of Vixia de Herbeira, the highest in Europe with a vertical drop of 612 m. The coastline from A Coruña (La Coruña) to Cabo Fisterra (Cabo Finisterre) — the Spanish equivalent of Land's End — is known as Costa de la Muerte (coast of death) an exposed and rocky stretch that regularly claims the lives of fishermen. Collectively the estuaries are known as the Rías Gallegas — the Rías Altas (upper inlets) lying on the north coast, with the Rías Bajas (lower inlets) on the western coast south of Cabo Fisterra.

These rías are an important interconnected system of feeding and resting grounds for a rich variety of wildfowl and waders that breed in northern Europe, Russia and the high Arctic yet winter in Spain or much further south in Africa. Because of its position on the western edge of Europe, north American waders also regularly turn up in late summer and early autumn — many overlooked given the sparse number of observers. Any of a number of these rías can attract a good range of wintering waders such as Little Stint, Dunlin, Sanderling, Ringed Plover, Black-winged Stilt, Avocet, Black-tailed Godwit and Jack Snipe although the Ría de Mino (G4), Umia–Grove (G2), Dunas de Corruebedo (G1) and Ría Ortigueira (G8) can be particularly productive areas. Purple Sandpiper is a species with restricted wintering distribution in Spain, but is quite common here in Galicia. Whimbrel, Marsh Sandpiper and Green Sandpiper are regular on passage, and if you are lucky something from across the ocean may turn up such as Pectoral Sandpiper or a Spotted Sandpiper, or something even rarer.

These are also good places in the winter, when the weather is stormy, for sheltering seabirds such as Common and Velvet Scoter, Black-necked Grebe, Great Northern Diver and auks such as Razorbill, and close views of these birds can be had from some of the rías. Alternatively, views can also be had from the many of the rocky coastal headlands sprinkled along the coast, such as Cabo de Corrubedo (G1) and Cabo Fisterra on the west coast, or Cabo Prior, Cabo Ortegal and Cabo de Bares (G9) on the northern coast. Birdwatching from these headlands can, in addition to the species listed above, also turn up Great Skua, Cory's Shearwater, Sooty Shearwater, Gannet and Sabine's Gull.

Galicia is also of interest for its breeding Kittiwake population, found in Spain only in this region, with now around 235 pairs (most of which breed on las Islas Sisargas off the north coast immediately to the west of A Coruña), although small numbers also breed on Islas Cíes (G3). Also at Islas Cíes there is a colony of Lesser Black-backed Gull, one of the most southerly in the world and a handful of Guillemot (the Spanish race — *Uria aalgae ibericus*). Numbers of Guillemot have dropped substantially here over the last 40 years, from around 400 to three or four! Indeed there are now only around a dozen pairs at most in Spain (all in Galicia) and there is a definite chance that the species may soon cease to breed in Iberia. Other coastal species of importance in Galicia are the Atlantic race of Storm Petrel, *Hydrobates pelagicus pelagicus*, and Shag, where Galicia has around 1,900 pairs out of a total 3,000–3,150 breeding in Spain, with particular strongholds on Islas Cíes and Islas de Ons (G12). It is also possible to see Raven, Peregrine and Red-billed Chough on these islands and other rocky coasts.

The coastline is also richly studded with many good beaches and tiny coves, which are generally empty (of people that is), although the further south you go the more populous they become, especially in summer. There are some particularly impressive dunes to be seen at Corruebedo.

Inland Galicia is lush and heavily wooded, a patchwork of tiny fields where every bit of cultivatable land is farmed. As the scale of farming is small and not intensive, there is much variety of bird habitat with species representative of northern Spain such as Bullfinch, Red-backed Shrike and Yellowhammer rubbing shoulders with Hoopoe, Sardinian Warbler and Golden Oriole.

Move further east and you reach the far western edge of the Cordillera Cantabrica mountain range with some mountains soaring as high as 1800–1900 m in the massifs of Ancares (G7) and Caurel (G6), and shared with the neighbouring region of Castile-León. Here Black Woodpecker, Capercaillie and Grey Partridge have their western outposts, and their is even a chance of Middle Spotted Woodpecker and, on the highest ground, Alpine Accentor.

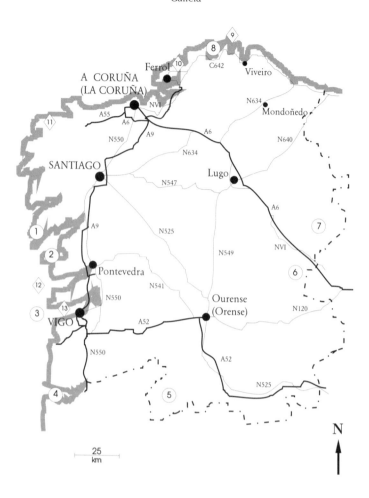

Main sites

1 G1 Dunas de Corruebedo
2 G2 Umia–Grove
3 G3 Islas Cíes
4 G4 Ría De Miño
5 G5 Baixa Limia–Serra (Sierra) De Xurés
6 G6 Serra (Sierra) de Caurel
7 G7 Serra (Sierra) de Ancares
8 G8 Ría de Ortigueira y Ladrido

Other sites worth visiting

9   G9   Cabo de Bares
10 G10 Laguna de Frouxeira
11 G11 Laguna de Traba
12 G12 Islas de Ons
13 G13 Ría de Vigo

G1 DUNAS DE CORRUBEDO

Status: Parque Natural and Ramsar site (550 ha).

Site description

Corrubedo is one of the most important coastal wetlands in Galicia, and sited around a wide bay that is sandwiched in between the headlands of Cabo de Corrubedo to the north and a series of small headlands to the south, the furthest being Punta Perico. Within this whole area there are a number of key habitats important for birds. The bay is made up of an impressive dune system, some 1 km long, 250 m wide and 12–15 m high, behind which there are areas of marsh, the main areas concentrated around Carregal lagoon and the three rivers, ríos Longo, Sirves and Artes, that flow into the bay at the northern part of the site. Two lagoons (Vixán and Carregal) are found at the southerly end of the site, which is also separated from the sea by a sandspit, and has well-developed reedbeds, damp meadows and woods of pine and eucalyptus.

Species

The interest of the site varies with the seasons, with the beach and bay important in the winter for Great Northern Diver, Razorbill, Common Scoter and Scaup while the lagoons and marshes are important for duck such as Teal, Shoveler and Gadwall and waders such as Dunlin, Grey Plover and Bar-tailed Godwit.

Given the great variety of habitats, the passage and breeding season make the dunes a very attractive proposition for a day's birding if one is staying in the area. Kentish Plover, Crested Lark, Cuckoo, Water Rail and Great Reed Warbler are regular breeding species, with Sandwich Tern, Marsh Harrier and Whimbrel all regular on passage, along with many other waders.

The dunes have a much wider interest than just birds with, for example, ten species of amphibian and 14 species of reptile.

Timing

Winter for duck, divers, auks and waders, and spring for a variety of species, particularly waders.

Access

From Santiago take the C543 to Noia, Porto do Son and finally Santa Uxía de Ribeira. Alternatively take the N550 to Padrona, then the C550 to Ribeira. The area of interest is split in two by the river system and marshland, so that to explore the area it is necessary to visit these two discrete zones.

Southern area Start at the new visitor centre at the park, CIELGA (*Centro de Interpretacíon do Ecosistema Litoral de Galicia*), situated almost in the centre of the park — from Ribeira take the road to Carreira and Vilar, then having passed these villages take a track to your left to the visitor centre. There is a car park here. Information boards are also placed at a number of sites in the park. From here it is possible to walk to the south and Vixán lagoon (2 km round trip), or to the north to the dunes and marshes and Carregal lagoon (4 km round trip).

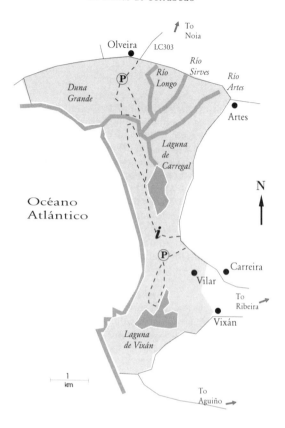

Northern area To visit the northern part of the site, which also has a car park, return to the main road and turn left to Olveira and Corrubedo. Near Olveira and almost opposite the LC303 road that takes you on to the C550; a track to the left leads to the dunes where there is another car park. This area has some of the largest dunes.

Calendar

All year: Goshawk, Water Rail, Kentish Plover, Stone Curlew, Barn Owl, Kingfisher, Stonechat, Fan-tailed Warbler, Cetti's Warbler, Crested Lark, Serin.

Breeding season: Hobby, Common Sandpiper, Cuckoo, Hoopoe, Tree Pipit, Great Reed Warbler, Reed Warbler, Melodious Warbler.

Winter: Red-throated Diver, Great Northern Diver, Great Crested Grebe, Black-necked Grebe, Cormorant, Grey Heron, Mallard, Teal, Gadwall, Shoveler, Pochard, Tufted Duck, Common Scoter, Merlin, Coot, Oyster-catcher, Grey Plover, Dunlin, Jack Snipe, Curlew, Greenshank, Great Black-backed Gull, Razorbill.

Passage periods: Cory's Shearwater, Gannet, Little Bittern, Purple Heron, Spotted Crake, Marsh Harrier, Sanderling, Bar-tailed Godwit, Whimbrel, Sandwich Tern, Yellow Wagtail, Nightingale, Whinchat.

G2 UMIA–GROVE

Status: Espacio Natural Régimen Protección General, ZEPA and Ramsar site (2561 ha).

Site description

The main interest here is a sheltered shallow inlet with extensive areas of intertidal sands and muds, saltmarsh and a number of small islands. The largest island of A Toxa (La Toja) is situated at the head of the inlet to the north and is connected by a causeway. This inlet is separated from the sea on its westward boundary by a spit of sand, and the beach of A Lanzada.

Species

This is one of the most important sites in Galicia for wintering waders with a long list of species that make use of the intertidal areas for feeding and roosting (particularly large numbers of Dunlin). The general area does, however, have more interest depending on the time of year of your visit, with ducks, grebes, and auks making use of the bay and inlet in winter, and waders, terns and gulls found regularly on passage.

Timing

Winter is the time of greatest interest, although waders do hang on into spring, and the intertidal flats, saltmarsh and associated habitats attract birds on passage. If you making only a brief visit to the area then the tide tables should be checked to make the most of your time here. The area can be very popular at weekends in the summer and on public holidays.

Access

From Pontevedra take the C550 westwards towards Sanxenco and O Grove at the head of the promontory. It is a very scenic drive and there

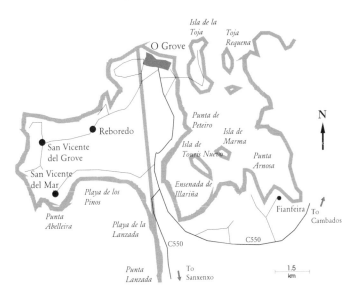

are many opportunites to stop and birdwatch with views across the Ría de Pontevedra and across to Isla de Ons. Most of the best areas are, however, situated on and around the peninsula (also sometimes known as O Grove) itself.

Playa de la Lanzada The bay facing the sea between the headlands Punta Lanzada and Punta Abelleira, containing the beaches Playa de la Lanzada and Playa de los Pinos is the first focus, and is good for duck and grebe in the winter, and waders and terns on passage.

Ensenada O Grove The second focus is the inlet itself on the landward side of the sandspit, which is the key area for wintering and passage waders. It is relatively easy to get good views into and across the inlet from a variety of points, and roads enable you to reach these areas very easily. At the north end good views are possible from Isla de la Toja, and the headland Punta de Peteiro. Excellent views of waders can also be had in the bay of Ensenada de Illariña (also known as O Bao) from the road itself. Roads also lead to the southern section at Punta Arnosa and at Fianteira where further views are possible.

Calendar

All year: Little Grebe, Mallard, Goshawk, Sparrowhawk, Buzzard, Kestrel, Peregrine, Water Rail, Moorhen, Coot, Barn Owl, Little Owl, Tawny Owl, Green Woodpecker, Crested Lark, Woodlark, Fan-tailed Warbler, Dartford Warbler, Sardinian Warbler, Serin, Cirl Bunting.

Breeding season: Kentish Plover, Redshank, Common Sandpiper, Nightjar, Alpine Swift, Swift, Hoopoe, House Martin, Melodious Warbler, Whitethroat.

Winter: Black-throated Diver, Great Northern Diver, Great Crestd Grebe, Cormorant, Shag, Little Egret, Grey Heron, Spoonbill, Shelduck, Wigeon, Gadwall, Teal, Pintail, Shoveler, Pochard, Tufted Duck, Scaup, Common Scoter, Eider, Hen Harrier, Merlin, Oystercatcher, Ringed Plover, Grey Plover, Dunlin, Bar-tailed Godwit, Black-tailed Godwit, Jack Snipe, Snipe, Curlew, Redshank, Greenshank, Turnstone, Mediterranean Gull, Little Gull, Black-headed Gull, Common Gull, Great Black-backed Gull, Razorbill, Guillemot.

Passage periods: Cory's Shearwater, Yelkouan Shearwater, Storm Petrel, Gannet, Montagu's Harrier, Hobby, Sanderling, Bar-tailed Godwit, Whimbrel, Spotted Redshank, Sandwich Tern, Common Tern, Little Tern, Whiskered Tern.

G3 ISLAS CÍES

Status: Parque Natural and ZEPA (433 ha).

Site description

A group of three small islands lying close to the mainland opposite the mouth of the Ría de Vigo (G12) and famous for its seabird colonies. The islands' shores contrast: the western shores steep, while the eastern shores that face the mainland are sandy, with dunes. Las Islas Cíes have three main islands, with two northern ones linked by a road and a sand bar: from north to south Illa do Monte Agudo, Illa do Faro and Illa de San Martiño. They lie around 15 km from the city of Vigo. The whole archipelago also consists of many other smaller islets and rocky outcrops.

The area was designated a natural park in 1980. Much of the interior consists of pine and eucalypt plantations which, although planted, have a relatively natural understorey, and can provide welcome shelter for birds on migration.

Species

The largest colony of Shag in Spain, with an estimated 400 breeding pairs, was one of the main reasons for the area's designation as a natural park. The islands also support one of the most southerly sites in the world for breeding Lesser Black-backed Gull. The Spanish race of Guillemot, *Uria aalge ibericus,* just hangs on here. In the early 1960s, 400 pairs bred on the islands, by 1975 there were around a dozen and now only two to three pairs breed here each year.

Timing

Spring and summer, although visits will be determined by the weather, availability of boats and, if planning to stay on the island, the opening of the campsite.

Cory's Shearwaters

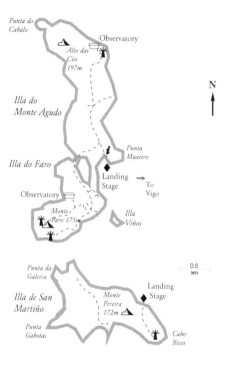

Access

Organised boats run regulary in spring and summer from the middle of June to the middle of September, although trips are also made during Easter and in spring at weekends when the weather is good. Boats leave from the Estación Marítima de Ría in Vigo which is close to the tourist office. It is also possible to arrange private trips if required outside these periods, and there is no restriction to visits at any time of year provided the group is no more than ten in number.

Once on the island there are numerous paths that lead across the islands, although access is limited in certain areas, particularly to the precipitous western cliffs. There are two bird observatories, Observatorio del Faro do Peito (Illa do Monte Agudo) and Observatorio de la Campana (Illa do Faro), and a campsite (Illa do Faro) which is open during summer months. There is an information centre on the island.

Calendar

All year: Shag, Peregrine, Kentish Plover, Yellow-legged Gull, Guillemot, Rock Dove, Stonechat, Black Redstart, Blackbird, Dartford Warbler, Sardinian Warbler, Red-billed Chough, Raven.

Breeding season: Cory's Shearwater, Lesser Black-backed Gull, Nightjar, Alpine Swift, Tree Pipit.

Winter: Great Northern Diver, Red-throated Diver, Black-throated Diver, Gannet, Cormorant, Great Skua, Sandwich Tern, Razorbill, Puffin, Kittiwake.

Passage periods: Manx Shearwater, Cory's Shearwater, Great Shearwater, Sooty Shearwater, Gannet, Common Scoter, Velvet Scoter, Great Skua, Pomerine Skua, Sandwich Tern, Common Tern, Little Tern, Turtle Dove, Nightingale, Redstart, Whinchat, Wheatear.

G4 RÍA DE MIÑO

Status: Part game refuge (900 ha).

Site description
Found in the south of the region, on the border with Portugal, this is one of many rías or estuaries of Galicia and so typical of the region. The river has a good variety of habitats, with sandbanks, mudflats, saltmarshes, reedbeds, bankside woodlands and a number of riverine islands.

Species
Mainly a site for species on passage or wintering, although a good range of species does breed in and around the river. Large numbers of duck are present in winter on the river including Shelduck, Mallard, Tufted Duck and Scaup but also present can be Great Northern Diver, Black-necked Grebe, Red-breasted Merganser and Razorbill, especially during periods when the weather is rough and shelter is needed.

The hides can be some of the best places for viewing waders including Grey Plover, Avocet, Ringed Plover and the occasional North American rarity. The reeds and associated vegetation in this area can also produce a number of breeding and passage warblers, and birds of prey including Marsh Harrier and Red Kite.

It is worth searching the dunes, scrub and woodland on both sides of the estuary for passage migrants.

Timing
Autumn through to spring is the most productive time, with September/October and April/May being the best times for migrants, and November to March the best time to visit for wintering birds. Summer can be particularly busy on the river, and the estuary is also affected by shooting interests at certain times of the year, at weekends and on public holidays.

Access
Most of the interest of the site centres on the mouth of the river, south of A Guarda (La Guardia) on the headland, where you can get good views out to sea as well as across the river mouth itself. From Vigo take the N120 to Porrino and then N550 southwards towards the Portuguese border, and the C550 to A Guarda. A more pleasant approach, however, is to follow the C550 out of Vigo south along the coast to Baiona and onwards to A Guarda.

At A Guarda the C550 runs in a loop, continue on this road to La Playa de Camposancos where it is worth walking and birdwatching along both coast and river shores. Return back onto the C550, but shortly afterwards, after about 250 m, a track off to the right takes you closer to the shore of

the river through Pasaxe and eventually to two hides near the campsite of *Camping Santa Tecla*. This track rejoins the C550 to A Guarda.

Depending on the distribution of the birds in the estuary and available time, it can be worth making a special detour into Portugal either by driving across at the head of the estuary through Tui, or by taking the ferry across the Miño from Goían (almost halfway from A Guarda to Tui) across to Vila Nova de Cerveira. Then take the N13 southwest wards towards Caminha and the mouth of the river, and a large pine wood and dune system.

Calendar

All year: Cormorant, Shag, Mallard, Shelduck, Red Kite, Marsh Harrier, Goshawk, Sparrowhawk, Buzzard, Peregrine, Water Rail, Moorhen, Coot, Woodpigeon, Little Owl, Kingfisher, Green Woodpecker, Great Spotted Woodpecker, Crested Lark, Woodlark, Skylark, White Wagtail, Grey Wagtail, Dipper, Stonechat, Fan-tailed Warbler, Sardinian Warbler, Crested Tit, Red-billed Chough, Tree Sparrow.

Breeding season: Hobby, Quail, Little Ringed Plover, Kentish Plover, Common Sandpiper, Little Tern, Cuckoo, Turtle Dove, Scops Owl, Nightjar, Alpine Swift, Swift, Hoopoe, Swallow, Crag Martin, Yellow Wagtail, Great Reed Warbler, Golden Oriole.

Winter: Great Northern Diver, Red-throated Diver, Great Crested Grebe, Black-necked Grebe, Gannet, Red-breasted Merganser, Little Egret, Common Scoter, Velvet Scoter, Tufted Duck, Scaup, Eider, Long-tailed Duck, Hen Harrier, Oystercatcher, Black-winged Stilt, Ringed Plover, Little Stint, Jack Snipe, Snipe, Black-tailed Godwit, Purple Sandpiper, Turnstone, Razorbill, Guillemot, Great Skua, Arctic Skua, Mediterranean Gull, Little Gull, Sabine's Gull.

Passage: Cory's Shearwater, Yelkouan Shearwater, Spoonbill, Osprey, Marsh Harrier, Avocet, Ringed Plover, Bar-tailed Godwit, Redshank, Wood Sandpiper, Kittiwake, Sandwich Tern.

G5 BAIXA LIMIA–SERRA (SIERRA) DE XURÉS

Status: Parque Natural (20,920 ha).

Site description

The Natural Park of Baixa Limia–Serra Xurés is located in the southwest of the Galician province of Ourense, on its border with Portugal. The area was designated a natural park in 1992 and is a huge area of contrasting landscape and scenery, with a corresponding variety of bird habitats. The massif is mainly granite, although one of the park's most obvious features is the *'bolos'*, rock deposits left behind after glacial erosion. Two main river systems drain the area, the Río Limia and the Río Salas, although many other stream and rivers feed into these two rivers. Three reservoirs also add to the interest, the Encoro de Salas, Encoro das Conchas, and Encoro de Lindosa, although they do not all fall within the park's boundaries.

Like other sierras in Galicia, Serra de Xurés also has contrasting Atlantic and Mediterranean vegetation, with areas of decidous trees of oak and beech, and maquis type scrub with cork oak and strawberry tree. Farming is generally small scale, of low intensity and mainly pasture-based, with parts of the park terraced for agricultural use. The reservoirs have limited marginal vegetation although there are some reedbeds, and there are some good riverine woods along some sections of river. The area is also of considerable archaeological interest, including many ancient burial sites scattered through the valley of the River Salas and adjoining mountains.

Species

The park does have a good variety of habitat and species, and over 140 species of bird have been recorded. The species list below gives some idea of the wide range of birds likely to to be encountered, with at least

Crested Tit

ten species of warbler breeding in the area, and the possibility of three species of shrike. Some species such as Goldcrest, Yellowhammer and Sardinian Warbler are on the edge of their range here, and breeding species such as Snipe and Redshank are quite rare in Spain. It is also reasonable to expect to see species that are rare in the UK but occur here in good numbers including Woodlark, Golden Oriole and Cirl Bunting.

Timing
Spring through into summer.

Access
Take the N540 south out of Ourense, through Celanova and Bande, and it is this road that takes you through the centre of the park. Many side roads off the N540 take you higher up into the sierra and are worth exploring. There are also a number of paths throughout the area; try the one from the village of Quegas, a round walk of around 6–7 km, which goes through some oak and sweet chestnut woods, scrub and farmland. Other routes do exist, but some can be quite difficult for those not used to walking along rough mountain paths.

Calendar
All year: Little Grebe, Great Crested Grebe, Goshawk, Sparrowhawk, Buzzard, Red-legged Partridge, Stock Dove, Barn Owl, Little Owl, Tawny Owl, Green Woodpecker, Grey Wagtail, White Wagtail, Dipper, Black Redstart, Blue Rock Thrush, Cetti's Warbler, Fan-tailed Warbler, Dartford Warbler, Sardinian Warbler, Godcrest, Firecrest, Crested Tit, Great Grey Shrike, Red-billed Chough, Tree Sparrow, Cirl Bunting, Rock Bunting, Corn Bunting.

Breeding season: White Stork, Black Kite, Quail, Little Ringed Plover, Snipe, Redshank, Common Sandpiper, Turtle Dove, Cuckoo, Swift, Hoopoe, Woodlark, Sand Martin, House Martin, Yellow Wagtail, Nightingale, Whinchat, Melodious Warbler, Subalpine Warbler, Bonelli's Warbler, Golden Oriole, Red-backed Shrike, Woodchat Shrike.

G6 SERRA (SIERRA) DE CAUREL

Status: Unprotected.

Site description

Another mountainous area in the far eastern hinterland of Galicia that sees few tourists and is very well wooded. Immediately south of Serra de Ancares (G7), it has much in common with its neighbour. It is part of a sparsely populated fringe of the Cordillera Cantabrica that traverses almost the whole of northern Spain's coast from the Basque Country in the east through to Galicia, with its most popular area, the Picos de Europa (AS6), the main attraction. While similar to Ancares with its steep wooded valleys and cliff faces it has more of a Mediterranean influence with associated scrub vegetation, and has a greater variety of geological features and consequently rock types and soils, giving it greater diversity. The highest point of the Caurel range is Piapaxaro at 1607 m.

Species

As this upland block forms the western edge of the Cordillera Cantabrica, it has some of the species that occur in Galicia at the western edge of their range, namely Black Woodpecker, Capercaillie and Grey Partridge. It is also possible to find Middle Spotted Woodpecker. The woodland avifauna is also very rich here, like the Serra de Ancares, with a similar list of breeding species, the key ones being Honey Buzzard, Short-toed Eagle, Woodcock, Redstart and Marsh Tit.

Timing

Spring and early summer.

Access

Take the NVI southeast out of Lugo as far as Pedrafita do Cebreiro, where you take a right along the very scenic LU651, which crosses the best area for birds (and scenery), and eventually joins the N120 at the

Honey Buzzard

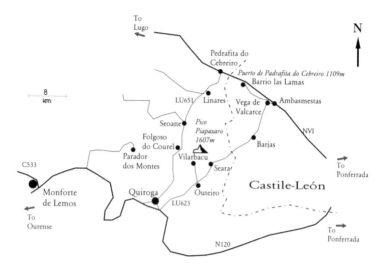

southern end of the site near Quiroga. From Ourense take the N120 to Monforte and continue to Quiroga where you turn left and take the same road, the LU651. There is another road to the south which needs care when driving, and stretches from Vega de Valearce off the NVI to Fistéus and Quiroga, and lies off the N120 to the south. Both roads offer plenty of opportunities to stop and explore the countryside and woodlands.

Calendar

All year: Hen Harrier, Goshawk, Sparrowhawk, Golden Eagle, Grey Partridge, Woodcock, Great Spotted Woodpecker, Middle Spotted Woodpecker, Crag Martin, Dipper, Blue Rock Thrush, Dartford Warbler, Firecrest, Goldcrest, Crested Tit, Nuthatch, Bullfinch, Cirl Bunting, Rock Bunting.

Breeding season: Honey Buzzard, Short-toed Eagle, Montagu's Harrier, Hobby, Red-backed Shrike, Rock Thrush, Subalpine Warbler, Melodious Warbler, Bonelli's Warbler, Spotted Flycatcher.

G7 SERRA (SIERRA) DE ANCARES

Status: Unprotected; although in Castile-León the sierra forms part of the Reserva Nacional de los Ancares Leoneses.

Site description

A sparsely populated and wooded mountainous area in the far eastern part of Galicia, on the borders with the regions of Asturias and Castile-

León, that forms the far western end of the Cordillera Cantabrica mountain range. There is some difference between the north- and south-facing slopes, with a more Atlantic woodland community on the northern slopes, mainly oak, silver birch and sweet chestnut, and Mediterranean maquis-type scrub on the southern.

Species

Much of the interest is focused on those species at the western edge of their range and which are mostly found in the eastern parts of the Cordillera Cantabrica or the Pyrenees, namely Black Woodpecker, Capercaillie, Grey Partridge and Middle Spotted Woodpecker. The woodland avifauna is also very rich with Woodcock, Honey Buzzard, Short-toed Eagle and Marsh Tit. In the rockier areas there is a chance of Rock Thrush, and at higher altitudes there is an outside chance of Alpine Accentor.

Wild cat, wild boar, beech marten and red squirrel all occur.

Timing

Spring and early summer

Access

Take the NVI southeast out of Lugo as far as Becerreá. Turn left here on the C535 road towards San Román. You are now on the western boundary of the area and there are many opportunities to explore by road, either northwards along the LU722 to Navia de Suarna and then onto minor roads, or higher into the mountains towards Rao. Apart from San Román the other main alternative to reach the heart of the sierra is to take the LU723 towards Portelo, and at Villanueva take a left turn onto mountain roads to Degrada, Robledo and Donis. Whichever route you decide to take there are many places to stop and take short walks across the range or through the woodlands.

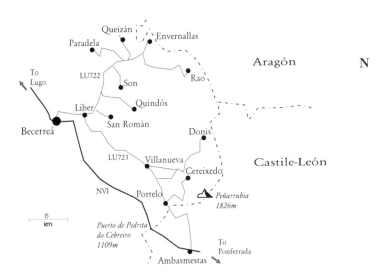

Calendar

All year: Hen Harrier, Goshawk, Sparrowhawk, Buzzard, Golden Eagle, Capercaillie, Grey Partridge, Woodcock, Tawny Owl, Black Woodpecker, Great Spotted Woodpecker, Middle Spotted Woodpecker, Water Pipit, Dunnock, Alpine Accentor, Goldcrest, Firecrest, Marsh Tit, Bullfinch.

Breeding season: Honey Buzzard, Short-toed Eagle, Wryneck, Redstart, Rock Thrush, Blackcap, Bonelli's Warbler, Long-tailed Tit, Short-toed Treecreeper, Jay, Red-backed Shrike.

G8 RÍA DE ORTIGUEIRA Y LADRIDO

Status: ZEPA and Ramsar site (2940 ha).

Site description

Spectacular scenery on the northwesternmost point of Spain provides the backdrop for this estuary situated in between the headlands of Cabo Ortegal to the west and Punta de Estaca de Bares in the east. The outer part of this wide tidal estuary is deep, with a rocky coastline and cliffs, whilst the inner two arms either side of the village of Ortigueira are much shallower and sheltered. There are large areas of intertidal muds and sands, extensives areas of saltmarsh and sand dunes, with occasional pine and eucalyptus plantations.

Species

The inner estuary is the main focus of attention with large numbers of wintering and passage duck — Wigeon, Teal, Pochard, Mallard, Pintail and Shoveler — and waders including Grey Plover, Bar-tailed Godwit, Turnstone, Oystercatcher and Sanderling. There are good numbers of Dunlin and Curlew in particular. Kentish Plover breeds here.

The outer parts of the estuary and seawatching from Cabo Ortegal can bring views of large numbers of Gannet, Manx Shearwater and Yelkouan Shearwater, occasional Great Northern Diver and more commonly Guillemot, Razorbill and sometimes Puffin.

There are breeding Storm Petrel (Atlantic race *pelagicus*) on some of the offshore islands and rocky cliffs, which also hold Peregrine, Raven and Red-billed Chough.

Timing

Throughout the year, with winter important for wintering duck and waders, and spring and the area is important as a passage site for waders.

Access

The estuary lies north of the C642 from Ferrol. Much of the estuary can be seen from roads that follow both the left and right banks.

The deeper areas of the estuary are best viewed on the western bank from the road leading from the village of Cariño northwards to the

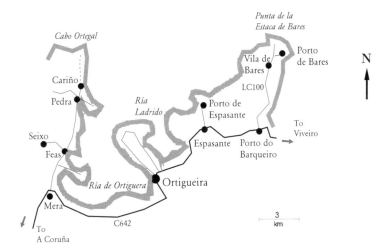

lighthouse at Cabo Ortegal, which is also good for seawatching. On the eastern side the section between Punta do Bandeixa and Punta do Tallo, which has various minor roads leading you to the sea off the main C642.

The sheltered shallow areas with mudflats and saltmarsh are also skirted by roads. From the Ría Ladrido (interesting in its own right) take the C642 and follow the estuary and saltmarsh westwards. This route can give good views onto the marsh, at various viewpoints. After a few kilometres turn right towards Cariño for further views.

Closer views can also be obtained from the village of Ortigueira, where roads lead down to the beach and harbour, and to the shore of the Ladrido estuary.

Calendar

All year: Shag, Buzzard, Peregrine, Kestrel, Yellow-legged Gull, Barn Owl, Kingfisher, Grey Wagtail, Stonechat, Black Redstart, Blue Rock Thrush, Cetti's Warbler, Fan-tailed Warbler, Dartford Warbler, Firecrest, Crested Tit, Red-billed Chough, Raven, Spotless Starling, Tree Sparrow, Serin, Cirl Bunting, Rock Bunting.

Breeding season: Storm Petrel, Hobby, Kentish Plover, Common Sandpiper, Cuckoo, Alpine Swift, Pallid Swift, House Martin, Yellow Wagtail, Wheatear, Grasshopper Warbler, Reed Warbler, Melodious Warbler, Whitethroat, Blackcap, Chiffchaff.

Winter: Great Northern Diver, Red-breasted Merganser, Wigeon, Teal, Mallard, Pintail, Shoveler, Pochard, Common Scoter, Merlin, Oystercatcher, Ringed Plover, Grey Plover, Curlew, Dunlin, Bar-tailed Godwit, Jack Snipe, Razorbill, Guillemot, Puffin.

Passage periods: Gannet, Manx Shearwater, Yelkouan Shearwater, Redshank, Spotted Redshank, Greenshank, Common Sandpiper, Nightjar, Tree Pipit, Red-backed Shrike.

OTHER SITES WORTH VISITING

G9 Cabo de Bares

Immediately east of Ría de Ortigueira (G8), and the northernmost point of mainland Spain. Well known as a seabird observation station and particularly good in the autumn period. Simple accommodation in the bird observatory. Take the C642 from Ferrol to Viviero, and about halfway between Ortigueira and Viveiro, take a left turn at Porto de Barquiero on the LC100 towards the headland, taking another left turn instead of following the road into Porto de Bares.

G10 Laguna de Frouxeira

A shallow lagoon with reedbeds and linked to the sea on the north coast. Duck and waders in winter. Marsh Harrier and passage species including warblers. C646 north from Ferrol and the lagoon lies to the left of the road.

G11 Laguna de Traba

Small coastal lagoon with breeding Water Rail, Great Reed Warbler. Can be excellent for passage waders in both spring and autumn, with the possibility of transatlantic migrants in late summer through into autumn. From A Coruña take the C552 to Carballo and then LC414 to Buño, LC422 to Ponte-Ceso, LC430/431 to Laxe. Take the LC433 and some 4–5 km out of Laxe take a right to Pedreña and Boaño. Track at end of road to lagoon.

G12 Islas de Ons

An island of around 450 ha with breeding seabirds. Reached by boat from Portonovo on the north coast of the Ría de Pontevedra just off the C550 near the town of Sanxenxo. Tracks across the island and limited accomodation.

G13 Ría de Vigo

A wide estuary, one of the largest in Galicia — and in Spain. The whole of the estuary can be interesting, although the area around Vigo is developed and some others are heavily visited. Take the C550 for views to the north and south at the mouth of the estuary, closest to the Islas Cíes (G3) offshore. The innermost section, Ensenada de San Simón, is best viewed from the western side along the N554 which follows the shore. Birds similar to Rio Miño (G4).

MADRID

It will come as no surprise to people that the region of Madrid is domi-nated by the Spanish capital, but not without a little competition from its beautiful and stunning neighbours. Although the capital of Spain, it lacks the architecture of some other European cities and the charm, history and splendour of Segovia, Toledo, Ávila and Cuenca — not to mention the nearby palaces of Aranjuez. What the city does have are wide boulevards, some great museums and a superb selection of tapas bars and nightlife — the locals claiming very proudly that their city stays up later than any other in Europe!

However, many visitors to Spain coming in search of birds, moun-tains and wild flowers and flying in to Madrid as the gateway to the country choose to ignore the city and its environs completely, and head directly east or south in search of the birds offered by Extremadura or Andalucia. However, stay awhile sampling the late nights and the sur-rounding countryside and you will see Black Vulture, Spanish Imperial Eagle, Black Stork, Great Bustard, Little Bustard, Black-bellied Sand-grouse, Alpine Accentor, Citril Finch and Bluethroat within a very short space of time, and perhaps even wonder if you really need to drive those long distances.

To the north of the city there is a very high mountain range, the Sierra de Guadarrama (MA1) part of the Sistema Central and reaching heights of well over 2000 m, with the highest peak of 2429 m at Peñalara. Plentiful snow in the winter means there are ski runs with a few ski resorts, and the mountains are high enough even for Alpine Accentor, one of the few breeding sites away from the main northern mountain ranges — the other two being the Sierra Gredos and the Sierra Nevada. Unfortunately no Wallcreeper or Alpine Chough though — they stay well and truly in the north in the Pyrenees and Cordillera Cantabrica.

Other species that the open mountain habitats have to offer include Black Vulture (which along with the population in the Sierra Gredos has one of the largest breeding concentrations in Spain of 110–130 pairs), Griffon Vulture, Golden Eagle, Water Pipit, Bluethroat, Black Redstart, Rock Thrush and Red-billed Chough. There is no shortage of pine woods and decidous woodland in the mounatins and its foothills. Citril finch occurs at higher levels, in addition to species such as Booted Eagle, Goshawk, Redstart, Bonelli's Warbler and Pied Flycatcher.

Come down the mountain and back towards the city and soon you begin to encounter more Griffon Vulture, with a good colony at La Pedriza del Manzanares (MA2), Thekla Lark, Bee-eater, Red-rumped Swallow, Blue Rock Thrush, Sardinian Warbler and Subalpine Warbler.

Lower on the plain there are still some remnants of the *dehesa* type holm oak that would at one time have covered substantial areas but is now best represented to the west of the city on the way to Extremadura, and at El Pardo (MA3) which fortunately has had some measure of protection. This open landscape is special for Black Vulture, Spanish Imperial Eagle, Black Stork (with small numbers in Madrid region, normally in single figures), Red Kite, Red-necked Nightjar, Azure-winged Magpie, Orphean Warbler and Spanish Sparrow.

Extensive areas of cereal cultivation are found to the east of the city of Madrid, and whose interest and importance has been recognised by the designation of 33,520 ha as a ZEPA, the *Estepas cerealistas de los Ríos Jarama y Henares* (MA5). Despite being close to the city they support breeding Montagu's Harrier, Lesser Kestrel, Great Bustard, Little Bustard, Black-bellied Sandgrouse, Pin-tailed Sandgrouse, Stone Curlew, Short-toed Lark and Calandra Lark.

Wetland interest focuses around the rivers and some of the reservoirs in the region. All the main rivers — Henares, Jarama, Tajuña and Tajo are of note with their *'sotos'*, riverine woods and river cliffs. Some stretches have heron colonies of Night Heron and Cattle Egret, such as the Río Tajo (MA7), with the additional attraction of Little Bittern, Purple Heron, Cetti's Warbler, Bearded Tit, Penduline Tit and Golden Oriole. The reservoirs also have some of these species as well as Water Rail, but are also of importance in winter, spring and autumn during passage. One of the best reservoirs is the Embalse de Santillana (MA3) below the Sierra de Guadarrama, which is good for wintering duck, passage waders and terns. The flooded pits to the south of Madrid, Los Albardales (MA6), an ornithological reserve of SEO, is also important for wintering birds.

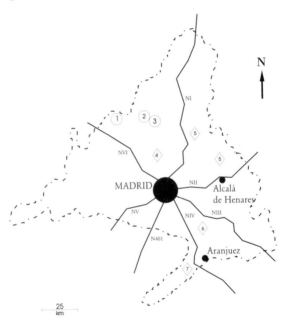

Main sites

1   MA1   Sierra de Guadarrama
2   MA2   La Pedriza del Manzanares
3   MA3   Embalse de Santillana

Other sites worth visiting

4   MA4   El Pardo
5   MA5   Estepas de los Ríos Jarama y Henares
6   MA6   Los Albardales
7   MA7   Río Tajo

MA1   SIERRA DE GUADARRAMA

Status: Part of Parque Natural.

Site description

The Sierra de Guadarrama to the northwest of Madrid, stretches for around 100 km from the Pico del Lobo and the Puerto de Somosierra in the north to El Escorial and beyond in the south. The seven peaks 'Siete Picos', occur between the passes of Navacerrada and Fuenfría, but the highest peak in the sierra is Peñalara at 2,429 m, right on the border of the regions between Madrid and Castile-León. While one would encourage exploration of the whole range, much of the interest is concentrated in the central portion between Miraflores de la Sierra in the east and Navacerrada in the west. Scots pine forest covers the mountain slopes interspersed with a mixture of shrub species including whin, juniper, *Cistus*, lavender and tree heather. The River Lozoya which has good riverine woodland cuts the mountain range in half, and a number of mountain lakes occur.

The mountains receive much snow, and attract skiers in season.

Species

Excellent for birds of prey, with a list almost as long as the mountain range itself and the potential of seeing around 17 species not including any harriers that you may happen to come across. As a bonus, if that is not enough there are six species of owl, and it is an excellent site for both Black Vulture and Spanish Imperial Eagle.

The high ground and meadows and scrub should reveal Alpine Accentor, Water Pipit, Bluethroat and Citril Finch, with species such as Rock Thrush, Wheatear and Ortolan Bunting also possible. Pine woods have Crested Tit, Crossbill and Goldcrest.

Timing

As the mountains are so close to Madrid they are very popular, and not surprisingly they can be very busy at weekends.

Access

Signs on the roads indicate whether the mountain passes are clear of snow and open to traffic. Take the M607 north out of the city to Colmenar Viejo and beyond. To reach the eastern section take the M609 right, soon after Colmenar, which takes you to Miraflores de La Sierra. At Miraflores turn left towards the Puerto de la Morucuera (Morucuera pass).

To reach the western section continue along the M607 past Colmenar to Cerceda, then stright on towards Collado-Mediano on the M623, at which you take a right onto the M601 to Navacerrada and eventually the Puerto de Navacerrada (Navacerrada pass).

At the Puerto de los Cotos (on the M604 between the two mountain passes of Navacerrada and Morcuera), there is a chairlift that takes you up part of the way to the summit of Peñalara, near the ski resort of Valdesquí (which is worth exploring in its own right for some key high-altitude grassland and scrub species). Alternatively, you can walk up the path!

There are various viewpoints around the mountains and refuges if you are interested in more serious walking, and there are numerous tracks and paths across the mountains for exploration.

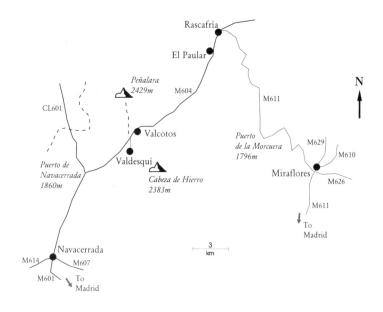

Calendar

All year: Red Kite, Griffon Vulture, Black Vulture, Goshawk, Sparrow-hawk. Buzzard, Golden Eagle, Spanish Imperial Eagle, Bonelli's Eagle, Kestrel, Peregrine, Rock Dove, Barn Owl, Scops Owl, Eagle Owl, Little Owl, Tawny Owl, Long-eared Owl, Great Spotted Woodpecker, Alpine Accentor, Black Redstart, Blue Rock Thrush, Dartford Warbler, Gold-crest, Crested Tit, Nuthatch, Great Grey Shrike, Red-billed Chough, Raven, Rock Sparrow, Citril Finch, Crossbill, Rock Bunting.

Breeding season: White Stork, Black Stork, Honey Buzzard, Black Kite, Egyptian Vulture, Short-toed Eagle, Booted Eagle, Hobby, Quail, Hoopoe, Crag Martin, Red-rumped Swallow, Water Pipit, Bluethroat, Redstart, Black-eared Wheatear, Rock Thrush, Melodious Warbler, Bonelli's Warbler, Pied Flycatcher, Woodchat Shrike, Ortolan Bunting.

MA2   LA PEDRIZA DEL MANZANARES

Status: Part of La Cuenca Alta del Manzanares Parque Natural (4000 ha total).

Site description

One of the most spectacular 'boulder fields' in Spain and which forms part of the La Cuenca Alta del Manzanares. This natural park is made up of a range of limestone mountains that have been eroded into an amazing variety of strange shapes, and which has become known more widely as the Pedriza del Manzanares. Vegetation is sparse, but

Scops Owl

there is some tree growth, albeit stunted on the lower slopes, and some juniper and planted pine on the upper slopes, for example in the Sierra de los Porrones. However, this is one of those sites where the geology and the rock formations steal the show. The rock formations have been compared to an open air art gallery, but that comparison does not seem to stop Griffon Vultures building their nests on them, and covering parts of the massive statues with their 'guano'. As it lies only 50 km from Madrid it has become a very popular weekend excursion area.

Species
While the rock formations may be the stars at this site, there are many distractions in the bird world. Griffon Vulture, mentioned earlier, build their nests on the craggy outcrops and the area is paradise for species that make their homes on cliffs or nest in rocky terrain: Eagle Owl, Crag Martin, Blue Rock Thrush, Rock Thrush, Red-billed Chough and Wheatear. Other interesting sightings to look out for include Bluethroat and Water Pipit, and a number of warblers that breed in the scrubby areas.

Timing
Spring (although early spring can still be very cold) and early summer. Definitely avoid the weekends and public holidays as it is a very popular site. Sometimes there are restrictions on the number of cars entering the park (during peak visiting times).

Access
Like the Santillana reservoir take the M607 north out of Madrid towards Colmenar Viejo, and carry on to Cerceda. Turn right here on the M608 to Manzanares, about 0.5–1 km before the village a signed road leads to the control post at the gates of La Pedriza, and up through the mountain pass of Collado de Quebrantaherraduras (horse-shoe breakers' pass), and ends at a parking area next to the river at the Canto Chico. Many steep paths take you up the valley from

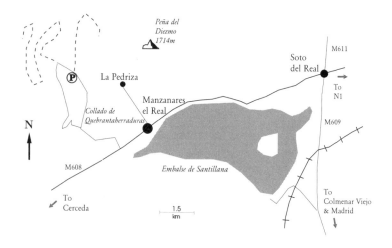

the Arroyo de la Dehsilla to the high ground of La Pedriza, and there are many opportunities for walking in the area.

Take care over the fallen boulders that sometimes block the paths, or at the very least can make walking difficult.

Calendar

All year: Red Kite, Griffon Vulture, Buzzard, Golden Eagle, Peregrine, Red-legged Partridge, Rock Dove, Barn Owl, Eagle Owl, Little Owl, Long-eared Owl, Crested Lark, Thekla Lark, Woodlark, Skylark, Crag Martin, Water Pipit, Dipper, White Wagtail, Blue Rock Thrush, Dartford Warbler, Sardinian Warbler, Azure-winged Magpie, Red-billed Chough, Raven, Rock Bunting.

Breeding season: Black Kite, Booted Eagle, Hobby, Cuckoo, Scops Owl, Swift, Bee-eater, Hoopoe, Red-rumped Swallow, Tawny Pipit, Bluethroat, Wheatear, Black-eared Wheatear, Rock Thrush, Subalpine Warbler, Orphean Warbler, Woodchat Shrike, Ortolan Bunting.

MA3   EMBALSE DE SANTILLANA

Status: Parque Natural.

Site description

This large reservoir receives water from the River Manzanares and two seasonal streams, the Samburiel and the Mediano. There are considerable variations in water level in the reservoir — as is the case with many others in Spain. The immediate area around the reservoir can be quite interesting with farmland, small stands of trees, scrub and well-developed bankside vegetation along the watercourses. The area of the reservoir to the east is more shallowly shelving so can be attractive to roosting ducks, feeding herons, egrets and storks.

Species

Cattle and Little Egrets feed around the shores. Although there is relatively little cover around the margins of the lake, small numbers of duck breed as does Water Rail and Little Grebe. Its main importance, however, is during winter when large numbers of duck congregate, and it also attracts large gull roosts. During the autumn large numbers of White Stork roost and feed on the shallow shores of the reservoir, and the wetland can be very good during spring passge for a wide variety of migrants.

The surrounding area is perhaps more interesting during the breeding season with species such as Thekla Lark, Spectacled Warbler and Azure-winged Magpie all likely. The latter is a relatively recent addition to the breeding birds of the area. The areas of dry farmland to the east of the reservoir in particular are also attractive to Little Bustard in the latter part of the summer, and while they do not breed immediately next to the reservoir they occur in the general area, along with Great Bustard, although Great are not normally seen here.

Manzanares has a good population of breeding White Stork.

Timing

All year.

Access

(See map on page 216.) Take the M607 north out of Madrid towards Colmenar Viejo, and carry on to Cerceda. Turn right here on the M608 to Manzanares and the reservoir. Alternatively, after Colmenar take a right towards Soto del Real which will bring you to the right-hand side of the reservoir. There are hides on the north shore but these have fallen into disrepair.

Calendar

All year: Little Grebe, Great Crested Grebe, White Stork, Little Egret, Gadwall, Mallard, Shoveler, Pochard, Coot, Moorhen, Water Rail, Thekla Lark, Fan-tailed Warbler, Dartford Warbler, Sardinian Warbler, Azure-winged Magpie.

Breeding season: Little Bustard, Cattle Egret, Black-winged Stilt, Stone Curlew, Great Spotted Cuckoo, Red-necked Nightjar, Bee-eater, Short-toed Lark, Yellow Wagtail, Melodious Warbler, Subalpine Warbler, Spectacled Warbler, Woodchat Shrike.

Winter: Black-necked Grebe, Cormorant, Grey Heron, Wigeon, Teal, Pintail, Red-crested Pochard, Black-headed Gull, Lesser Black-backed Gull.

Passage periods: Purple Heron, Night Heron, Black Stork, Montagu's Harrier, Osprey, Hobby, Little Bustard, Avocet, Black-tailed Godwit, Bar-tailed Godwit, Redshank, Greenshank, Common Sandpiper, Black Tern, Whiskered Tern.

OTHER SITES WORTH VISITING

MA4 El Pardo

A *dehesa* (grassland with holm oak) very close to the city with Black Vulture and Spanish Imperial Eagle, and the added interest of a reservoir that attracts wintering duck. Also Crane and Black Stork outside breeding season, and passage terns. Restricted access. On edge of northern periphery of city, take the M601 off the main NVI road to El Pardo.

MA5 Estepas de los Ríos Jarama y Henares

Cereal growing area to the east of the city, with hills and some holm oak woodland. Steppe birds with Montagu's Harrier, Lesser Kestrel, Great and Little Bustard, Black-bellied and Pin-tailed Sandgrouse, Roller and larks. Take the NII–E90 east out of the city to Alcalá de Henares, then a left on the M119 and best area north of Camarma de Esteruelas. For other area (Río Jarama), take the M100 from Alcalá to Cobeña and north (right) onto M103. Best area between Valdetorres de Jarama and Talamanca de Jarama.

MA6 Los Albardales

SEO reserve near the River Jarama halfway between Madrid and Aranjuez. Take the NIV south out of Madrid, and around 20 km take a left to San Martin de la Vega on the M506, and just to the north of the village. Lagoon important for wintering birds. Contact SEO (see page 10) for visiting details.

MA7 Río Tajo

Stretch of river and plains between Aranjuez and Toledo, with mixed habitat of river, reedbeds, riverine woodlands, cliffs, farmland and parkland. Range of species including Pin-tailed Sandgrouse, Penduline Tit, Little Bittern, Roller and Night Heron. Main interest at the Aranjuez end and sandwiched between the CM4001 to the north and the N400 to the south.

MURCIA

Between Catalunya in the north and Andalucia in the south lies a tract of coastal Spain made up of Valencia and Murcia and popularly known as the Levante. Murcia is a small region which boasts 320 sunny days per year, and the Murcian coast (or *Costa Cálida* — 'the warm coast') has its share of holiday-makers, many of whom are concentrated around the semi-inland sea, the Mar Menor, with its high-rise hotels dominating the seaward horizon. However, it is not just the sea and the sun that attract people to Murcia, some return year after year to coat themselves in its therapeutic mud, a product of the salt-pans behind Mar Menor and reputedly good for both skin and rheumatism!

Murcia's history, when Cartagena was the major city of the Cartaginians in Spain and it had an important silver- and gold-mining industry tend to be overlooked by modern sun worshippers. Most also do not look twice at its countryside or are put off by first appearances. Lying in a rain shadow area behind the Cordilleras Béticas mountain range it has an uncompromisingly arid appearance with its dry, rugged bare mountain slopes and gullies with expanses of esparto grass.

The coast is where the rugged landscape of the mountains reaches the sea's edge, and with it comes an horizon of oleander, prickly pear and dwarf palm and the occasional ruined watchtower, reminding everyone of the days when pirates were a real danger.

The higher sierras are typically covered in pine woods, but these areas are now restricted to the far northwest part of the region, and as altitude decreases and you get closer to the coast these forests disappear to be replaced by scrub. In many areas not even scrub is present and the ground is mostly bare and eroded. Those areas with a covering of trees have respectable woodland bird communities with birds of prey well represented including Short-toed Eagle, Goshawk, Sparrowhawk, Buzzard, Booted Eagle and Hobby, and also with Crested Tit, Crossbill and Bonelli's Warbler. A good example, but perhaps atypical, is the Sierra de Espuña (MU1) — an upland area that was systematically cleared of its trees and subsequently suffered horrendous erosion, but has been successfully reforested.

The more widely distributed bare and eroded areas of countryside, with rocks, gullies and gorges are, however, certainly not without their bird interest. While Murcia is one of the few areas of Spain not to have any species of vulture, it does have good populations of both Golden Eagle and Bonelli's Eagle. Luckily one does not have to travel far to see these species as they are not restricted to the higher sierras but found widely in the region and at low levels. In addition, species such as Alpine Swift, Crag Martin, Black Wheatear, Black-eared Wheatear, Blue Rock Thrush, Red-billed Chough and Raven, along with Rock Sparrow and Rock Bunting are also likely to be encountered. These habitats are common enough, even on the coast, where there is the added bonus of a good site for Trumpeter Finch (in the north of the region in the Sierra de la Fausilla (MU4) just south of Mar Menor). Pallid Swift and Storm Petrel also breed along the coast, and good views can be had of passing Cory's Shearwater and Audouin's Gull from many of the rocky headlands, such as Cabo Cope and Cabo Tiñoso.

In areas where there is at least some vegetation and scrub warblers can be well represented including Sardinian, Subalpine, Spectacled and Dartford Warblers and Whitethroat, with Orphean Warbler in those areas with taller scrub or young pine plantations.

Steppe areas in Murcia are now few and far between, most lost through cultivation and irrigation and now cereal production, with almonds, fruit and vines alongside. Most of the species are present with the exception of Great Bustard (although there are occasional sightings in the far northeast of the region) and little chance of Pin-tailed Sandgrouse. Montagu's Harrier, Little Bustard, Stone Curlew, Black-bellied Sandgrouse and all eight species of lark are more widely found in the remaining areas. Of particular note is the presence of breeding sites for Dupont's Lark on the lower slopes of the Sierra de Espuña (MU1) and strong populations of Lesser Short-toed Lark and Thekla Lark, found for example on the salt steppes of Los Solares de Río Guardalentín (MU2) and the farmed land around the Alfonso XIII reservoir (MU5). Other open-country species such as Lesser Kestrel, Roller, Stock Dove, Great Spotted Cuckoo and Red-rumped Swallow are all possible while Spanish Sparrow occurs in the far northwest.

Murcia also has many of the 'typical' Mediterranean species, especially in river valleys (even if they are commonly dry!) and on the cultivated and irrigated land between the sierras and the coast, such as Hoopoe, Bee-eater, Nightingale, Golden Oriole and Woodchat Shrike. These areas should also be checked for Rufous Bush Chat and Olivaceous Warbler.

Wetlands are at a premium in Murcia given the low rainfall and the region's predeliction for irrigation. Most of the rivers have suffered as a consequence, although there are some reservoirs, the best being Embalse de Alfonso XIII (MU5), that are of interest with species such as Water Rail, Great Reed Warbler, and some wader interest with Black-winged Stilt. However, the region is dominated by one site, the Mar Menor (MU3), the largest coastal lagoon in Spain and supporting a huge range of species — breeding, wintering and passage. While this lagoon does not attract the vast numbers of birds found at Spain's other coastal wetland gems, it does make up for this by having an amazing variety of species and some key ones to boot, including Bittern, Purple Gallinule, Bearded Tit, Audouin's Gull, Gull-billed Tern and Marbled Duck. It is also the largest wintering site in Spain for Red-breasted Merganser.

All in all, although one's first impressions of Murcia may be disappointing, with a little delving it has a range of species to match any other region in Spain, and most are within easy reach of each other. What it lacks in vultures it makes up for in Rufous Bush Chat and Purple Gallinule!

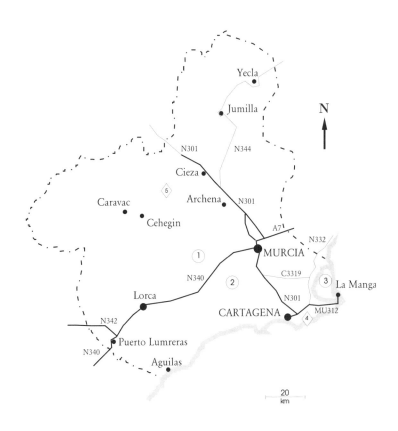

Main Sites

1   MU1   Sierra de Espuña
2   MU2   Los Solares de Río Guadalentín
3   MU3   Mar Menor y Salinas de San Pedro del Pinatar

Other sites worth visiting

4   MU4   Sierra de la Fausilla
5   MU5   Embalse de Alfonso XIII

MU1 SIERRA DE ESPUÑA

Status: Parque Natural (13,855 ha) and Reserva Nacional de Caza (14,181 ha).

Site description

Part of the eastern section of the Andalusian mountain chain (Cordillera Aubbética), which stretches form the bay of Cádiz to Cape La Nao in Alicante. Its highest point is El Morrón de Espuña (1584 m), with another two peaks surpassing 1500 m, and despite its southerly position regularly receives at least some snow each year. The area consists of four separate mountain blocks each separated from the other by flood valleys and ravines, and there is a considerable area of pine forest on the slopes with areas of scrub.

Much of the area is now covered with replanted pine, and where trees do not cover the landscape then large rocky limestone formations dominate the scenery. The River Espuña and the river flowing through the Enmiedo Ravine are the most important watercourses. The former has its origin in Collado Bermejo (1207 m) and flows into the Guadalentín 100 m above sea level, after only 19 km. This gives some idea of the steep slopes it has to negotiate on its way.

The history of this area is alarming. Deforestation along with torrential rainstorms washed away large areas of soil, exposing the bedrock and causing regular floods in the valleys of Totana and Alhama de Murcia. After one of the worst catastrophes (in 1879) susbstantial replanting was undertaken of a variety of trees, covering at least 7000 ha. The replanting has been such a success that the area has been designated both as a game reserve, and a natural park. Maquis scrub still forms important areas within the sierra, including plants such as thyme, lavender, rosemary and chamomile. Esparto grass is found in areas where the soil quality is very poor.

Species

Three main habitats in the park need to be explored to produce a wide range of species. Cliffs and rocky faces hold large birds of prey including Golden and Bonelli's Eagle, Peregrine and Eagle Owl, but also Blue Rock Thrush. Typical forest species such as Goshawk, Crossbill, Booted Eagle and Bonelli's Warbler can be found, and those of grassland and open country habitats, especially of semi-arid ground, including Black Wheatear and larks (including Thekla, Lesser Short-toed and Dupont's). A regular breeding area for Dupont's Lark is situated in the grassland area immediately around the junction with the MU503 and the road that goes off right into the sierra. Scrub can also be good for Subalpine, Dartford and Spectacled Warbler.

One of the most interesting mammals in the park is red squirrel, a subspecies of which has a much lighter coloured coat than normal. The arruí, or moufflon from the Atlas Mountains was introduced in the early 1960s to increase the game species in the area. The introduction programme using animals from Casablanca and Frankfurt zoos has been very successful.

Timing

April through to June. Weekends can be busy, and the area is popular with climbers.

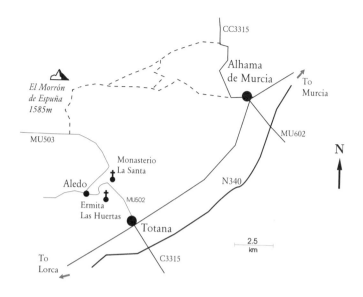

Access

Within easy reach of the coast and Murcia. Take the N340 (E15) south-west out of Murcia and depending on which part of the sierra you wish to visit, leave the main road at Alhama de Murcia or Totana a further 10 km along the road. From Totana take the MU502 which leads to the heart of the park, turning right at the village of Aledo, along the MU503, and then right into the park and back down to Alhama. The lower slopes of the park are less forested, and one should look out for a variety of grassland and open-country species (see above).

From Alhama de Murcia initially take the C3315, but after a few kilometres take a left turn into the sierra towards Mula or La Perdiz.

There are many tracks through the sierra, although most of these are unmarked, and a number of mountain refuges (permission is required to use these).

Calendar

All year: Goshawk, Sparrowhawk, Buzzard, Golden Eagle, Bonelli's Eagle, Peregrine, Tawny Owl, Dupont's Lark, Lesser Short-toed Lark, Thekla Lark, Woodlark, Crag Martin, Black Wheatear, Blue Rock Thrush, Dartford Warbler, Sardinian Warbler, Red-billed Chough, Crossbill, Rock Bunting.

Breeding season: Short-toed Eagle, Booted Eagle, Great Spotted Cuckoo, Alpine Swift, Bee-eater, Red-rumped Swallow, Subalpine Warbler, Spectacled Warbler, Orphean Warbler, Bonelli's Warbler.

MU2 LOS SOLARES DE RÍO GUADALENTÍN

Status: Unprotected.

Site description

A restricted area of salt steppe or 'saltmarsh' alongside the River Guada-lentín, that is partly cultivated for cereals and has scattered trees and shrubs. One of the few areas of steppe vegetation remaining in Murcia and definitely worthy of a visit, especially given its proximity to the coast, where most visitors stay during their holiday, and the town of Murcia itself.

Species

A very good spectrum of open steppe and grassland species and espe-cially good for Stone Curlew, Black-bellied Sandgrouse and Montagu's Harrier. Also very good for larks and a rich variety of open-country birds including Bee-eater, Roller, Black Wheatear, Black-eared Wheatear, Great Grey Shrike and Woodchat Shrike. Ocassional Golden Eagle and Bonelli's Eagle drift over the area.

Hoopoe

Timing

Spring and early summer.

Access

Take the N340 westwards out of Murcia and turn left onto the MU602 towards Cartagena, or the following exit onto the C3315 towards Mazarrón. The main interest of the area lies between these two roads on either side of the river Guadalentín, and the best one to follow is the MU603 which links these two roads. Once on the MU602, at the first crossroads, after around 7 km, turn right and shortly afterwards tracks lead into the area. A particularly well-known path leads off from the petrol station on this road.

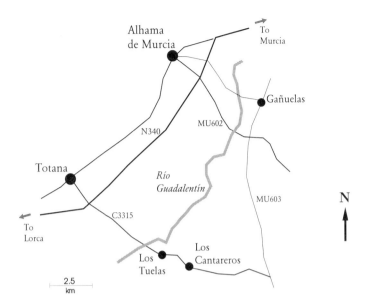

Calendar

All year: Kestrel, Red-legged Partridge, Stone Curlew, Black-bellied Sandgrouse, Stock Dove, Scops Owl, Little Owl, Hoopoe, Calandra Lark, Lesser Short-toed Lark, Stonechat, Black Wheatear, Dartford warbler, Great Grey Shrike, Rock Sparrow, Corn Bunting.

Breeding season: Marsh Harrier, Montagu's Harrier, Little Bustard, Quail, Turtle Dove, Red-rumped Swallow, Great Spotted Cuckoo, Bee-eater, Roller, Short-toed Lark, Black-eared Wheatear, Spectacled Warbler, Subalpine Warbler, Spotted Flycatcher, Woodchat Shrike.

MU3   MAR MENOR Y SALINAS DE SAN PEDRO DEL PINATAR

Status: Ramsar site (14,933 ha).

Site description

The largest coastal lagoon in Spain and one of the largest in the Mediterranean, measuring 21 km long and 10 km wide. It is separated from the Mediterranean by a long coastal sand spit known as *La Manga* ('The Sleeve') which is 24 km long and 900 m wide at its broadest point. Mar Menor was originally a bay but La Manga began to progressively close it off to the point where today only a system of canals and sluices keep the Mar Menor in direct contact with the open sea.

The waters are incredibly saline and as a consequence have produced a very specialised habitat for birds. While much of the immediate surrounds to the lagoon have been developed there are areas of saltpans, most especially to the north at San Pedro del Pinatar, sometimes also known as Salinas de Cotorillo. Together with a line of sand dunes which separate them from the Mediterranaean they cover an area of 800 ha. There are also saltpans to the south but these are relatively small areas at Marchamalo. In addition, there are also sandy areas and dunes, some saltmarsh and areas of reedbed, irrigation ponds, farmland and a number of islands, mainly within the lagoon but also some outside, the largest being Isla Perdiguera and Isla Mayor. The southern portion of the site ends in the Cabo de Palos headland.

Species

Huge interest throughout the year with wintering duck and Red-breasted Merganser in particular. This is a regular wintering site for the latter and is one of the largest wintering sites in the whole of Spain. Many species of wader and most other birds can turn up on passage, including a good range of waders, terns, gulls and much more besides. Greater Flamingo are present for most of the year, apart from the spring, but do not breed here, although they do so over the border in Valencia. The lagoons and associated habitats have a very respectable breeding list including Black-winged Stilt, Avocet, Kentish Plover, Stone Curlew and a good array of larks including Calandra, Short-toed and Lesser Short-toed Lark. A sizeable colony of around 300 pairs of Little Tern is present. In addition, the site does have some specialities. A few pairs of Purple Gallinule breed here, Storm Petrel breed on the offshore islands along with Audouin's Gull, for example on the small island of Isla Grosa on the seaward side of Mar Menor. In addition, Bittern, Baillon's Crake and Bearded Tit are also present during the breeding season. The saltpans can have large roosts of Audouin's Gull.

Timing

Throughout the year, although high summer can be very busy, and heat haze is a problem during the hottest parts of the day in spring and summer. Windsurfing can cause disturbance from time to time.

Access

Immediately south of the border with the neighbouring region of Valencia. From Murcia take the N301 south towards Cartagena, but at Baños y Mendigo, turn left onto the C3319 to San Javier. From Alicante take the N332 south to San Pedro del Pinatar, and beyond. As the site is very large there are a number of birdwatching opportunities in and around the margins of the site.

For the northern saltpans head for San Pedro del Pinatar, and then take the road signed for the port and saltpans (*Puerto y Salinas*). It is not possible to visit the whole area but there are good views from the road and a small number of paths. A track between the saltpans and the Mar Menor leads to a windmill, further views are available here and, although it is not possible to drive further, one can walk to the end of the spit at Punta de Algas.

Further views across the Mar Menor and adjoining saltmarsh and associated habitats can be obtained from the coastal road in the south where it follows closely the boundary of the lagoon. From the northern

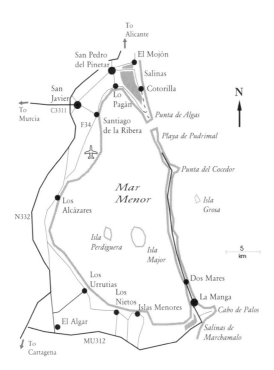

end join the F34 minor road that passes next to the Aeropuerto de San Javier, and follow it through Los Alcázares where the road hugs the shore, and continue southwards stopping every so often. This eventually joins the main road (MU312) where you turn left if you want to explore the southern saltpans at Marchamalo. As with the northern part of the site, access is not allowed directly onto the pans but good views can be had from the road.

Another road follows the seaward spit (now covered with high-rise holiday developments) and almost encloses the lagoon, giving further views right across the lagoon, and can be particularly good in winter. The road runs along almost the entire length of the spit (some 24 km) and after the first 6 km or so the hotels begin to disappear and the scene becomes a little more tranquil up to Punta del Cocedor and beyond to the beach of Playa de Pudrimal.

Calendar

All year: Little Grebe, Greater Flamingo, Little Egret, Shelduck, Mallard, Moorhen, Coot, Avocet, Stone Curlew, Kentish Plover, Yellow-legged Gull, Scops Owl, Kingfisher, Calandra Lark, Lesser Short-toed Lark, Crested Lark, Black Wheatear, Fan-tailed Warbler, Dartford Warbler, Rock Sparrow.

Breeding season: Storm Petrel, Bittern, Marbled Teal, Purple Gallinule, Black-winged Stilt, Little Tern, Black-headed Gull, Audouin's Gull, Common Tern, Quail, Gull-billed Tern, Whiskered Tern, Black Tern, Pallid Swift, Short-toed Lark, Spanish Sparrow, Spectacled Warbler.

Winter: Black-necked Grebe, Cormorant, Grey Heron, Red-breasted Merganser, Black-headed Gull, Audouin's Gull, Ringed Plover, Grey Plover, Golden Plover.

Passage periods: Grey Heron, Quail, Baillon's Crake, Redshank, Common Sandpiper, Great Spotted Cuckoo, Wryneck, Red-rumped Swallow, Knot, Little Stint, Temminck's Stint, Ruff, Spotted Redshank, Green Sandpiper, White-winged Black Tern.

OTHER SITES WORTH VISITING

MU4 Sierra de la Fausilla
A series of low coastal hills. Trumpeter Finch and Bonelli's Eagle with Cory's Shearwater, terns and Audouin's Gull off Cabo del Agua. From Cartagena take the N332 towards La Unión, taking a right turn at Alumbres on the N343 to Escombreras. The hills lie between Escombreras and the sea.

MU5 Embalse de Alfonso XIII
A reservoir with adjacent farmed but arid areas. Red-crested Pochard, Water Rail and Marsh Harrier mingle with Black-bellied Sandgrouse, Montagu's Harrier and Thekla Lark. North of Murcia on the N301 past Cieza, then a left onto the C3314 towards Calasparra. Take MU552 south towards the reservoir and the plains.

NAVARRA

Navarra comes tumbling down from the Pyrenees; moist, misty, full of legends and influenced by the proximity of the Bay of Biscay. With the vast beech and silver fir forests of Irati spreading out into the foothills and lower sierras, via the largest Griffon Vulture colony in Spain, it quickly transforms itself into a different climate and the semi-arid and strange landscapes of the Bardenas 'desert'. Navarra is a region of contrasts. There is also the contrast between town and country, and while Navarra has few large towns or cities, Pamplona dominates the scene (the second largest town is Tudela with only 30,000 inhabitants). Pamplona, the capital of the region, is now most famous for *Los Sanfermines*, a manic festival in July where there is much celebration and partying, and in which the celebrated bull-running through the streets plays only a small part.

The Pyrenees stand as the natural border with France, along a 163-km stretch, but the mountains of Navarra are gentler, less rugged, and do not reach such great heights — at least in the west — as the rest of the Pyrenees. They are also far less developed, and there is not as yet a single ski lift in the region. However, in the far east of the region at the head of the Roncal valley (N2) we have the beginning of the higher Pyrenees, with peaks over 2000 m and this is by far the most rugged part of Navarra. Lammergeier, Alpine Chough and Citril Finch are fairly widely distributed in the region's mountains, but many high-altitude birds are restricted to this far-eastern corner of the region. Come here if you want the chance of Ptarmigan, Capercaillie, Grey Partridge, Tengmalm's Owl, Alpine Accentor, Wallcreeper and Snow Finch.

What the western end lacks in alpine species, it makes up for by its importance as a migration route, and there are a number of passes such as at Collado de Urquiaga (N1) that are regularly used. The Urgatz bird observatory (N1) north of Roncevalles studies the post-breeding migration of birds across the Pyrenees. In addition to some of the commoner species one also stands a reasonable chance of Black Stork, Crane, Honey Buzzard, Short-toed Eagle and Booted Eagle, if you are prepared to put in the time.

Another feature of the Navarrese Pyrenees is its woodlands, most of which are dominated by beech and silver fir, and hugely important (not just for the bird communities), with the most extensive forests at Quinto Real and Irati — the largest ancient forest in the Pyrenees at around 6250 ha (N1). It is possible to get all seven species of woodpecker, and the forests hold strong populations of both Black and White-backed Woodpecker. Navarra is *the* region for White-backed Woodpecker, holding almost all of the 60–70 pairs thought to breed in Spain — it is *the* bird of Navarra. The woods and forests have much more besides, with excellent numbers of birds of prey — Honey Buzzard, Goshawk, Booted Eagle and Hobby — and other species such as Redstart, Pied Flycatcher and Hawfinch.

Moving south down the picturesque valleys of Salazar and Roncal (N2) and into the sierras there are some very impressive gorges, especially in the east of the region. Large colonies of Griffon Vulture in particular occur, being most numerous at Foz de Burgui — part of the Roncal valley (N2) — and at the Foz de Arbayún and Lumbier (N3) — part of the Sierra de Leyre. The spectacular 300 m sheer walls of the Arbayún Gorge are home to the largest Griffon Vulture colony not just in Navarra but the whole of Spain with something approaching 250 nests. Other cliff-nesting species also vie for attention — Egyptian Vulture, Bonelli's Eagle, Peregrine and Red-billed Chough, but get closer in and other species such as Crag Martin, Blue Rock Thrush and Rock Sparrow appear. Other sierras with their gorges, rivers and woodlands are also worth seeking out such as Monte del Conde (N10) and the Sierra de Urbasa in the west of the region (N8).

South of Pamplona, the country changes rapidly. The mountains and wooded hills are left behind and the 'monotonous plain' so characteristic of central Spain begins to open out. This area is extremely important for its steppe species and dominated by the open expanse of Las Bardenas Reales (N7) where bustards, sandgrouse, larks and wheatears are found within the eerie, eroded, lunar-like landscape. Threatened by intensive cultivation — made possible through unsustainable irrigation projects — the species hang on, helped by the establishment of three nature reserves. All of the typical species are present: Montagu's Harrier, Little Bustard, Great Bustard, Stone Curlew, Black-bellied Sandgrouse and Pin-tailed Sandgrouse — and with greater numbers of larks, including good numbers of Dupont's, Calandra, Thekla and Lesser Short-toed Lark. Lesser Kestrel and Black-eared Wheatear are also found.

Once the arid landscape of Bardenas gets too much for you then you do not have far to look for some wetland interest. While open water is reasonably rare in Navarra, the riverine woodlands of the Aragón and Ebro valleys (N6) have Night and Purple Heron, Nightingale, Penduline Tit and Golden Oriole. This is a very rare and threatened habitat across the whole of Europe, with few extensive areas now remaining. Other than rivers the two most important wetlands are Laguna de las Cañas (N4) and Laguna de Pitallas (N5) — both with extensive reedbeds, especially at Pitallas, with breeding Bittern, Little Bittern, Night and Purple Heron, Garganey, Red-crested Pochard, Savi's Warbler, Olivaceous Warbler, Bearded Tit and Reed Bunting.

Main sites

1 N1 Western Pyrenees
2 N2 Valle de Roncal
3 N3 Foz de Arbayún y Foz de Lumbier
4 N4 Laguna de las Cañas
5 N5 Laguna de Pitallas
6 N6 Sotos de Río Aragón y Río Ebro
7 N7 Las Bardenas Reales

Other sites worth visiting

8   N8   Sierra de Urbasa
9   N9   Peñas de Echauri
10 N10 Monte del Conde

N1 WESTERN PYRENEES

Status: Part Coto Nacional de Caza, and nature reserves. Also both Aritzakun–Urrizate–Gorramendi (5909 ha) and Selva de Irati–Roncesvalles (18,684 ha) are ZEPA.

Site description

This area includes the far western end of the Pyrenees with most of the highest peaks in this section between 1000 and 1500 m. They do, however, reach above 2000 m at the eastern end of Irati Forest and the Sierra de Abodi, but this is not typical. There are three distinct areas in this part of the Pyrenees, gradually increasing in altitude from west to east, but what they do share apart from their altitude, mountain peaks, rocky gorges and cliffs are the forests, which are extensive and cover considerable areas of the mountain slopes on both the French and Spanish sides. Quinto Real and Bosque de Irati have the greatest areas of forest.

Pico Gorramakil (Gorramendi) The first area, nearest the coast, is Pico Gorramakil, a mountainous region just topping 1000 m (at 1090 m) and close to the French border with cliffs, rocky bluffs and wet pasture intermingling with small beech woods, with scattered farms and sheep and goat grazing.

Kintoa (Quinto Real) Further south and slightly east is the Coto Nacional Kintoa (Quinto Real) an extensive and mature beech woodland, which is at the western fringe of the vast Irati Forest, but which has more open countryside and higher levels of pasture, heather and scrub. This game reserve is the westernmost reserve in the Pyrenees, and is centred around the peak of Monte Adi (1458 m) and covers some 5982 ha of relatively gentle mountain slopes just south of the frontier with France.

Roncesvalles–Bosque de Irati–Sierra de Abodi This area is further east still and is perhaps the most important, stretching from around Roncesvalles and east to the Bosque de Irati and the Sierra de Abodi. This sparsely populated mountainous area, rising up to the peak of Orhi (2017 m) on the French border, has further extensive areas of mixed beech woods and silver fir, and the forest at Monte de la Cuestión, part of the Bosque de Irati, is the largest beech forest in Spain. Irati is supposedly haunted by the ghost of Jeanne d'Albret, the queen of Navarra and mother of Henri IV, who was poisoned in 1572 and who revisits her old 'haunts' on windy nights. This vast forest extends over the border into France where it becomes known as Forêt d'Iraty. The historic battlefield at Roncesvalles is part of this area, and is where the rearguard of Charlemagne's army was massacred by the Basques in 778 AD while retreating into France. There is another important forest near here, this time of oak, at Garralda.

Urgatz bird observatory north of Roncevalles studies the post-breeding migration of birds across the Pyrenees.

Species

It is the beech and silver fir woods that are the most important habitat, and very important for birds and the only area in Spain where, luck permitting, you can get all seven species of Woodpecker —

Black Woodpecker

Green, Black, Great Spotted, Lesser Spotted, Middle Spotted, White-backed, Lesser Spotted and Wryneck. This is the main area in Spain for White-backed Woodpecker, and almost all of the 60–70 pairs thought to breed in Spain come from Navarra (a small number are found over the border in Aragón). It is not just woodpeckers that make the forests important, although they are indicators of the health and conservation value of the area. Other species of note include Honey Buzzard, Goshawk, Woodcock, Redstart, Marsh Tit, Treecreeper, Pied Flycatcher and Hawfinch.

One should not forget the other birds of interest though, especially when that includes Lammergeier, Griffon Vulture, Egyptian Vulture, Golden Eagle and Alpine Chough on the crags and ledges, and on the higher pastures Water Pipit and Citril Finch. The westernmost section is, however, missing some of the species that you will begin to pick up as you go further east — these include Capercaillie, the Spanish race of Grey Partridge, Ptarmigan and Wallcreeper. It is possible to find both Alpine Accentor and Snow Finch in the easternmost part of the Sierra de Abodi, when the altitude increases.

Timing
As the mountains do not reach such great heights here, and there is the ameliorating effect of the nearby Bay of Biscay on temperatures, winters are milder and spring can begin earlier. Mid-April to late June is the best time, although some of the raptors and vultures are obvious earlier in the year (February). February onwards can also be a good time to track down woodpeckers as they are very vocal from February to April. Spring and autumn can be good for passage. Take care at certain times of year with hunters.

Access
Pico Gorramakil (Gorramendi) This area is to the south of the crossing into France at Danxarinea, on the N121B. From Pamplona take the N121A north for around 34 km, passing through a couple of tunnels and turning right after Almandoz onto the N254/N121B. A route to the

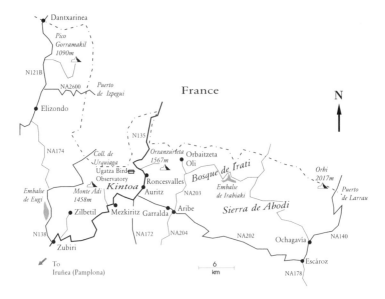

right after 16 km (NA2600) to the border at Puerto de Izpegui is possible and can be good for Golden Eagle and other birds of prey. Both the road and the next right turn up to the Pico Gorramakil have some stunning scenery. Instead of turning right at Puerto de Otxondo you can also carry on to the French border at Dantxarinea.

Kintoa (Quinto Real) From Pamplona take the N135 to Zubiri and just outside the town turn left onto the N138. This road goes through Urtasuri and Eugi, and along the right-hand side of the Eugi reservoir climbing up to the Collada de Urquiaga — the mountain pass that takes you into France. If you have not already stopped on the way it is possible to explore the woods and pastures here with tracks going into and through the forest along the ridge. Another route that is good for forest birds is also off to the left of the N135. From Zubiri carry on for around 15 km and turn left onto a minor road for Casa Establo. If you have reached Mezkiritz you have gone past the turning.

Roncevalles–Bosque de Irati–Sierra de Abodi From Pamplona take the N135, but carry on past Zubiri again and the Bosque de Irati (main forest area) lies east of Roncesvalles. There are a large number of alternatives for exploring this vast forest and lower mountain slopes. The southern areas are best approached along the NA202 (right off the N135 before you reach Auritz (Burgete)). Along this road you take a number of left turns into the core areas, these include the NA203 from Aribe (Arive) which heads north to Orbaitzeta. From Ochagavía (33 km from the N135) a track takes you up to the village of Irati close to the French border. Carry on from Ochagavía on the NA203 will take you to the border with France again and the Puerto de Larrau where it is possible to get Alpine Accentor and Snow Finch at their western most site in the Pyrenees.

A road also takes you up the forested slopes north of Roncesvalles. About 2 km out of the town turn left up to slopes of Orzanzurieta (1567 m) which can be good for Citril Finch.

234

Urgatz bird observatory The Urgatz bird observatory is situated around 3 km west of the N135 from the Alto De Ibañeta, north of Roncevalles. This is open from July to November to study the post-breeding migration of birds across the Pyrennes (tel: 948 301289, 948 210746 or contact Jarauta, 16–3º Izda, Iruña).

Calendar

All year: Red Kite, Lammergeier, Griffon Vulture, Goshawk, Sparrowhawk, Buzzard, Golden Eagle, Peregrine, Eagle Owl, Long-eared Owl, Tawny Owl, Woodcock, Green Woodpecker, Black Woodpecker, Middle Spotted Woodpecker, White-backed Woodpecker, Lesser Spotted Woodpecker, Woodlark, Crag Martin, Water Pipit, Grey Wagtail, Dipper, Blue Rock Thrush, Song Thrush, Garden Warbler, Blackcap, Goldcrest, Firecrest, Marsh Tit, Crested Tit, Nuthatch, Treecreeper, Jay, Red-billed Chough, Alpine Chough, Raven, Citril Finch, Bullfinch, Cirl Bunting, Rock Bunting.

Breeding season: Black Kite, Honey Buzzard, Egyptian Vulture, Short-toed Eagle, Hen Harrier, Wryneck, Nightjar, Hoopoe, Tree Pipit, Redstart, Rock Thrush, Subalpine Warbler, Melodious Warbler, Bonelli's Warbler, Red-backed Shrike, Ortolan Bunting.

Passage periods: Black Stork, White Stork, Honey Buzzard, Black Kite, Short-toed Eagle, Marsh Harrier, Montagu's Harrier, Booted Eagle, Crane, Stock Dove, Mistle Thrush.

N2   VALLE DE RONCAL

Status: Foz de Burgui and other sites (Reserva Natural). Foz de Burgui-Sierra de Illòn ZEPA (4619 ha); Larra-Aztaparreta ZEPA (3767 ha); Sierra de San Miguel ZEPA (2987 ha).

Site description

Roncal is the most easterly valley in Navarra and the most 'alpine' area in the region, with the head of the valley being the western extremity of what is known as the high Pyrenees. It has much in common with its adjoining valleys in Aragón — Valle de Ansó (AR1) and the Valle de Hecho (AR17). The lower parts of the valley have pastures and hay meadows, small woods, and the river itself with side tributaries, rocky outcrops and gorges. The most famous of these gorges is the Foz de Burgui, but there are others — Sigüés, Roncal and Urzainqui. The pastures gradually become more alpine as one reaches the higher parts of the valley, containing many wet flushes rich in plants, extensive woods and forest of mountain pine, beech and silver fir and the high peaks and rocky crags.

In the lower reaches of the valley is Foz de Burgui, a deep limestone gorge formed by the River Esca and on the border between Navarra and Aragón.

Species

A very rich valley for birds from Embalse de Yesa right up to the French border. This site is also very good for woodpeckers, including Black and White-backed Woodpecker; it also has species of high altitude, notably Lammergeier, Alpine Accentor, Alpine Chough, Snow Finch and the elusive Wallcreeper. This is the most western site for the high-altitude forest species — Tengmalm's Owl. Tree Pipit, Red-backed Shrike and Yellowhammer are common in the lower valley.

Foz de Burgui One of the biggest vulture colonies in Navarra and Spain after Foz de Arbayún (N3) with around 130–150 birds, plus other cliff-nesting species such as Egyptian Vulture, Golden Eagle, Peregrine, Eagle Owl, Red-billed Chough and Blue Rock Thrush. Also good in winter with Alpine Accentor, Alpine Chough and Wallcreeper.

Middle and lower valley Pasture, hay fields and small woods with Sparrowhawk, Red-legged Partridge, Quail, Wryneck, Green Woodpecker, White-backed Woodpecker, Grey Wagtail, Dipper, Tree Pipit, Redstart, Stonechat, Dartford Warbler, Subalpine Warbler, Firecrest, Treecreeper, Red-backed Shrike, Woodchat Shrike, Serin, Bullfinch, Yellowhammer, Cirl Bunting.

Belagua refuge Scenic mixture of open and forested habitats with a very rich flora and birds including Capercaillie, Grey Partridge, Woodcock, Tengmalm's Owl, Nightjar, Water Pipit, Black Woodpecker, White-backed Woodpecker, Goldcrest, Treecreeper, Alpine Chough, Citril Finch and Crossbill.

Collado de la Piedra San Martín (French border) Alpine pastures, coniferous forest in places with rocky outcrops and crags. Lammergeier, Ptarmigan, Water Pipit, Alpine Accentor, Ring Ouzel, Wallcreeper, Alpine Chough and Snow Finch.

Timing

The best time of year for birdwatching is late spring, during May and June. However, some of the alpine species can be seen at lower altitudes in the winter months.

Access

From Pamplona (Iruñea) take the N240 eastwards up to Embalse de Yesa, and its abandoned hilltop villages. You are now in Aragón. Take a left turning into Roncal Valley along the AR137–NA137 two-thirds along the length of the reservoir.

Foz de Burgui The NA137 follows the gorge and provides a good opportunity for birdwatching from one of a number of stopping points. Views are also possible from the chapel of La Virgen de la Peña above the gorge, which is reached up a track to the right about 1 km before the gorge starts.

Belagua refuge Continue on through Foz de Burgui and past Roncal and Isaba into the highest parts of the valley. The refuge is about 18 km from Isaba after a series of hairpin-type bends. There is plenty of car parking at the refuge, and refreshments, along with a plan and details of

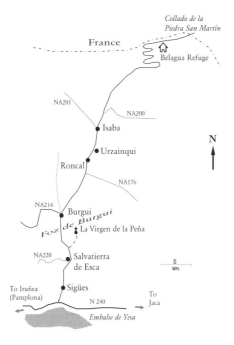

walking and cross-country skiing itineraries from the refuge. You can walk striaght out from the refuge into rich pasture and forest.

Collado de la Piedra San Martín (French Border) Continue on the NA137 from the Belagua refuge up to the pass at 1760 m and into France where there are plenty of opportunities on the border for exploration, although some of the paths across the Sierra de Añalara and up to the peaks are only suitable for experienced mountain walkers.

If you continue over the French border you reach Forêt D'Isseaux, which is very beautiful and also good for woodpeckers.

Calendar

All year: Red Kite, Lammergeier, Griffon Vulture, Goshawk, Sparrowhawk, Buzzard, Golden Eagle, Kestrel, Peregrine, Ptarmigan, Capercaillie, Red-legged Partridge, Grey Partridge, Woodcock, Eagle Owl, Tawny Owl, Tengmalm's Owl, Kingfisher, Black Woodpecker, Great Spotted Woodpecker, White-backed Woodpecker, Crag Martin, Water Pipit, Grey Wagtail, Dipper, Dunnock, Alpine Accentor, Black Redstart, Blue Rock Thrush, Goldcrest, Wallcreeper, Treecreeper, Red-billed Chough, Alpine Chough, Snow Finch, Citril Finch, Crossbill, Yellowhammer, Cirl Bunting.

Breeding season: Black Kite, Egyptian Vulture, Short-toed Eagle, Hen Harrier, Booted Eagle, Quail, Common Sandpiper, Wryneck, Alpine Swift, House Martin, Tawny Pipit, Tree Pipit, Ring Ouzel, Bonelli's Warbler, Spotted Flaycatcher.

Passage periods: Black Stork, Black Kite, Honey Buzzard, Woodpigeon, Rock Thrush.

N3 FOZ DE ARBAYÚN Y FOZ DE LUMBIER

Status: Foz de Arbayún Reserva Natural (1164 ha). Foz de Arbayún-Sierra de Leyre ZEPA (9020 ha).

Site description

There are two spectacular limestone river gorges found in the Sierra de Leyre, a small range of mountains rising to 1356 m, in the foothills of the Pyrenees. The rivers Salazar (Arbayún) and Irati (Lumbier) have carved out these impressively deep gorges, and are unspoiled partly due to their relative inaccessibilty. Both gorges have been declared nature reserves and are famed for their vulture colonies.

Foz de Arbayún is one of the most dramatic gorges in Spain and was declared a nature reserve in 1987. The gorge is 6 km long and 385 m deep from the edge of the cliff to the river Salazar. There is scrub and woodland on the valley floor of oak, maple, ash, willow, hazel, Kermes oak and box.

Foz de Lumbier is a smaller gorge near the village from which it takes its name, but it is no less dramatic, especially as it possible to walk along the gorge floor alongside the river.

Species

The general area has very large numbers of breeding Griffon Vultures, approaching 1,000 in total. Foz de Arbayún is particularly notable as it is the largest Griffon Vulture colony in Spain, with around 240 nests. It is more than just a home for Griffon Vultures, and both gorges are extremely important for other cliff-nesting birds including Egyptian Vulture, Golden Eagle, Peregrine, Eagle Owl, Alpine Swift, Blue Rock Thrush, Red-billed Chough, Jackdaw and Raven.

Egyptian Vulture and Griffon Vulture

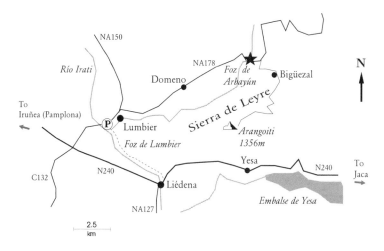

Timing
Generally April through to late June when immature vultures will be on the nest site. Come earlier in the year for displaying raptors and vultures. Vulture activity will depend on the time of day and the weather, and there is more likely to be activity in the morning around the colony before the vultures drift off in search of food.

Access
Around 30 km east of Pamplona off the N240, turning left onto the NA178 towards Lumbier and beyond.

Foz de Lumbier Soon after this turning (0.5 km) there is a vulture-feeding site on the right with viewing facilities. Carry on up towards Lumbier and turn right just before the village, which takes you to the start of the gorge and a car park. It is then possible to walk along a disused railway line alongside the river and on the floor of the gorge. Vultures can sometimes drift past at low levels here. Take a torch with you to go through the now disused railway tunnel, and the old track continues along a very good valley with Nightingale and Bee-eater and eventually takes you down to the next village of Liédena.

Foz de Arbayún
Carry on past Lumbier village, staying on the NA178 towards Navascués. Opposite a 'hill' on the left, about 15 km from the main road, is a *mirador* or viewing platform suspended above the gorge. Amazing views are possible down into this spectacular gorge — and remember to take a telescope for views into the nests. The scrub around the platform can be good for warblers.

Calendar
All year: Lammergeier, Griffon Vulture, Goshawk, Sparrowhawk, Golden Eagle, Bonelli's Eagle, Peregrine, Rock Dove, Eagle Owl, Long-eared Owl, Grey Wagtail, Dipper, Wren, Stonechat, Black Redstart, Blue Rock Thrush, Dartford Warbler, Sardinian Warbler, Great Grey Shrike, Crested Tit, Red-billed Chough, Jackdaw, Raven, Rock Sparrow, Crossbill, Cirl Bunting, Rock Bunting.

Breeding season: Red Kite, Black Kite, Honey Buzzard, Egyptian Vulture, Short-toed Eagle, Booted Eagle, Alpine Swift, Hoopoe, Crag Martin, House Martin, Red-backed Shrike, Subalpine Warbler, Melodious Warbler, Golden Oriole.

Winter: Alpine Accentor, Wallcreeper, Alpine Chough.

N4   LAGUNA DE LAS CAÑAS

Status: Reserva Natural, ZEPA and Ramsar site (101 ha).

Site description

One of the best wetland sites in Navarra — a lake dammed for irrigation of the surrounding farmland. It is situated near the River Ebro, close to the city of Logroño in a cereal, vine and horticultural area with some industry on the periphery of the city. The lake, although dammed, has a well-developed fringe of emergent vegetation including reedbeds and surrounding trees and scrub including willow, black poplar and tamarisk.

Species

Laguna de las Cañas has one of the relatively few heronries in Navarra region and is important for this alone. There are around 70 pairs of Night Heron but much smaller numbers of Purple Heron. Other species that occur at this wetland are Grey Heron, Little Bittern, Cattle Egret (only breeding site in Navarra) and Little Egret. Bittern has bred in the past and still occasionally occurs on passage. Other breeding species of note are Black-necked Grebe, Garganey, Red-crested Pochard (only site in Navarra), Savi's Warbler and Olivaceous Warbler, Bearded Tit and Reed Bunting (uncommon and widely dispersed in Spain). There is a good selection of wildfowl on the reservoir during winter, and it is also of interest for species on passage but it is during the breeding season that the site comes into its own.

Timing

Spring and autumn are the best times of year.

Access

From Logroño take the NIII toward Viana. The lake is around 3 km before you reach Viana, along a unsurfaced track behind a pine wood and on the boundary with the neighbouring region of La Rioja. There is a path around the lake.

Calendar

All year: Great Crested Grebe, Black-necked Grebe, Little Grebe, Grey Heron, Gadwall, Mallard, Marsh Harrier, Water Rail, Moorhen, Coot, Cetti's Warbler, Fan-tailed Warbler, Reed Bunting.

Breeding season: Little Bittern, Night Heron, Cattle Egret, Little Egret, Purple Heron, White Stork, Garganey, Red-crested Pochard, Black Kite,

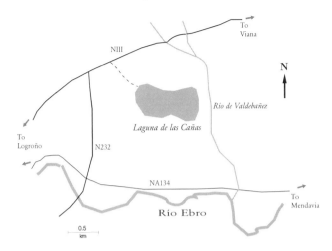

Black-winged Stilt, Little Ringed Plover, Bee-eater, Nightingale, Savi's Warbler, Reed Warbler, Great Reed Warbler, Melodious Warbler, Oliva-ceous Warbler, Bearded Tit, Penduline Tit, Golden Oriole.

Winter: Cormorant, Shelduck, Wigeon, Teal, Pintail, Shoveler, Pochard, Tufted Duck, Jack Snipe.

Passage periods: Bittern, Black Stork, Greylag Goose, Garganey, Ferrugi-nous Duck, Red Kite, Osprey, Little Crake, Black-winged Stilt, Avocet, Ringed Plover, Ruff, Snipe, Black-tailed Godwit, Whimbrel, Curlew, Green-shank, Green Sandpiper, Black-headed Gull, Whiskered Tern, Black Tern.

N5   LAGUNA DE PITALLAS

Status: Reserva Natural (300 ha), ZEPA and Ramsar site (215 ha).

Site description

Laguna de Pitallas is situated in a cereal-growing area in the valley of a tributary of the Río Cidacos, itself a tributary of the Aragón river. Along with Laguna de las Cañas (N4) this is the other wetland site in Navarra that is of comparable importance. It is over twice the size of Cañas and the largest of the natural wetlands in Navarra. It is very shallow with the consequence that there is little visible open water apart from occa-sional channels, with most of the surface covered in reed. Management has included the maintenance of water levels and the planting on the periphery of the site of a variety of trees and shrubs as both nesting habi-tat and screening vegetation.

Species

As with Lagunas de las Cañas this site supports a number of breeding herons including Little Bittern, Night Heron, Grey Heron and Purple

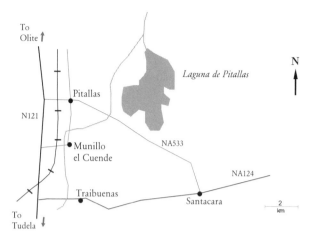

Heron, although the most noteworthy species is Bittern with only a handful of other breeding sites in the whole of Spain. Little Crake and Baillon's Crake may also breed at Pitallas. Outside Las Cañas, this is the only known breeding site for Savi's Warbler.

The lagoon also has some passage and wintering interest, for instance large numbers of Marsh Harrier winter here.

The adjacent fields around the lagoon have Montagu's Harrier, Little Bustard, Stone Curlew, Black-bellied Sandgrouse, Calandra Lark and Tawny Pipit.

Timing
Throughout the year.

Access
From Tafalla take the N121 towards Tudela. After 13 km turn left onto the local road for Pitallas. Three km after the village of Pitallas a track leads to the dyke of the lake. You can leave your vehicle here.

A wire fence marks the boundary of the protected area and access is not allowed. It is possible to walk around the periphery of the lake on the outside of the fence.

Calendar
All year: Little Grebe, Great Crested Grebe, Little Egret, Grey Heron, Mallard, Red-crested Pochard, Marsh Harrier, Water Rail, Cetti's Warbler, Reed Bunting.

Breeding season: Bittern, Little Bittern, Night Heron, Purple Heron, Garganey, Black Kite, Little Crake, Baillon's Crake, Black-winged Stilt, Lapwing, Redshank, Common Sandpiper, Sand Martin, Savi's Warbler, Reed Warbler, Great Reed Warbler, Melodious Warbler, Penduline Tit, Golden Oriole.

Winter: Wigeon, Teal, Pintail, Shoveler, Pochard, Tufted Duck.

Passage periods: Black Stork, Glossy Ibis, Greylag Goose, Shelduck, Garganey, Osprey, Crane, Snipe, Green Sandpiper, Whiskered Tern.

N6 SOTOS DE RÍO ARAGÓN Y RÍO EBRO

Status: A number of riverine woodlands are declared Enclaves Naturales and Reservas Naturales.

Site description

This site comprises riverside woodland of poplar and willow — *sotos* — in the Ebro and the lower reaches of the River Aragón and its tributaries, the Cidacos and the Arga. These narrow belts of woodland normally occur on both sides of the riverbank but have a restricted distribution. Where they do occur they support a rich bird community. The *sotos* differ slightly from site to site, for example on the Ebro the woodland tends to be a little more mature with a more varied mix of trees and shrubs, and is more extensive.

Because they are both rare and important for birds many areas have been designated as reserves; those *sotos* that are reserves are listed below. There are also a number of other reserves, mainly small woods or lagoons, also found in the general area.

Rada: Sotos de Rada. **Río Arga:** Sotos y cortados de Falces a Peralta, Sotos de Funes. **Río Aragón:** Sotos de Aragón desde Mélida a Caparroso, Sotos y cortados de Caparosso, Sotos y cortados de Funes y Milagro. **Río Ebro:** Sotos de Castejón a Tudela.

There are other *sotos* on the Río Cidacos, and the stretch of river south of Olite is good. The Laguna de Pitillas (N5) is also close by.

Species

The *sotos* are especially important for nesting Penduline Tit and Golden Oriole, species that are closely associated with poplars, and for small colonies of Night Heron and Purple Heron. The trees are also used by roosting herons and egrets, and in autumn by swallows. Nightingale and Cetti's Warbler are typically abundant and their songs can be particularly deafening at times, although both species can be very difficult to see well. *Cortados*, or sandbanks, also occur along some sections of the rivers and have strong colonies of Sand Martins and Bee-eaters.

Timing

Spring, especially from late March through into June.

Access

From Pamplona take the N121 south towards Tudela. The *sotos* occur on either side of this road along the Aragón and its tributaries, south of the town of Olite. The main *soto* on the Ebro is further south near Tudela.

Rada *Sotos de Rada.* Carry on past Olite and take a left turn opposite Caparrosso along the NA550. There is a right turn to Rada after 4–5 km, and the woodland is past the village along tracks to the Acequila de Navarra.

Río Arga *Sotos y cortados de Falces a Peralta.* Carry on past Olite for 16 km and take a right turn on the NA128 to Peralta. The nearby village of Falces is to the north, and roads cross over the river with views into the *sotos*.

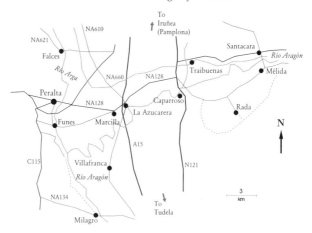

Sotos de Funes. As before, but when you reach Peralta a minor road goes south to the next village of Funes where the woodland and river are to the left of the road.

Río Aragón *Sotos y cortados de Caparosso.* Carry on past Olite on the N121 and turn off right into the village of Caparroso. In Caparrosso there are paths that lead into the sotos, both to the north and south of the river.

Sotos de Aragón desde Mélida a Caparroso. Pass Olite on the N121 for about 14 km and turn left onto the NA124 to Santacara. A track takes you to the river if you turn right in the first village of Traibuenas. Back on the N124 carry on to Santacara and the village on the other side of the river Mélida, to get good views and explore the area from both sides of the river.

Sotos y cortados de Funes y Milagro. Take the NA128 turning 16 km off the main NA121 south of Olite towards Peralta. Instead of going into Peralta wait until this road joins the C115 and turn left (south) for 3 km past the turning for Funes but taking the next left to Milagro where the road follows the river and its woodland for most of the journey.

Try also the river between the villages of Murillo el Fruto and Carcastillo.

Río Ebro *Sotos de Castejón a Tudela.* Carry on from Olite down the N121 until it joins the NA134 left for Tudela. Continue into the centre of Tudela

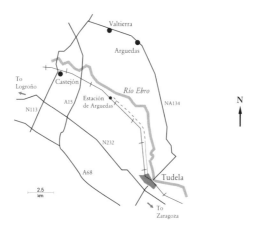

and immediately after you have crossed the River Ebro to enter the town turn right onto a track that follows the railway and the river. There are plenty of opportunities to explore the river and its woodland off this track.

There are other *sotos* on the Río Cidacos, along the stretch of river south of Olite, on minor roads through Beire, Pitallas and Murillo el Cuende.

Calendar

All year: Little Grebe, Great Crested Grebe, Little Egret, Red Kite, Sparrowhawk, Common Sandpiper, Barn Owl, Kingfisher, Green Woodpecker, Great Spotted Woodpecker, White Wagtail, Cetti's Warbler, Fan-tailed Warbler, Long-tailed Tit, Tree Sparrow, Cirl Bunting.

Breeding season: Night Heron, Purple Heron, White Stork, Black Kite, Egyptian Vulture, Booted Eagle, Hobby, Little Ringed Plover, Turtle Dove, Scops Owl, Bee-eater, Wryneck, Hoopoe, Sand Martin, Yellow Wagtail, Nightingale, Reed Warbler, Great Reed Warbler, Melodious Warbler, Penduline Tit, Golden Oriole, Woodchat Shrike.

N7   LAS BARDENAS REALES

Status: Part of the area is protected as Reservas Naturales–Vedado de Eguaros (500 ha), Rincon del Bú (460 ha) and Caídas de la Negra (1926 ha), but large areas remain unprotected.

Site description

This spectacular desert-like area with its large number of ravines and cliffs cuts though a flat-topped plateau or *mesa* and is one of the most important steppe areas in the Ebro Valley and in Spain. The gypsum, marl and clay landscape is a very strange one, with what appear to be stranded eroded islands standing in a semi-arid desert sea.

Within this 'desert' of dry grassland and scrub of albardine, rosemary, thyme and Kermes oak there are extensive areas of cereals and other crops, including rice, which exist by means of irrigation, which has threatened birdlife by opening up areas to increasing cultivation. There are also stands of pine scattered through the site.

Part of the area is a military firing range, and there are three nature reserves within Las Bardenas Reales: Vedado de Eguaros, Rincon del Bú and Caídas de la Negra. There are current proposals to turn the whole area into a parque natural covering much of the plain of 42,500 ha.

The landscape is also home to a sprinkling of castles, now mostly ruined, but which add to the atmosphere of the plain. The north of Bardenas Reales is normally referred to as La Gran Meseta or El Plano de Bardenas and comprises the central area, or La Bardena Blanca, in which two of the reserves are found, and the southern section, La Bardena Negra, in which the reserve of Caídas de la Negra is situated.

Species

The Ebro Valley is very important for steppe birds in general, and Bardenas Reales is no exception. All of the typical steppe species are present with large numbers especially of Dupont's Lark (>500 pairs), Calandra Lark (>1,000 pairs) and Lesser Short-toed Lark (1,000 pairs). Given the size of the area and difficulty of accurately censusing populations, it is likely that these figures could be a bare minimum and we may find that numbers have been greatly underestimated. In addition to larks there are around at least 50 pairs each of Black-bellied Sandgrouse and Pin-tailed Sandgrouse, and smaller numbers of Great and Little Bustard, and Stone Curlew.

The area is also well known for its vultures and bird of prey populations, with the cliffs home to Egyptian Vulture, Griffon Vulture, Golden Eagle and Bonelli's Eagle. Eagle Owl is also resident.

Short-toed Eagles nest in the more wooded parts, such as at Caídas de la Negra. There is also the largest known summer roost — mainly in pines — of Egyptian Vulture in Spain, with over 200 birds.

Timing

Visiting in the summer will not be very rewarding. If you visit the area between May and September it is worthwhile visiting the rice fields at Arguedas if you wish to see a wider range of species. Black-bellied and Pin-tailed Sandgrouse can often be found flying in small flocks in the evenings, heading for some of the many small lagoons that dot the landscape between the months of October and April.

Winter is cold, but not usually so frosty as in other parts of the Ebro Valley. By mid-April the warmer weather and summer visitors have arrived.

Access

As Bardenas Reales covers a substantial area there are many routes into this eerie landscape. Having said that, the area is not well served with roads, although there are many tracks and one of the best ways of seeing the countryside without getting lost is to use the GR13 long-distance path which crosses the central part of Bardenas Reales from the Hermitage of the Virgen del Yugo.

From Tudela take the NA134 north for 3 km and turn right onto the NA125 towards Ejea de los Caballeros which crosses a good part of Bardenas Reales. To the north of this road is the reserve of Rincon del Bú with a number of tracks off to the left. To the south of this road is the reserve of Caídas de la Negra. One good option is to take the track to the right almost on the border with Aragón and which takes you to the chapel of Sancho Abarca, close to the 'peak' of Loma Negra (646 m). This can also be approached from the Aragón side off the A127 at Tauste.

A couple of alternatives also exist from Arguedas north of Tudela on the NA134. A minor road leading southeast from Arguedas goes to the firing range, and a track follows the boundary of the range and passes through some good habitats, but is not possible to enter at the range. Another minor road leads north out of Arguedas, taking you past Nuestra Señora del Yugo chapel (4 km) and after around 8 km turns right (explore the plains here) and which after a further 6 km leads to Castillo de Peñafor which is within the Venada de Eguaros reserve.

Calendar

All year: Griffon Vulture, Golden Eagle, Bonelli's Eagle, Peregrine, Little Bustard, Great Bustard, Stone Curlew, Black-bellied Sandgrouse, Pintailed Sandgrouse, Dupont's Lark, Calandra Lark, Lesser Short-toed Lark, Crested Lark, Thekla Lark, Black Wheatear, Blue Rock Thrush, Dartford Warbler, Red-billed Chough, Rock Sparrow.

Breeding season: White Stork, Egyptian Vulture, Montagu's Harrier, Lesser Kestrel, Great Spotted Cuckoo, Red-necked Nightjar, Alpine Swift, Bee-eater, Short-toed Lark, Tawny Pipit, Wheatear, Black-eared Wheatear, Spectacled Warbler.

Winter: Red Kite, Merlin, Short-eared Owl.

OTHER SITES WORTH VISITING

N8 Sierra de Urbasa

Designated a reserva natural in 1987. An upland sierra with deep gorges and limestone cliffs, wood, fast flowing streams and cultivated land. Griffon Vulture, birds of prey, Eagle Owl, Red-billed Chough, Dipper. NIII southwest out of Pamplona for 43 km as far as Estella (Lizarra). Turn right onto minor roads to Puerto de Urbasa and Altstasu.

N9 Peñas de Echauri

A small sierra with a 200-m high limestone cliff escarpment and limestone cliffs with scrub and oak woodland. An important area for Griffon Vulture; also Egyptian Vulture, Bonelli's Eagle, Alpine Chough, Blue Rock Thrush and Crag Martin. From Pamplona take the minor road west to Ororbia and Echauri. The cliffs begin 2–3 km outside the village; there is car parking.

N10 Monte del Conde

A Mediterranean oak woodland and reserva natural. Breeding Goshawk, Short-toed Eagle, Booted Eagle and a good range of other woodland species. South of Pamplona on the the N121 for 28 km, turn left onto the NA500 towards Olleta. The woodland is on the right-hand side of the road about 2 km after leaving the main road. Tracks through the woodland.

LA RIOJA

The smallest region in Spain (and one of Europe's smallest), and for most people famous for producing some of the best Spanish red wines, but less well known for its dinosaurs — the only reminders of their presence now being their erstwhile huge footprints seen along *La Ruta de los Dinosaurios* (R8).

Surprisingly the region is not named after a grape variety, but from the name one of the tributaries of the River Ebro (the Río Oja) which forms its northern boundary.

Wine though is at the very heart of La Rioja's identity and the region is about the heart of the modern Castilian language. Some of the earliest words in Castilian Spanish (the modern language of much of Spain) are lines of verse written by a monk from a Riojan monastery and which contain the words *un vaso de bon vino* ('a glass of good wine')! The growing of vines and winemaking were certainly practised before the Romans, and today the industry is as strong as ever with the main centre of production focused on the area around Haro, a town some 40 km north of Logroño, the capital of the region. The area now under vines is just under 50,000 ha, and most wine comes from three zones in the region — Rioja Alta, Rioja Alavesa and Rioja Baja.

With good wine all around, this seems an ideal region in Spain to combine one's interest in birds and grapes, and although small, the region does have its wide plains, gorges, mountains (Sistemo Ibérico Norte) and riverine woodlands, but they are all at a scale that makes the region seem much more human and accessible.

Much more compact than its neighbours, it still offers many opportunities to see a wide diversity of species in a relatively small geographical area. The mountainous areas that form part of the Sistemo Ibérico Norte, rising to over 2000 m, in turn form the Sierra de la Demanda (R1). Although not so rich in species as the Pyrenees, they do hold similar species including Grey Partridge, Alpine Swift, Water Pipit, Citril Finch and, more rarely, Alpine Accentor.

Interestingly, because of the geographical position of La Rioja and its wooded hill landscapes, a number of species occur here at the edge of their range in Spain or are much rarer further south. If you are heading for Castile-La Mancha or further south still, then this may be your last chance for species such as Hen Harrier, Woodcock, Marsh Tit, Red-backed Shrike and Yellowhammer.

The greatest interest for birdwatchers in La Rioja, apart from the wine, is probably contained in the wooded open country with its occasional deep ravines, gorges and cliffs, holding important populations of Griffon and Egyptian Vultures as at the gorges of Peñas de Iregua and Leza y Jubera (R2). Other sites such as Peñas de Arnedillo, Isasa y Turruncún (R3) and the Sierra de Alcrama y Río Alhama (R4) also have vulture colonies, along with many other cliff-nesting species such as Bonelli's Eagle, Eagle Owl, Crag Martin, Blue Rock Thrush, Red-billed Chough and Rock Sparrow.

Its plains may not be so wide as in other parts of Spain, but in the east of the region, in the Ebro Valley, there are pockets of suitable habitat where small numbers of both species of bustard and sandgrouse are present along with other species such as Montagu's Harrier, Stone Curlew and Great Spotted Cuckoo. Semi-arid rocky areas also occur in the east of the region, such as the Sierra de Alcrama y Río Alhama (R4), and should be visited for Thekla Lark, Tawny Pipit, Black Wheatear, Black-eared Wheatear and Spectacled Warbler.

Wetland interest is very definitely limited in La Rioja, with most of what there is confined to the rivers and the Río Ebro itself, especially those riverine woodlands found along its banks, composed of poplar and willows and known locally as *sotos*. The best example is Sotos de Alfaro (R5), situated right in the far northeastern corner of La Rioja and close to its border with Navarra. These woodlands are good for Night Heron, Purple Heron, Penduline Tit, and perhaps, most interestingly, Olivaceous Warbler — a species with very restricted distribution in Spain.

While small, La Rioja is famous for something rather large, its dinosaur footprints in the gullies of that part of the region known as Rioja Baja, near Enciso (R8). This site, *La Ruta de los Dinosaurios*, obviously should not be missed, but it also offers an introduction to birds that are more widespread in the region, and you may come across, quite unexpectedly, White Stork, Black Kite, Quail, Hoopoe, Dartford Warbler, Melodious Warbler and Woodchat Shrike.

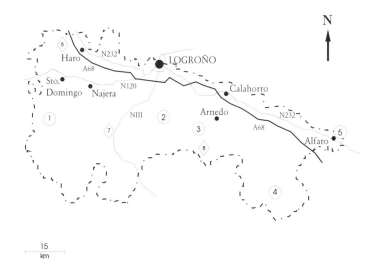

Main sites

1   R1   Sierra de la Demanda
2   R2   Peñas de Iregua, Leza y Jubera
3   R3   Peñas de Arnedillo, Isasa y Turruncún
4   R4   Sierra de Alcarama y Río Alhama
5   R5   Sotos de Alfaro

Other sites worth visiting

6   R6   Sierras de Urbión, Cebollera y Cameros
7   R7   Obarenes–Sierra de Cantabria
8   R8   Enciso: La Ruta de los Dinosaurios

R1 SIERRA DE LA DEMANDA

Status: Coto Nacional de Caza de Ezcaray and ZEPA (56,350 ha).

Site description

A mountainous area rising to over 2000 m with extensive deciduous woodland of oak and beech, areas of maquis scrub, alpine pasture and river valleys. Afforestation of parts of the area with Scots pine has taken place, and the whole site is very imposing with the high peaks of 2271 m (San Lorenzo) and 2131 m (San Millán). The area is little visited, especially by birdwatchers, and there is probably much that is overlooked. It forms part of the mountain system known as Sistema Ibérico Norte and there is a ski resort at Valdezcaray.

Species

One of the few sites for Alpine Accentor outside its main breeding areas in the Pyrenees and the Cordillera Cantabrica, and also good for other upland species such as Water Pipit and Citril Finch. The other main attraction is the birds of its woodlands, especially birds of prey which include Goshawk, Sparrowhawk, Honey Buzzard, Booted Eagle and Short-toed Eagle. Hen Harrier also breeds here as does Egyptian Vulture. This is a very good birdwatching area in a wooded mountainous landscape.

This area is particularly interesting as it holds southern outliers of breeding Grey Partridge (120–150 pairs) and Woodcock, plus a population of Pied Flycatcher, which is relatively thinly distributed in Spain. Surprisingly perhaps, the area is well known for its Woodpigeon passage although other species such as Honey Buzzard, Red Kite and Crane are also regularly observed.

The road along Turza Valley, and Tobiá Valley can produce similar species including Egyptian Vulture, Short-toed Eagle, Woodcock, Rock Thrush, Red-backed Shrike, Bullfinch and both species of treecreeper.

Subalpine Warbler

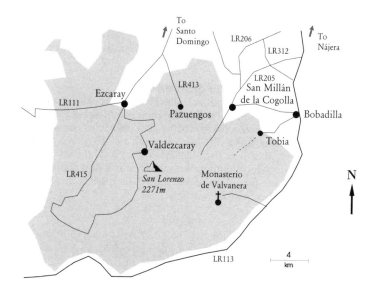

Timing

May and June are best times of year to visit this reserve.

Access

From Logroño take the N120 towards Burgos. There are two main points of entry into the sierra off this road.

Around 25 km out of Logroño take the left turn on the LR113 at Nájera a Salas de los Infantes. This road follows the eastern and southern boundaries of the reserve, so you need to take one of a number of right turns into the core of the area, for example: at Bobadilla to San Millán de la Cogolla (Cárdenas Valley), or again at Bobadilla to Tobiá (Tobiá Valley), or further down the main Najerilla Valley on the LR113 another right turn (LR435) to Monasterio de Valvanera (Valvanera Valley). From each of these destinations roads, tracks and paths lead you higher up each of the respective valleys. The road that leads up Cárdenas Valley from San Millán is especially noteworthy: very isolated, quiet and leading to one of the most impressive areas of beech wood in La Rioja, and good for Woodcock and Honey Buzzard.

The other main entry point in the area has equally stunning views. Take a left turn off the N120 to Santo Domingo de la Calzada, and then onto a minor road, the LR111, to Ezcaray, from here it is possible to drive around the sierra in a circular route with many opportunities for birdwatching. This is also the route to the ski resort in the Sierra de la Demanda at Valdezcaray. A path leads up to the peak of San Lorenzo (2271 m) and this provides the best opportunity for species of higher altitudes such as Water Pipit and Alpine Accentor.

At Ezcaray there is an established walk along the old road to the village of Turza, which starts near the old railway station.

Calendar

All year: Hen Harrier, Goshawk, Sparrowhawk, Buzzard, Golden Eagle, Peregrine, Grey Partridge, Red-legged Partridge, Woodcock, Eagle Owl,

Tawny Owl, Green Woodpecker, Great Spotted Woodpecker, Skylark, Crag Martin, Water Pipit, Alpine Accentor, Blue Rock Thrush, Dartford Warbler, Marsh Tit, Crested Tit, Nuthatch, Short-toed Treecreeper, Treecreeper, Red-billed Chough, Citril Finch, Bullfinch, Yellowhammer, Cirl Bunting, Rock Bunting.

Breeding season: White Stork, Black Kite, Honey Buzzard, Egyptian Vulture, Short-toed Eagle, Booted Eagle, Tree Pipit, Redstart, Wheatear, Subalpine Warbler, Melodious Warbler, Bonelli's Warbler, Pied Flycatcher, Red-backed Shrike.

Passage periods: Red Kite, Honey Buzzard, Crane, Woodpigeon.

R2 PEÑAS DE IREGUA, LEZA Y JUBERA

Status: ZEPA (7840 ha).

Site description

These are precipitous gorges that have been cut into the limestone by tributaries of the River Ebro. The gorges are situated to the south of Logroño, where the Ebro Valley flows through the Sistema Ibérico Norte, an inland mountain range. The site includes parts of the rivers Iregua, Leza and Jugera and the gorges through which they flow. Deciduous woodland and open country occurs between the three gorges.

Species

Griffon Vulture (over 100 pairs), Golden Eagle and Eagle Owl are the main reasons for its designation as a ZEPA. In recent years there have been regular sightings of immature Lammergeier, possibly dispersing from their natal sites in the Pyrenees. Lammergeier formerly bred at this site in the past but suffered from persecution and later became extinct.

Obviously the main attraction of this site are the gorges and their cliff-nesters, and in addition to the above-named species include Kestrel, both Crag and House Martin, Black Redstart, Rock Thrush and Blue Rock Thrush, Red-billed Chough, Raven, Jackdaw and Rock Sparrow.

The woodlands between the gorges should not be overlooked and have Short-toed and Booted Eagle, Tawny Owl and Great Spotted Woodpecker.

Timing

Spring and summer.

Access

Peña Iregua For Iregua Gorge take the N111 south out of Logroño, which goes through the gorge at its greatest depth, between the villages of Islallana, Viguera and Panzanes.

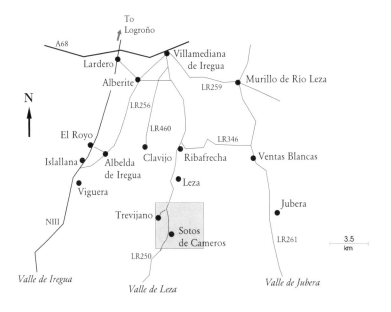

Peña Leza For Leza Gorge take the local road, LR250, out of Logroño towards Laguna de Cameros, and the gorge is between the villages of Leza and Soto de Cameros. The view from the road along the Río Leza is wonderful. It is recommended that you stop in Sotos de Cameros and walk from the Hermitage along the top of the gorge along the Camino de Peña la Mota.

Peña Jubera For Jubera Gorge, use the same local road out of Logroño but take a left turn at Villamediana de Iregua along the LR259 to Murillo de Río Leza. From here take the LR261 that follows the river south, and the gorge can be seen from the village of Jubera itself.

The country around is most easily explored by taking one of the many minor roads that run off the roads described above — N111, LR250 or LR259.

Calendar

All year: Griffon Vulture, Golden Eagle, Bonelli's Eagle, Kestrel, Peregrine, Red-legged Partridge, Rock Dove, Eagle Owl, Tawny Owl, Great Spotted Woodpecker, Thekla Lark, Crag Martin, Black Redstart, Blue Rock Thrush, Dartford Warbler, Fan-tailed Warbler, Red-billed Chough, Spotless Starling, Raven, Jackdaw, Rock Sparrow, Serin, Cirl Bunting, Rock Bunting.

Breeding season: Egyptian Vulture, Short-toed Eagle, Booted Eagle, Scops Owl, Alpine Swift, Bee-eater, House Martin, Tawny Pipit, Rock Thrush, Melodious Warbler, Bonelli's Warbler.

R3   PEÑAS DE ARNEDILLO, ISASA Y TURRUNCÚN

Status: ZEPA (2400 ha).

Site description

An area of cliffs and rocky outcrops in an area of rugged hills which has been extensively deforested. There are many cliffs, largely limestone, of varying sizes. The vegetation consists largely of scrub with small copses of oak and various other species on some slopes.

Species

Griffon Vulture and Eagle Owl are the reasons for the designation of this site as a ZEPA. A very varied area which, despite its history of deforestation, now has a wide range of bird species in the valley and breeding on the cliffs. While the cliff-nesters are the main focus, with both Griffon Vulture and Egyptian Vulture, the cliffs and rocks support much more besides, including Crag Martin, Peregrine, Alpine Swift and Blue Rock Thrush.

Exploration of the countryside around, both open ground and scrub, can be very rewarding with species such as Bee-eater, Tawny Pipit, Black and Black-eared Wheatear, Ortolan Bunting, and Dartford and Subalpine Warbler in the oak scrub.

Timing

Spring and early summer.

Access

From Logroño take the NA134 east following the Ebro to Lodosa. Turn right here on to the LR123 to the town of Arnedo. The great interest lies in the triangle between Arnedo in the east, Arnedillo in the west (along the LR115) and Préjano in the south (take the LR123 out of Arnedo and then shortly after leaving take a right turn along the LR382 to the Monasterio de Vico and Prejano. A minor road does take you to Arnedillo but its condition can vary from year to year. It is along this route that you will see the Peñalmonte cliffs which have both Egyptian and Griffon Vultures.

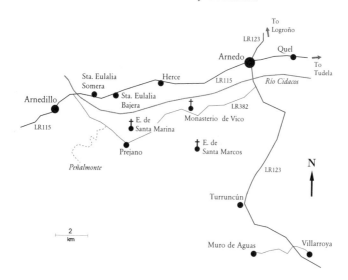

There is another walk from the Monasterio de Vico near the Río Cidacos, through pines and groves to the Ermita de San Marcos, where you may see those scrub and open-country species listed above.

Calendar

All year: Griffon Vulture, Bonelli's Eagle, Peregrine, Red-legged Partridge, Rock Dove, Eagle Owl, Little Owl, Thekla Lark, Crag Martin, Black Redstart, Black Wheatear, Blue Rock Thrush, Dartford Warbler, Fantailed Warbler, Red-billed Chough, Carrion Crow, Jackdaw, Spotless Starling, Rock Sparrow, Cirl Bunting, Rock Bunting, Corn Bunting.

Breeding season: Egyptian Vulture, Short-toed Eagle, Scops Owl, Alpine Swift, Bee-eater, Hoopoe, House Martin, Tawny Pipit, Nightingale, Black-eared Wheatear, Rock Thrush, Subalpine Warbler, Woodchat Shrike, Ortolan Bunting.

R4 SIERRA DE ALCARAMA Y RÍO ALHAMA

Status: ZEPA (8780 ha).

Site description

Tucked away in the southeast corner of La Rioja this is a deforested area of open country with Mediterranean scrub of rosemary, genista, juniper and thyme, with scattered trees including Kermes oak, and willows and poplars along the rivers. Gullies and cliffs are important features and the impressive river gorge below the village of Valdegatur houses an impressive array of cliff-nesting species, and is a must when visiting the area.

255

Serin

Species

Another important area for vultures and other birds of prey, with more than 100 pairs of Griffon Vulture. The area is also important for Egyptian Vulture, Short-toed Eagle, Peregrine and Eagle Owl. Other species associated with the rocks and cliff faces include Kestrel, Black Wheatear, Rock Sparrow, Black-eared Wheatear, Rock Thrush and Blue Rock Thrush, Red-billed Chough, Rock Dove, Crag Martin and Black Redstart.

The cultivated areas in the valleys and riverine woodlands are also of interest, and contain Nightingale, Cetti's Warbler, Sardinian Warbler and Serin.

Timing

Spring and early summer.

Access

From Soria take the N122 east towards Tarazona. Around 15 km from Tarazona take a left turn northwards onto the N113, and after 13 km

another left (LR123) to Cabretón and Cervera del Río Alhama. No specific walks are recommended, but much of the area is easily explored by investigating the many local tracks in the countryside. It is worth driving to Valdemadera, and also Valdegutur, this latter destination being the main gorge with breeding vultures and associated cliff-nesting species. This is approached from Cabretón. A track from the village of Valdegutur leads to the gorge.

Calendar

All year: Griffon Vulture, Bonelli's Eagle, Kestrel, Peregrine, Eagle Owl, Red-legged Partridge, Rock Dove, Great Spotted Woodpecker, Thekla Lark, Black Redstart, Black Wheatear, Blue Rock Thrush, Cetti's Warbler, Sardinian Warbler, Dartford Warbler, Red-billed Chough, Raven, Rock Sparrow, Serin, Rock Bunting.

Breeding season: Egyptian Vulture, Short-toed Eagle, Alpine Swift, Bee-eater, Wryneck, Crag Martin, Black-eared Wheatear, Rock Thrush, Spectacled Warbler, Subalpine Warbler, Nightingale, Golden Oriole, Red-backed Shrike.

R5 SOTOS DE ALFARO

Status: Unprotected

Site description

Riverine woodland on the banks of the River Ebro, mainly black poplar but containing other species including willow and tamarisk. Much more extensive in the past and now restricted to small pockets along the Ebro.

Species

Despite its small size this riverine woodland is extremely important with many species typical of the habitat still present, including Purple Heron, Night Heron, Melodious Warbler and Penduline Tit. The Olivaceous Warbler is probably the most interesting feature as it is a very rare bird outside south and southeast Spain. Lesser Spotted Woodpecker is another uncommon species, particularly away from the north coast woodlands.

The village of Alfaro is well worth a visit in its own right with a large colony of White Stork, with over 100 breeding pairs.

Timing

Spring.

Access

Take the N232 eastwards out of Logroño and follow the River Ebro to the village of Alfaro. In Alfaro head for the railway station, but before reaching the station bear left, cross the lines and park at the old sugar mills (*Antigua azucarera*), a path takes you to and from the river, via poplar plantations.

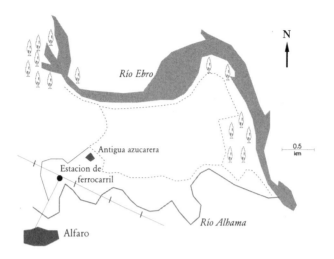

Calendar

All year: Red Kite, Common Sandpiper, Barn Owl, Kingfisher, Green Woodpecker, Lesser Spotted Woodpecker, Cetti's Warbler, Fan-tailed Warbler, Firecrest, Short-toed Treecreeper, Penduline Tit, Spotless Starling, Serin, Cirl Bunting.

Breeding season: White Stork, Purple Heron, Night Heron, Black Kite, Hobby, Turtle Dove, Scops Owl, Bee-eater, Hoopoe, Wryneck, Sand Martin, Nightingale, Great Reed Warbler, Melodious Warbler, Olivaceous Warbler, Woodchat Shrike, Golden Oriole.

OTHER SITES WORTH VISITING

R6 Sierras de Urbión, Cebollera y Cameros
Large (80,000 ha) massif rising to heights above 2000 m and is covered by large areas of forest with excellent bird communities. Very good for owls — Eagle Owl, Tawny Owl, Short-eared Owl and Long-eared Owl. Many tracks through area. NIII Logroño–Soria road runs through the area.

R7 Obarenes–Sierra de Cantabria
Mid-altitude sierra, partly deforested but with mixed maquis scrub and some remnant forest. Cliffs and ravines. Griffon and Egyptian Vulture. Head for Arroyo de Santa Olalla, between Miranda and Tirgo on the LR301 opposite the Convento de San Miguel, for an introduction to the area.

R8 Enciso: La Ruta de los Dinosaurios
Exciting site with dinosaur fossils and footprints in rocks. Plenty to see in the way of living birds as well with Bee-eater, Golden Oriole and Melodious Warbler. South of the region, from the village of Enciso on the C115 between Arnedo and Soria. Track begins on opposite side of Río Cidacos between two hermitages.

VALENCIA

This long but relatively narrow coastal region stretches for over 300 km, from its border with Murcia in the south up to Catalunya in the north. It is one of the most fertile areas in Europe — the 'land of oranges and rice' and home of Spain's national dish, paella. Despite intensification of agriculture and the ravages of the tourist industry with its focus on the Costa Blanca, and Benidorm its most famous resort, there is much to interest birdwatchers in its nationally important coastal wetlands.

The inland sierras have escaped the fate of the coastline and are a million miles away from the excesses of package holidays. Many of the hills and mountains are of limestone with peaks and gorges, but most are also well clothed in a variety of woodland and scrub. As a result, they are home to diverse range of species with birds of prey being well represented and including both Golden Eagle and Bonelli's Eagle, along with Eagle Owl. The uplands of the south and north of the region do, however, differ, with some species mainly restricted to the north. These include both Griffon and Egyptian Vulture, Dipper, Great Spotted Woodpecker, Dunnock, Redstart, Rock Thrush, Nuthatch, Citril Finch and Ortolan Bunting. Nightjar also has a strong population in the north.

It is, however, to the coast that the majority of birdwatchers will be drawn, both as a base for their holiday perhaps, and also because Valencia still, perhaps surprisingly, has some very fine coastal marshes, lagoons and saltpans. Whilst these wetlands are now much smaller and heavily fragmented, and have suffered further from recent years of low rainfall they are still of immense value to birds. There are wetlands down the whole of the coastal strip, but the most famous of all the sites is L'Albufera de Valencia (V4). One of the most important sites in Spain for wintering wildfowl, especially Shelduck and Red-crested Pochard, it also supports a huge range of other species throughout the year. There are good numbers of herons and egrets in particular, and especially noteworthy is its large population (> 100 pairs) of breeding Squacco Heron, and also breeding terns, Collared Pratincole and Bearded Tit. While other sites in the northern half of the region are not as extensive as L'Albufera, they do hold a similar range of species, and some sites, for example, El Prat de Cabanes (V2), has a larger pratincole colony.

The sites in the far south are different in character — most are salt-pans, some still operational, and the birds they support form a different community. They are particularly important for two globally threatened species, Marbled Teal and White-headed Duck. Marbled Teal has a very small European population and in Spain numbers have declined dramatically this century. Whilst the main population is found in Andalucia, there is an important breeding population in southern Valencia at around four sites, with El Hondo (V9) the most important site in Europe. El Hondo also has a small population of White-headed Duck whose future is being threatened by hybridisation with Ruddy Duck, an introduced species that is increasing in numbers in Spain. Shooting is still very much an issue here and at other sites such as Santa Pola (V10), and this activity is causing considerable concern over the long-term future of both species. These two sites along with others in the area such as Las Salinas de la Mata–Torrevieja (V11) are also important for Red-crested Pochard, Kentish Plover and terns such as Whiskered Tern, Little Tern and Gull-billed Tern. Greater Flamingo, a typical bird of salt-pans, occurs but does not breed, but is present for most of the year in varying numbers. Passage can be very exciting with phalaropes and rarer gulls being recorded in recent years, in addition to many different species of wildfowl and waders.

Cliffs are almost absent from the coast apart from the area around the Parque Natural de Montgó (V6) and the Peñón de Ifach (V8), which in addition to being good seawatching and migration locations, are also home to breeding Pallid Swift. The latter also has a sea-cliff nesting pair of Peregrine.

While the south of the Valencia is semi-arid in nature, it lacks the steppe habitats and the birds that go with them. Certain species typical of steppe, such as Short-toed Lark, Lesser Short-toed Lark and Stone Curlew can be found associated with areas of saltpans. The more general countryside holds species typical of the general area with, for example, Little Owl, Hoopoe, Red-rumped Swallow, Black Wheatear and Woodchat Shrike.

Two species often found in open countryside are well represented in Valencia, Olivaceous Warbler and Rufous Bushchat, and both species are not always found on 'listed' sites. Valencia is the region in which you are most likely to see Olivaceous Warbler (outside Andalucia). Rufous Bushchat is fairly widely distributed in the south of Alicante province but it is elusive and you will probably have more luck searching the undergrowth of fruit orchards for this species rather than the sites described in the following pages.

Main sites

Other sites worth visiting

V1 ELS PORTS–MAESTRAT

Status: No special protection.

Site description

The El Ports and Maestrat districts comprise a very attractive low mountain range of between 700 and 1400 m, found in the northern-most corner of the region of Valencia, where forestry and sheep production are the main land uses. While the area has a relatively good infrastructure, there are only scattered villages and the population density is fairly low.

The hillsides and mountain slopes are clothed in Aleppo pine, small mixed oak woods and smaller amounts of beech, box, holly and juniper, but large expanses of holm oak scrub. Riverside woodland is also well represented, and cliffs and river gorges are common. Within the forest complex is a complicated mosaic of pasture, craggy peaks, cliffs and river gorges, with occasional hermitages and sleepy mountain villages. Numerous religious monuments also reflect the historical importance of these towns and villages in medieval times.

The Tinença de Benifassár area in particular has been appreciated for its natural beauty for centuries, and is little changed in many ways. The celebrated local botanist and naturalist Cavanilles described the Tinença de Benifassár as an area 'surrounded and closed in on all sides by tall calcareous mountains, snow-covered in winter, which penetrate to the midst of it, alternating with deep gorges...'

Species

Given the great variety of land form, altitude, land management and habitat, it is easy to appreciate that the whole area offers a correspondingly wide range of bird species. El Ports–Maestrat is a very good upland area for birds of prey with around half a dozen pairs of Bonelli's Eagle, resident Golden Eagle and Eagle Owl. The wood-

Ortolan Bunting

lands add to this diversity with breeding Goshawk, Booted Eagle and Short-toed Eagle, and passerines such as Bonelli's Warbler. The more open areas of woodland support Wryneck and Scops Owl, while the scrub areas hold Dartford and Spectacled Warbler. Cliff faces, rivers and gorges criss-cross the area, with Alpine Swift, Crag Martin and Dipper occurring. This is one of the few areas in Valencia for breeding Egyptian Vulture, along with a number of other species not found in the southern sierras of Valencia, such as Griffon Vulture, Rock Thrush, Nuthatch, Redstart and Ortolan Bunting. Lower altitudes hold Golden Oriole, Red-backed Shrike, Great Spotted Cuckoo and Bee-eater.

The area is noted for its population of Spanish ibex, and also has wild cat and wild boar.

Timing

Of interest throughout the year, but best in spring, from April onwards into June. Some of the tracks through the forests and alongside gorges can get a little tricky after periods of rain, in early spring and autumn particularly.

Access

From the coast take the N232 from Vinaròs towards Zaragoza, and specifically Morella 64 km distant and at the heart of the region. If travelling south along the coastal A7 motorway leave at exit 42 for Vinaròs. There are various points of access once within the area but Morella can be used as the focal point, as there are a number of good roads and tracks that radiate out from here. The capital of the Els Ports district, Morella, dominates the horizon for miles around, with 'cubist-like' houses clinging to its steep slopes, and crowned by a rocky summit bearing the remains of the town's castle.

Tinença de Benifassár can easily be reached from Morella, where you continue along the N232 towards the Aragón border and more specifically the Puerto de Torre Miró, where you take a right turn along the minor road CV105 to Castell de Cabres, El Boixar, Fredes and La Pobla de Benifassár.

There are many long-distance and short-distance routes in this area. The GR7 (long-distance with red and white painted posts) crosses the district and links to various towns such as Fredes, El Boixar, Vallibona, Morella, Ares del Maestre, Benesal and Culla. The section between Morella and Ares del Maestre runs through terrain that is fairly easy to cover and with a great variety of habitat and bird species, and the section between Morella to the Coll del Peiró Trencat (towards Vallibona) is also worth trying, with both open and wooded areas including a section alongside the River Cèrvol.

The GR7 branches off into a series of shorter routes signposted as PRs (recognised by yellow and white painted posts). For example, the PRV2 from Morella descends along the Costa del Nogueral and crosses the River Bergantes to climb to the Mola de la Garumba (1144 m), winding to the top of the summit and offering impressive views over Morella, the area being good for birds of prey, and then descends to the town of Forcall. PRV16, another short-distance route, connects Fredes to the Ulldecona Dam, and then passes through the spectacular Portell de l'Inferno ('the port of hell'); this route offers particularly scenic views and climbs up and down throughout its length.

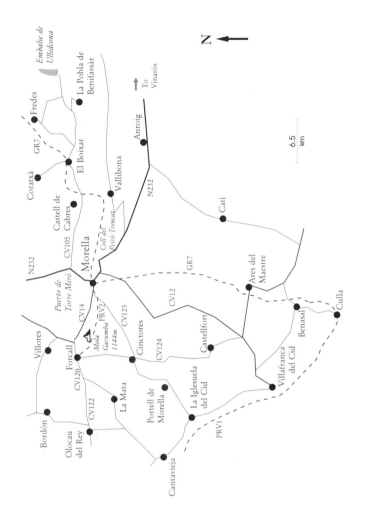

Calendar

All year: Griffon Vulture, Goshawk, Sparrowhawk, Golden Eagle, Bonelli's Eagle, Peregrine, Rock Dove, Eagle Owl, Tawny Owl, Long-eared Owl, Kingfisher, Dipper, Blue Rock Thrush, Dartford Warbler, Spectacled Warbler, Sardinian Warbler, Firecrest, Nuthatch, Red-billed Chough, Rock Sparrow, Rock Bunting.

Breeding season: Egyptian Vulture, Short-toed Eagle, Booted Eagle, Hobby, Great Spotted Cuckoo, Scops Owl, Red-necked Nightjar, Alpine Swift, Bee-eater, Wryneck, Short-toed Lark, Crag Martin, Redstart, Black-eared Wheatear, Rock Thrush, Olivaceous Warbler, Subalpine Warbler, Orphean Warbler, Ortolan Bunting.

V2 EL PRAT DE CABANES–TORREBLANCA

Status: Parque Natural, ZEPA and Ramsar site (812 ha).

Site description

The marshland of El Prat de Cabanes–Torreblanca, formerly known as *Albalat des Ànecs* (the home of the ducks), was declared a natural park in 1989. It extends south from Torreblanca for 7 km, and is only separated from the sea by a narrow stretch of shingle and sand dunes. This important coastal wetland area or *albufera* is 812 ha in size, and while this coastal saltwater lagoon has gradually silted up, the area has developed into a rich mixture of wetland habitats. Most of the area is now made up of wet rushy pasture with pockets of saltmarsh along the seaward boundary. Smaller areas of reedbed, scrub and open water also occur.

Much of the remaining area of open water is now at the northern end of the site and includes lagoons created from old peat workings; whilst the scrubby areas are found towards the south. The site is flooded during the winter, and some parts of the site retain open water into the summer.

Species

This coastal marsh is important for many wetland species, and is one of the best sites in Spain for seeing Collared Pratincole and Moustached Warbler. Around 30 pairs of pratincoles regularly breed here, although this can reach 50 pairs in some years, and indeed did support up to 100 pairs more recently. Good views can be had of this colonial breeder both on and around the nesting site as they feed on insects over open water, reed, scrub and in nearby rice fields. Moustached Warbler are mainly found in the wetter areas of reed, and while numbers also appear to have fallen by around half, up to 200 pairs still nest here. Their call can give them away, and care should be taken in the spring as Sedge Warbler do pass through the site.

El Prat de Cabanes is also very important for harriers, particularly Montagu's Harrier with over 20 breeding pairs and increasing. Marsh Harrier also breeds but these have become rarer in recent years. The importance of the site is further enhanced with up to 50 pairs each of Little Bittern and Black-winged Stilt, and 15 pairs of Red-crested Pochard and Kentish Plover. The reeds also hold good populations of other species of warbler, with 100–200 pairs each of Fan-tailed Warbler and Great Reed Warbler. This stretch of the coast can give good views of Audouin's Gull in the summer, and around 100 birds have been recorded in the past few years.

The area is good for passage migrants in spring and autumn, especially at the southern end of the site.

Timing

The site is of interest to birdwatchers all year round, although later in the year in the high summer there is little open water, and the beach is generally much busier. April and May are the most productive months when a visit combines the interest and excitement of birds on passage with those species that have begun to breed. The autumn may also be interesting.

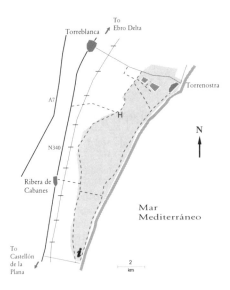

Access
Situated on the coast in the north of Valencia and north of the town of Castellón de la Plana, immediately off the N340 coast road at Torreblanca. There are four points of access to the site, although most visitors enter the site from the north. At Torreblanca take the road towards the coast, Torrenostra and Torrenostra Beach. Pass under the railway bridge and take the second right turn (2 km) which brings you to the northern end of the site and a nature trail. A track follows the inland boundary of the site southwards but this can be difficult for vehicles during the winter and early spring.

To visit the information centre, access is again from the N340 coast road immediately south of Ribera de Cabanes. It is not signposted, but take the road towards the coast at the 1001 km marker post. There is also a research centre — Torre la Sal, Centro Invetsigación CIBIMA.

For those not wishing to walk along the whole length of the site, then access is also possible from turnings off the N340, at tracks at the 1004 km and 1007.5 km markers (the latter near a restaurant). Some car parking is available at both access points.

Calendar
All year: Little Grebe, Great Crested Grebe, Cattle Egret, Little Egret, Red-crested Pochard, Marsh Harrier, Water Rail, Little Ringed Plover, Kentish Plover, Cetti's Warbler, Fan-tailed Warbler, Moustached Warbler, Reed Bunting.

Breeding season: Little Bittern, Purple Heron, Montagu's Harrier, Black-winged Stilt, Avocet, Collared Praticole, Audouin's Gull, Sandwich Tern, Little Tern, Short-toed Lark, Nightingale, Savi's Warbler, Reed Warbler, Great Reed Warbler, Melodious Warbler, Woodchat Shrike.

Winter: Black-necked Grebe, Marsh Harrier, Wigeon, Gadwall, Teal, Avocet, Audouin's Gull, Mediterranean Gull, Grey Plover, Little Stint, Kingfisher, Penduline Tit.

Passage periods: Greater Flamingo, Greylag Goose, Black-tailed Godwit, Curlew Sandpiper, Audouin's Gull, Mediterranean Gull, Bluethroat, Olivaceous Warbler.

V3   COASTAL WETLANDS BETWEEN CASTELLÓN DE LA PLANA AND VALENCIA

Status: Marjal del Moro — ZEPA (350 ha). No special protection for the other sites.

Site description

Valencia still has a number of coastal marshes and wetlands, despite widespread loss to tourist developments, road building and agricultural intensification. While many of the remaining sites are now small and fragmented and suffer from varying degrees of human pressure they are still of considerable importance, especially when looked at as a whole.

There are a number of these coastal sites between Castellón and Valencia, and the following four sites provide some of the most productive birdwatching. However, there are others and many smaller sites can be found with a little searching. From north to south they are: ***Marjal de Oropesa***, another coastal marshland and a smaller version of El Prat de Cabanes (2), immediately to the north. Further south past Castellón, ***Río Mijares*** is another wetland, now surrounded by cultivated ground, although it is fringed with reedbeds and other emergent vegetation. Other semi-natural habitats associated with and adjoining the river are also valuable to a range of birds, not merely wetland species.

Further south still, ***Marjal de Almenara*** is a coastal area of seasonally flooded ground. Ponds occupy part of the site and provide some open water throughout the year. These are supplied by underground water that finds its way to the surface here, and which has its origins in the Sierra de Espadan. Where these waters rise to the surface ponds are formed, with associated reed and emergent vegetation. A much larger area is flooded in the winter, but in the summer much of the area is relatively dry and intensively cultivated.

The final site, ***Marjal del Moro***, is perhaps one of the most important. Another small marsh but with an important range of species, which are described below.

Species

Small numbers of herons and egrets breed at most of the sites, with around 20 pairs breeding at both Marjal del Moro and Almenara. Marjal del Moro is also worth a visit for viewing a regular breeding site for Collared Pratincole, as well as being an occasional breeding site for one to two pairs of Marbled Teal. Other attractions within this suite of wetland sites include good populations of Black-winged Stilt and Moustached Warbler, and the area holds a remarkable range of passage waders and duck. The flooded areas at Almenara are certainly

Yellow 'Spanish' Wagtails

worth visiting in the winter for the large flocks of Red-crested Pochard, which can reach between 500 and 1,000 individuals.

Timing
Throughout the year, including the winter.

Access
Marjal de Oropesa Immediately to the south of El Prat de Cabanes (V2). From the north take a left turn to Oropesa off the main N340 coast road. Go to the end of the road and walk north (left) until you get to the marsh at the stream mouth.

Río Mijares The mouth of the Río Mijares is sited immediately to the south of Castellón. Take the CV18 south towards Burriana, after Almazora a road takes you to the beach and follows the northern bank of the river. Alternatively, continue on the CV18 for 1 km out of Almazora when you cross the river by bridge. Tracks and paths occur on both banks of the river between the road and the beach

Marjal de Almenara For Marjal de Almenara, take the N340 towards Almenara, a town to the north of Sagunt. From the town take the road towards the coast to Casa Blanca. Although the ponds lie to the south of this road, the land on both sides becomes flooded in the winter.

Marjal del Moro From Sagunt take the CV300 south to Puçol, then left to the beach, Platja de Puçol. There is marshy ground either side of this road but most is to the south (right).

Calendar
All year: Little Grebe, Mallard, Water Rail, Kentish Plover, Redshank, Cetti's Warbler, Fan-tailed Warbler, Moustached Warbler, Reed Bunting.

Breeding season: Bittern, Little Bittern, Marbled Teal, Black-winged Stilt, Collared Pratincole, Little Ringed Plover, Scops Owl, Lesser Short-toed Lark, Yellow Wagtail, Savi's Warbler, Reed Warbler, Great Reed Warbler, Melodious Warbler.

Winter: Great Crested Grebe, Black-necked Grebe, Cattle Egret, Little Egret, Grey Heron, Greylag Goose, Shelduck, Wigeon, Gadwall, Pintail,

To
Ebro Delta

Orpesa
● *Marjal de Oropesa*

A7
Benicàssim

Almazora ●
Castelló de la Plana
Río Majares

12
km

N340

Mar Mediterráneo

Almenara
●
● *Marjal de Almenara*
Platja de
Casa Blanca

Sagunt
el Port de Sagunt

Puçol ●
● *Marjal del Moro*
Platja de
Puçol

To
València

N

Teal, Red-crested Pochard, Pochard, Ferruginous Duck, Tufted Duck, Marsh Harrier, Coot, Avocet, Ringed Plover, Golden Plover, Grey Plover, Little Stint, Dunlin, Ruff, Jack Snipe, Snipe, Curlew, Greenshank, Common Sandpiper, Sandwich Tern, Kingfisher.

Passage periods: White Stork, Glossy Ibis, Night Heron, Squacco Heron, Purple Heron, Marsh Harrier, Osprey, Black-tailed Godwit, Little Gull.

V4 LA ALBUFERA DE VALENCIA

Status: Parque Natural, ZEPA and a Ramsar site (21,000 ha).

Site description

Lying 10 km to the south of the city of Valencia, this vast lagoon, the Albufera de Valencia is one of the largest remaining wetland areas and one of the most important ornithological sites in the whole of Spain. Its importance was recognised in its declaration as a natural park in 1986, which was also seen as a method of safeguarding the area from further developments and pollution.

Around 8,000 years ago the sandbank at what is now La Devesa cut off a portion of the sea, forming the inland *Albufera*. Originally covering some 30,000 ha, over the years it has progressively shrunk, partly as a result of natural sedimentation but also through land reclamation for agriculture and, more recently, for industrial, urban and tourist developments. The lagoon now covers only 2800 ha (including reedbeds and islands known as *matas*), although some additional 18,200 ha of marsh and sand dune are also included within the natural park. It is part of a complex hydrological system — the lake itself is very shallow, typically 1 m deep but up to only 2.5 m at its deepest. In the winter it fills up with freshwater from the Río Turia and the Acequia de-Rey. At the southern end of the Albufera there is a canal, the Perelló, which can be opened and closed to allow water to flow into the Mediterranean.

A narrow strip of relatively undamaged sand dunes protects the wetland area from the sea, on which a dense Mediterranean maquis shrub has developed, with occasional flooded saltwater hollows and saltmarsh vegetation. Three canals (or *golas*) with sluices (two natural and a third man-made) connect the lagoon and surrounding wetlands with the sea and each has its own characteristic flora and fauna. The park is surrounded by rice fields filled with water from the lagoon via irrigation ditches.

Besides its intrinsic value as an excellent example of a coastal lagoon, it is extremely important for birds. During the winter, the lagoon and surrounding rice paddies teem with thousands of waterfowl, and many of these species also nest here or use the area as a resting place on migration.

An information centre in Racó de l'Ollá, El Palmar carreterra (tel: 96 162 73 45) provides information on the site including details on access. The Spanish Ornithological Society (SEO) run a bird observatory at Avenida Los Pinares, 106, 46012 Valencia (tel: 96 161 08 47).

Species

Not only is La Albufera one of the most important sites in Spain for wintering wildfowl, it is also extremely important for breeding herons, with around 200 pairs of Little Bittern, 100–150 pairs of Night Heron, 1,100–1,400 pairs each of Cattle and Little Egrets, over 100 pairs of Squacco Heron, 300 pairs of Grey Heron and around 100 pairs of Purple Heron. In all, over 250 species have been recorded with around 90 breeding species, including around 30 pairs of Red-crested Pochard, 150–200 pairs of Black-winged Stilt, more than 100 pairs of Kentish Plover, and other key species of conservation importance such as half a dozen pairs of Collared Pratincole, Moustached Warbler and 50–70 pairs of Bearded Tit.

Tern numbers have fluctuated considerably but have generally been increasing. There are now around 100 pairs of Gull-billed Tern, 470 pairs of Sandwich Tern, 1,650 pairs of Common Tern (only 60 pairs in 1983), and 200 pairs of Little Tern. Whiskered Tern also breed.

It is in winter, however, that this site is most spectacular with tens of thousands of wildfowl. Wintering duck counts average between 40,000–60,000 birds, the most numerous species being Shoveler, whose numbers have peaked at over 30,000 birds, and Red-crested Pochard whose numbers can be over 10,000 individuals. Other wildfowl such as Mallard, Teal, Pintail, Gadwall and Pochard are also numerous. It is not surprising that given its situation and range of habitats it is also very good for passage migrants, particularly waders, with 1,000–2,000 Lapwing and up to 6,000 Black-tailed Godwit, and smaller numbers of, for example, Golden Plover, Sanderling, Snipe and Redshank.

Timing

Worthy of a visit at any time of year, although hunting during the months of October to February can cause some disturbance. For those visitors lucky enough to be in the area in the winter, La Albufera can hold massive flocks of wildfowl.

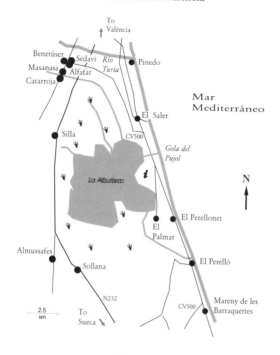

Access

Situated 10 km south of Valencia. Take the CV500 from Valencia towards El Saler, then continue southwards along the coast towards El Palmar and the information centre, where there are car parks at the north of the site. From the south, leave the A7 (at junction 59) or the N332 towards Callera. Then follow the CV502 to El Perolló. There are various routes once on site. The road between El Perolló and Sueca can be very good in the winter.

Calendar

All year: Great Crested Grebe, Cattle Egret, Little Egret, Greater Flamingo, Red-crested Pochard, Marsh Harrier, Avocet, Kentish Plover, Audouin's Gull, Whiskered Tern, Sandwich Tern, Kingfisher, Hoopoe, Lesser Short-toed Lark, Cetti's Warbler, Fan-tailed Warbler, Moustached Warbler, Sardinian Warbler, Bearded Tit.

Breeding season: Little Bittern, Night Heron, Squacco Heron, Purple Heron, Black-winged Stilt, Collared Pratincole, Gull-billed Tern, Common Tern, Little Tern, Bee-eater, Short-toed Lark, Nightingale, Savi's Warbler, Reed Warbler, Great Reed Warbler, Golden Oriole, Woodchat Shrike.

Winter: Yelkouan Shearwater, Black-necked Grebe, Cormorant, Shelduck, Gadwall, Teal, Mallard, Pintail, Marbled Teal, Pochard, Ferruginous Duck, Golden Plover, Sanderling, Snipe, Redshank, Lapwing, Great Skua, Mediterranean Gull, Little Gull, Short-eared Owl, Bluethroat, Penduline Tit.

Passage periods: Glossy Ibis, Garganey, Booted Eagle, Little Stint, Temminck's Stint, Curlew Sandpiper, Dunlin, Ruff, Spotted Redshank, Greenshank, Green Sandpiper, Black Tern, Nightjar, Pallid Swift, Water Pipit, Melodious Warbler.

V5 EL MARJAL DE PEGO–OLIVA

Status: Parque Natural, ZEPA and Ramsar site (1290 ha).

Site description

Another of Valencia's coastal marshes and one of the best of its wetland sites. These marshes occupy a sizable area of around 1300 ha, and are the remains of old rice fields now in disuse, but now support large expanses of reedbed and provide a very rich wetland habitat for many species of bird. The rivers Bullent and Racons, numerous small springs, a complicated network of drainage channels and irrigation ditches that lie between the two rivers, together form an interweaving matrix of watercourses that quarter and separate the fields, which now remain flooded for most of the year. The area's importance was recognised by its declaration as a Ramsar site in 1994 and parque natural in 1995.

Species

El Marjal de Pego–Oliva is especially important for herons and egrets with around 70 breeding pairs of Little Bittern and 20 pairs of Purple Heron. It is no less important for passage, with Night Heron and Squacco Heron regularly occurring and from time to time Bittern, which is a rare passage migrant. A colony of Cattle Egrets has established itself here in recent years. Also it is currently important for the small number of Marbled Teal which occur at the site, as they favour shallow water with extensive emergent and submerged vegetation. Marbled Teal is a species of 'global conservation concern', and this is one of the few sites in Spain, and indeed Europe, where it is found.

A small population of around 20 pairs of Red-crested Pochard also breed here, and Common Pratincole is also an irregular breeder. Another species which was once characteristic of this area was Purple Gallinule, but unfortunately it no longer occurs. Following declines throughout southern Spain, the population is now in recovery in Andalucia and has recently been reintroduced to another wetland site further north in Catalunya, Aiguamolls de l'Empordà (CAT4). Pego–Oliva must be a likely candidate for any further reintroductions.

Spotless Starlings

272

A non-native species, Common Waxbill was originally introduced and is now naturalised in this part of Spain and a feral flock of these birds can normally be found around the western part of the site.

Very good for passage and wintering species with Bluethroat and Penduline Tit both being regular visitors in winter.

Timing
Year-round interest, although the best times of year for visiting the area probably coincides with migration periods. Winter can be good for seabirds, including terns.

Access
Situated approximately halfway between Alicante and Valencia, approached either from the A7 motorway or the N332 and visible from the motorway. The site is also midway between the local towns aof Gandia and Dénia, and the marshes are best approached off the N332 which then crosses over the motorway. Tracks across the marsh can then be taken once the road has crossed one of the main ditches linking the two rivers. The road traverses the central part of the marsh for further views, whilst other views can be had along the western boundary along the CV715 from Pego to Oliva, or the eastern area by the CV700 from Pego to El Verger, and Dénia.

Information on access and other details from Centro de Información, C/Domenec, 2. 03780, Pego (tel: 96 640 02 51).

Calendar
All year: Little Grebe, Great Crested Grebe, Cattle Egret, Mallard, Water Rail, Moorhen, Coot, Kingfisher, Cetti's Warbler, Fan-tailed Warbler, Moustached Warbler, Common Waxbill.

Breeding season: Little Bittern, Purple Heron, Marbled Teal, Red-crested Pochard, Black-winged Stilt, Little Ringed Plover, Kentish Plover, Whiskered Tern, Little Tern, Short-toed Lark.

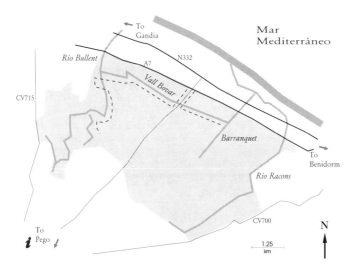

Winter: Little Egret, Grey Heron, Wigeon, Teal, Shoveler, Pochard, Marsh Harrier, Bluethroat, Penduline Tit.

Passage periods: Bittern, Night Heron, Squacco Heron, Spoonbill, Osprey, Garganey, Ringed Plover, Spotted Crake, Little Crake, Grey Plover, Little Stint, Curlew Sandpiper, Black-tailed Godwit, Ruff, Spotted Redshank, Caspian Tern, White-winged Black Tern, Sand Martin.

V6 MONTGÓ–CABO DE SAN ANTONIO

Status: Parque Natural (825 ha) and Reserva Natural (110 ha).

Site description

The Sierra de Montgó is a hilly coastal area that rises to 753 m and dominates the local landscape. As it reaches the coast on its northwest side it eventually ends up at the Cabo de San Antonio, an impressive rocky outcrop of 160 m with a lighthouse. Montgó is especially rocky with low-lying shrubby vegetation, and there are sheer cliffs on either side.

The scrubby maquis has rosemary, heather, lavender and Kermes oak together with some stands of juniper and holm oak. Planted woodland with Aleppo pine occurs on the hill slopes and there are many rock faces and outcrops. The sea cliffs and the prominent position of the site make it important for migration, and also for seawatching.

Species

While the principal interest here is for the cliff- and rock-nesting species, the area does have a wide range of habitats including scrub, open ground and woodland, and it is a good site for viewing a fair number of species in a day, especially during the spring. Bonelli's Eagle, Peregrine, Eagle Owl, Black Wheatear, Blue Rock Thrush, Red-billed Chough and Rock Bunting are all resident and naturally associated with the rocky nature of the site, and many of these are possible during a day's birdwatching here. Eagle Owl may be more difficult, but the general area is also good for other species of owl, including Barn, Scops, Tawny and Little.

The sea cliffs can yield Pallid Swift, which is one of the few breeding sites for this species in Valencia, and which also occurs at Peñón de Ifach (V8). The ground should also hold Black Redstart, and the scrub Dartford Warbler. The cliffs are particularly good in winter for watching seabirds such as Gannet and Arctic Skua, and occasionally Eleonora's Falcon is seen on passage.

Timing

Spring and autumn can be good for migration, and the winter period can also be good for seabirds.

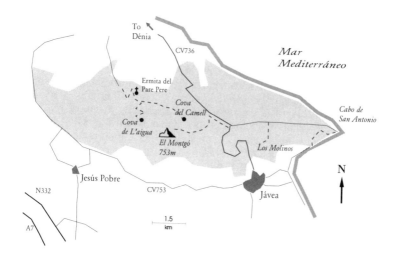

Access

Whether you are coming from Valencia or Alicante, take one of the turnings off the N332 for Jávea, Dénia or Benitachell. From here, minor roads lead respectively either to the headlands or inland to the hills.

The site is situated 75 km northwest of Alicante and reached via the A7 motorway or the parallel coastal road, the N332. Access to Montgó itself can be rather confusing as there are many paths that appear to lead up to the area but actually lead nowhere.

From the nearby towns of Dénia and Jávea walks up the mountain along marked paths can be attempted, and various nature trails can be followed in the park itself.

Calendar

All year: Bonelli's Eagle, Peregrine, Kestrel, Rock Dove, Barn Owl, Scops Owl, Eagle Owl, Little Owl, Tawny Owl, Hoopoe, Thekla Lark, Black Redstart, Stonechat, Black Wheatear, Dartford Warbler, Sardinian Warbler, Blue Rock Thrush, Firecrest, Long-tailed Tit, Crested Tit, Short-toed Treecreeper, Great Grey Shrike, Red-billed Chough, Raven, Spotless Starling, Serin, Crossbill, Rock Bunting.

Breeding season: Cory's Shearwater, Turtle Dove, Crag Martin, Pallid Swift.

Winter: Yelkouan Shearwater, Great Skua, Mediterranean Gull, Sandwich Tern, Razorbill.

Passage periods: Gannet, Cormorant, Shag, Eleonora's Falcon, Arctic Skua, Audouin's Gull, Hoopoe, Tree Pipit, Redstart, Black-eared Wheatear, Willow Warbler, Spotted Flycatcher.

V7 CARRASCAL DE LA FONT ROJA

Status: Parque Natural (2450 ha).

Site description

This park, occupying the Monejador Sierra, has some of the best pre-served Mediterranean forest remaining in Valencia. This range of mountains runs from east to west, reaching a maximum height of 1352 m, with relatively shallow southern slopes, and northern slopes that are are much steeper with gorges and screes. The vegetation on the southern slopes consists of rosemary, whin and the occasional stand of pine, while on the northern slopes above 1000 m there is mixed woodland. The lower slopes are covered in dense pine plantations.

Species

There are several interesting resident species including Bonelli's Eagle, Blue Rock Thrush, Cirl and Rock Bunting. The woodlands also have a good variety with Great Spotted Woodpecker, Bonelli's Warbler, Firecrest, Crossbill and Serin all relatively common. Some of the lower ground has Nightingale and Golden Oriole, with Hoopoe and Wood-chat Shrike found in the more open areas.

Timing

Spring and early summer, from early April through to June.

Access

From Valencia take the N430 south towards Albacete, and after around 50 km take a left turn on the CV40/N340 to Alcoy. To the south of the town take a right turn on the minor road to the parque natural and the Santuario de la Font Roja. The road goes as far as the information centre and then stops. From Alicante take the N332 coast road northwards to San Juan de Alicante where you turn left onto the N340 towards Alcoy. After 8 km, or 3 km before reaching Alcoy, take another left to the park.

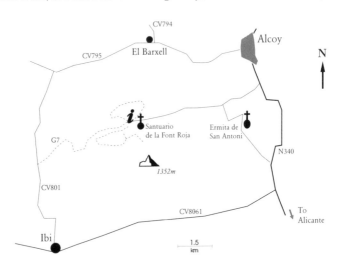

Various tracks and paths start at the information centre at the park — Centro de Información de la Font Roja (tel/fax: 96 533 76 20), and the long distance G7 path goes through the site. There are signposted routes providing a good range of walks through the full range of habitats, including woodland, scrub and open ground.

Calendar

All year: Bonelli's Eagle, Goshawk, Sparrowhawk, Eagle Owl, Little Owl, Great Spotted Woodpecker, Crag Martin, Robin, Stonechat, Black Wheatear, Blue Rock Thrush, Dartford Warbler, Firecrest, Crested Tit, Short-toed Treecreeper, Rock Sparrow, Serin, Crossbill, Cirl Bunting, Rock Bunting.

Breeding season: Nightjar, Hoopoe, Nightingale, Black-eared Wheatear, Subalpine Warbler, Blackcap, Bonelli's Warbler, Spotted Flycatcher, Golden Oriole, Red-backed Shrike, Woodchat Shrike.

V8   PEÑÓN DE IFACH Y LAS SALINAS DE CALPE

Status: Parque Natural (Peñón de Ifach only — 35 ha).

Site description

Joined to land via a narrow isthmus, the limestone rock of Ifach rises 332 m over the surrounding sea near Calpe and dominates the scenery all around. Its rock faces are covered in scrub with lavender, dwarf palm and juniper. The disused saltpans of Calpe, a small fishing port, are situated beneath the rock and right alongside the main road on the coast.

Species

Although right next to a developed part of the coast with many visitors, over 80 species of bird have been recorded at the site and it can be excellent for seawatching, especially in the winter when large numbers of Gannets feed off the coast. The rock itself has a pair of sea-cliff nesting Peregrines, and is one of the best places for Peregrine in Valencia. It is worth walking up the rock, for in addition to Peregrine, are breeding Pallid Swift, Blue Rock Thrush, Black Redstart, Crag Martin, Stonechat, Dartford Warbler and Raven. It is also worth checking the fields and scrub on the way up for migrants such as Wheatear.

The saltpans are back down at the coastal resort, and are some of the most easily accessible sites in Spain for viewing Audouin's Gull. In addition to breeding Avocet, Black-winged Stilt and Kentish Plover, the area can attract Greater Flamingo and a good mixture of terns and waders on passage.

Timing

Mainly spring and autumn.

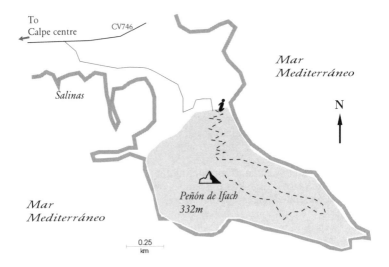

Access

Calpe is 21 km northeast from Benidorm and the saltpans are signposted within the town. The saltpans can be viewed by parking in a lay-by just off the main road (CV746) into town; all you need to do is stop by the roadside and look across to the old causeways of the old salt workings. A road goes partly up the rock past the harbour and up to the Information Centre, from here a track takes you further up the promontory.

Calendar

All year: Greater Flamingo, Grey Heron, Little Egret, Peregrine, Coot, Moorhen, Black-headed Gull, Yellow-legged Gull, Crested Lark, Crag Martin, Stonechat, Black Redstart, Blue Rock Thrush, Dartford Warbler, Sardinian Warbler, Raven, Serin.

Breeding season: Shag, Avocet, Black-winged Stilt, Kentish Plover, Audouin's Gull, Pallid Swift, Reed Warbler, Spectacled Warbler.

Winter: Gannet, Cormorant, Shag.

Passage periods: Black-necked Grebe, Hobby, Eleonora's Falcon, Common Sandpiper, Sandwich Tern, Common Tern, Little Tern, Whiskered Tern, Black Tern, Wheatear.

V9 EL HONDO

Status: Parque Natural, ZEPA and Ramsar site (2378 ha).

Site description

One of the most important wetland sites in southeast Spain despite it now being a fragment of what once was a vast area of marshland. Two irrigation reservoirs were constructed on a site of a former marshy lagoon, and large stands of reedbed and other emergent vegetation including rushes and saltmarsh have become established here. A number of other smaller brackish and freshwater waterbodies are also present. The two waterbodies are quite sizable, with the Embalse de Levante being 450 ha, and the Embalse de Poniente 650 ha, the total area of the site being 2378 ha. Shooting continues to be a severe problem here despite its designated status, and despite interventions by conservation organisations. However, there is currently a partial shooting ban on around 60% of the site. Other concerns are the potential problems of lead and insecticide poisoning, and in the autumn of 1997 over 80 Marbled Teal were found dead at El Hondo.

Species

El Hondo is the most important site in Europe for the globally threatened Marbled Teal, and at least 30 pairs breed. Small numbers of another globally threatened species also breed, White-headed Duck bred successfully here in 1991. Unfortunately Ruddy Duck has been recorded on the site and these along with hybrid birds (White-headed x Ruddy) have been shot to help conserve White-headed Duck.

One should not forget the other interest of the site which is substantial, with almost 200 species now recorded for this wetland. Herons are especially important with over 100 pairs of Little Bittern, 5–10 pairs of Squacco Heron, up to 50 pairs of Night Heron, 35 pairs of Purple Heron, 450 pairs of Cattle Egret, 200 pairs of Little Egret, up to 500 pairs of Red-crested Pochard, 350–450 pairs of Avocet, 200 pairs of Black-winged

Marbled Teal

Stilt, c 200 pairs of Kentish Plover, 50 pairs of Little Tern, and over 100 pairs of Whiskered Tern. This is the largest breeding colony of Whiskered Tern in Valencia.

Important also as a site for passage and wintering ducks and waders particularly Red-crested Pochard (average 700+ and a maximum of 1,500+); also with large flocks of Shoveler and large autumn passage roosts of Swallow and Starling. Bluethroat have normally arrived by early October or sometimes earlier, and Penduline Tit also winters. In summary, an excellent mix of species right through the year including non-wetland species on the drier areas (particularly in early autumn), with species such as Short-toed and Lesser Short-toed Larks, Crested Lark, Bee-eater, and Black-eared Wheatear.

Timing

Of considerable interest at any time of year, although shooting can be a problem in autumn and winter on certain days and on some parts of the site. As with many wetland sites heat haze can make viewing difficult during the middle of the day at the height of summer. The area can also be very good for raptors during winter months.

Access

From Alicante it is just over 40 km to El Hondo, and is best approached off the N340 from Alicante to Murcia. Take the N340 to Elche, and carry on through the town on the same road towards Crevillente. Two km out of Crevillente turn left on to the CV90 towards Dolores. Immediately after a railway line turn left through the village of El Realengo and this road will bring you to the site. If you miss this approach, after about 6 km turn left to San Felipe de Neri and drive through the village after which El Hondo is signposted; the road follows the northern boundary of the site. Alternatively, proceed through Catral and take a left turn immediately out of the town which will bring you along the southern

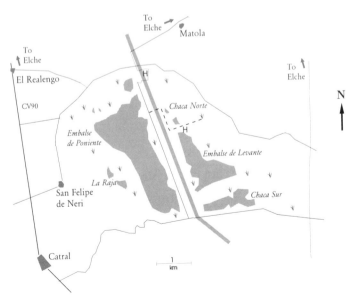

boundary. The site can be approached from Elche itself from the east, but directions are more complicated and it is easy to get lost!

Once at the site much can be seen from the road, but permits to enter the site and information on use of the hides are available from the information centre (see below). A track runs between the two main wetlands, the Embalse de Poniente and the Embalse de Levante. The areas at either end of Embalse de Levante are worth checking — Charca Norte and Charca Sur — as is La Raja immediately to the west of the Emabalse de Poniente. As the birds can make use of a large part of the site at different times of year it is worth looking extensively.

Information on the park (including visiting arrangements) can be obtained from Centro de Información del Parque Natural de El Hondo, Vereda de Sedres, Segunda Elevación. 03295, Elche (tel: 96 667 85 15).

Calendar

All year: Little Grebe, Great Crested Grebe, Cattle Egret, Little Egret, Greater Flamingo, Marbled Teal, White-headed Duck, Red-crested Pochard, Marsh Harrier, Water Rail, Moorhen Avocet, Kentish Plover, Kingfisher, Yellow-legged Gull, Fan-tailed Warbler, Moustached Warbler, Bearded Tit, Penduline Tit.

Breeding season: Black-necked Grebe, Little Bittern, Squacco Heron, Purple Heron, Garganey, Shelduck, Spotted Crake, Black-winged Stilt, Collared Pratincole, Whiskered Tern, Lesser Short-toed Lark, Savi's Warbler, Great Reed Warbler, Spectacled Warbler.

Winter: Black-necked Grebe, Cormorant, Grey Heron, Greylag Goose, Osprey, Wigeon, Teal, Pintail, Shoveler, Coot, Golden Plover, Crag Martin, Water Pipit, Bluethroat.

Passage periods: Glossy Ibis, Greater Flamingo, Crane, Garganey, Gadwall, Hobby, Golden Plover, Lapwing, Temminck's Stint, Dunlin, Black-tailed Godwit, Spotted Redshank, Mediterranean Gull, Little Gull, Black Tern, Swallow, Kingfisher, Nightjar, Grasshopper Warbler, Starling.

V10 LAS SALINAS DE SANTA POLA

Status: Parque Natural, ZEPA and a Ramsar site (2496 ha).

Site description

The saltpans are located in the former Albufera de Elche, a lagoon at the mouth of the River Vinalopó. The lagoon was drained at the end of the 19th Century, and the area now consists of saltpans, freshwater marshes with reedbeds, extensive saltmarshes, sand dunes and a beach some 5 km long. Several channels cross the landscape, draining through the original outlet of the lagoon into the sea. The dunes in the Pinet area also form part of the park. Areas are still being worked and these are also of value to birds, but the degree to which they are attractive depends on their current state of working.

This coastal wetland area was declared a natural park in 1988, and designated as a Ramsar site for its wintering populations of Greater Flamingo and Avocet and breeding Shelduck, Marbled Teal, Red-crested Pochard, Black-winged Stilt, Avocet, Kentish Plover and Little Tern.

Species

A former breeder, Greater Flamingo is still present throughout the year and up to 8,000 birds have been recorded on the saltpans. It is more normal for hundreds of birds to use the site in the winter, with numbers peaking in late summer, when there may be over 2,000 birds on site. Although breeding was recorded in the 1970s, there are no recent records.

There is sufficient cover in the marshes and reeds for Little Bittern to breed and the site regularly supports 10–15 pairs. Its main breeding interest focuses on wader, terns and Marbled Teal. Marbled Teal has spread out from its centre of population in Andalucia and now breeds regularly at a handful of sites in Valencia. This duck is a species of 'global conservation concern' and this site is therefore extremely important as part of the conservation measures being developed to safeguard its survival. The saltpans also prove very attractive to waders, and breeding species include 400–500 pairs of Avocet, around 200 pairs of Black-winged Stilt, 300 pairs of Kentish Plover and smaller numbers of other species. Five species of tern also breed, with Common Tern (200 pairs) and Little Tern (250 pairs) being the most numerous, although Whiskered Tern, Gull-billed Tern and Sandwich Tern (25 pairs) also breed. Slender-billed Gull are normally present and there are 25 pairs of Bearded Tit.

Large winter flocks of Coot (over 10,000 birds) and Black-headed Gull occur, and up to 2,000 Black-tailed Godwit have been recorded on the Salinas de Bonmati, with small numbers of Spoonbill and Slender-billed Gull and regular sightings of phalaropes. It is a very good passage site as can be seen from the species list, particularly for waders, but some of the rarer gulls also turn up. Slender-billed Gull winters regularly and has also recently bred.

Timing

The saltpans are good throughout the year but probably at their best in spring, although autumn and winter are also interesting.

Access

To the south of Alicante take the N332 and after approximately 20 km you come to the small resort of Santa Pola. The N332 passes for the most part on the east side of the saltpans and there are several places to pull over to get good views over the area, although the road is busy and not ideal for birdwatching.

A minor road (CV851) skirts the other edge of the salinas along with various tracks, and views of some of the more remote lagoons can be obtained.

Visits to the Santa Pola saltpans can be arranged from the Centro de Información de la Mata, Casa Forestral de la Mata, La Mata-Torrevieja (tel: 96 692 04 04) but permits are not really needed as almost everything can be seen from the roadside between the 22 and 24 km road markers.

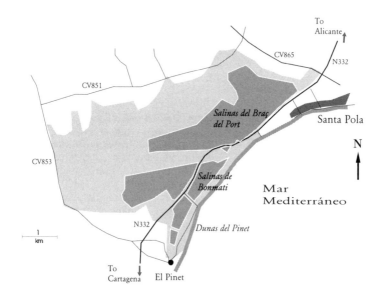

Calendar

All year: Great Crested Grebe, Little Egret, Greater Flamingo, Shelduck, Red-crested Pochard, Marsh Harrier, Avocet, Kentish Plover, Slender-billed Gull, Yellow-legged Gull, Sandwich Tern, Lesser Short-toed Lark, Fan-tailed Warbler, Cetti's Warbler, Moustached Warbler, Bearded Tit.

Breeding season: Little Bittern, Night Heron, Purple Heron, Marbled Teal, Montagu's Harrier, Black-winged Stilt, Little Tern, Common Tern, Gull-billed Tern, Whiskered Tern, Savi's Warbler, Great Reed Warbler.

Winter: Black-necked Grebe, Cormorant, Spoonbill, Grey Heron, Wigeon, Teal, Pintail, Shoveler, Pochard, Osprey, Ringed Plover, Golden Plover, Crag Martin, Water Pipit, larks, Reed Bunting.

Passage periods: Garganey, Spotted Crake, Grey Plover, Little Stint, Temminck's Stint, Curlew Sandpiper, Dunlin, Ruff, Black-tailed Godwit, Bar-tailed Godwit, Little Gull, Audouin's Gull, Caspian Tern, Black Tern, Kingfisher, Sand Martin.

V11 LAS SALINAS DE LA MATA Y TORREVIEJA

Status: Parque Natural, ZEPA and Ramsar site (3693 ha).

Site description

Two wide coastal lagoons which have been exploited for salt extraction, with a permanent saltwater supply from the sea. The two interconnected wetlands are still used for salt extraction, as they have been for many years. The Laguna de la Mata (700 ha) is used to regulate the water levels in the larger lagoon, Laguna de Torrevieja (1400 ha). Salt water is drawn from the Cabeç de la Sal in Pinoso and left to evaporate. The waters of Torrevieja consequently have a higher salinity than those of La Mata, and this has a direct influence on the use of the two sites by birds. Both areas have an important drier period in summer months. This saltworks complex is almost identical to the one that operates at nearby Santa Pola.

Salinas are one of the most inhospitable coastal habitats for both plants and birds. Not including those species that prefer more cover, generally most birds prefer to nest on islands within the salinas rather than around the edge of the pans. In summer, small fish provide important food for herons, gulls and terns, and during winter and on migration, numerous species congregate in significant numbers.

The shores of the lagoon run from muddy beaches to beds of reed, rushes and saltmarsh. The surrounding area is a mosaic of extensive pine plantations, vineyards and irrigated farmland.

Salinas de la Mata y Torrevieja form a very important wetland in their own right and from an ecological viewpoint are part of a much larger wetland complex that also includes the sites of El Hondo and Santa Pola.

Species

Important for small numbers of breeding Shelduck, which is very rare as a breeding bird in Spain, around 60 pairs of Black-winged Stilt, 100 pairs of Kentish Plover, 70 pairs of Little Tern, and around half a dozen pairs of Montagu's Harrier.

Outstanding concentrations in winter or during passage of Black-necked Grebe (average 800 with a maximum of 3,500), Greater Flamingo (1,000–2,000) and Red-crested Pochard (2,000–3,000). Water level is a critical factor governing the number of birds using the saltpans in winter, not only here but at other sites in the area. This is one of the most important sites in Spain for wintering Black-necked Grebe.

Timing

Throughout the year, and even into the winter when numbers of wildfowl can be particularly impressive. As with the other similar sites, heat haze in summer can make viewing very difficult.

Access

Located on the landward side of the main road, the N332 from Alicante to Cartagena. The CV90 from Torrevieja to Benijófar runs between the two lagoons and gives views over the wetlands, particularly Laguna de Torrevieja. However, they are not that easy to approach. La Mata, the

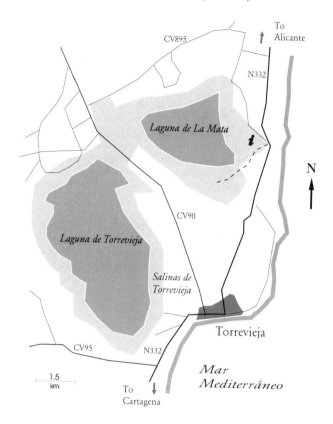

northernmost of the two, has access from the main N332 and a track runs along the southern shore and this is probably the best area for viewing waders, and warblers which breed in the reedbeds.

Private land surrounds Torrevieja and access is difficult.

An information centre is found on the site — Casa Forestal de la Mata, La Mata-Torrevieja — from where a number of routes to the south of the lake can be followed (tel: 96 692 04 04).

Calendar

All year: Greater Flamingo, Shelduck, Avocet, Stone Curlew, Kentish Plover, Lesser Short-toed Lark, Cetti's Warbler, Fan-tailed Warbler.

Breeding season: Montagu's Harrier, Black-winged Stilt, Common Tern, Little Tern, Yellow Wagtail, Rufous Bushchat, Spectacled Warbler, Reed Warbler, Great Reed Warbler, Black-eared Wheatear, Reed Bunting.

Winter: Black-necked Grebe, Pochard, Shoveler, Pintail, Mallard, Wigeon, Red-crested Pochard, Slender-billed Gull, Reed Bunting.

Passage periods: Garganey, Golden Plover, Little Stint, Lapwing, Marsh Sandpiper, Little Gull, Sedge Warbler, Rock Sparrow.

OTHER SITES WORTH VISITING

V12 Peñagolosa

Limestone mountain area rising up to over 1800 m with gorges and extensive pine forests. Golden Eagle, Short-toed Eagle, Eagle Owl, Red-billed Chough, Crossbill. Northwest from Castellón de la Plana towards Figueroles and Llucena on CV16/CV90. Massif between here and border with Aragón.

V13 El Alto Turia

Mountain area with gorges and extensive pine woods and scrub. Griffon Vulture, birds of prey and woodland species. Take CV35 northwest from Valencia towards Chelva. Tuéjar to the left after another 5–6 km where there is an information centre.

V14 Hoces del Cabriel y de Júcar

Mountain area with high densities of birds of prey including Golden, Bonelli's and Short-toed Eagles. Partly within a national game reserve. Take A3/E901 west from Valencia to Requeria and then N322 or N330 from Requenia.

V15 Isla de Tabarca

Small island 4 km offshore with breeding Pallid Swift and Audouin's Gull. Also good for migration. Boats from Alicante and Santa Pola. Marine reserve.

V16 Sierra de Aitana

Limestone mountain area with pine and oak woods. Golden Eagle, Bonelli's Eagle, Crested Tit, Red-billed Chough, Cirl Bunting. Inland and close to Benidorm. South of Benidorm on the N332 to Villajoyosa, turn right onto minor road CV770 to Sella and beyond. Road 12 km past Sella to right, and road to top of sierra.

V17 Laguna de Salinas

Natural lagoon with saltmarsh vegetation. Breeding Avocet and Black-winged Stilt, also larks and Stone Curlew. From Alicante N330 north towards Elda. Continue to Sax (7 km) and turn left into Sax for the CV830 to Salinas. Lagoon on the left before Salinas.

FURTHER READING

Bárcena F, Teixeira A M, and Bermejo A. 1984. Breeding seabird populations in the Atlantic sector of the Iberian peninsula. In: Croxhall J P, Evans P G H, and Screiber R W (eds). *Status and Conservation of the World's Seabirds*. ICBP Technical Publication No 2.

De Juana E. 1980. *Atlas Ornithológico de la Rioja*. Logroño: Instituto de Estudios Riojanos.

De Juana E. 1984. The status and conservation of seabirds in the Spanish Mediterranean. In: Croxhall J P, Evans P G H, and Screiber R W (eds). *Status and Conservation of the World's Seabirds*. ICBP Technical Publication No 2.

De Juana E, Santos T, Suárez F, and Tellería J L. 1988. Status and conservation of steppe birds and their habitats in Spain. In: Goriup P (ed.). *Ecology and Conservation of Grassland Birds*. Pp 113–123. ICBP, Cambridge.

De Juana E. 1990. *Areas Importantes para las Aves en España*. Sociedad Española de Ornitología.

Elósegui J. 1985. *Atlas de las Aves Nidificantes de Navarra*. Pamplona: Caja de Ahorros de Navarra.

Garcia E, and Paterson A. 1994. *Where to watch birds in Southern Spain*. Christopher Helm.

Gil-Degado J A. 1983. Breeding bird community in orange groves. In: Puuroy FJ (ed.). *Censos de aves en el Mediterraneo*. Proc. VII Int. Conf. Bird Census (IBCC) 1981 Univ. León.

Grimmett R F A, and Jones T A. 1989. *Important Bird Areas in Europe*. ICBP Technical Publication No 9.

Muñoz-Cobo J, and Purroy F J. 1980. Wintering bird communities in the olive tree plantations of Spain. In: Oelke H (ed.). *Bird Census work and nature conservation*. Pp 185–189 Gottingen.

Polunin O, and Smythies B E. 1988. *Flowers of South-West Europe: a field guide*. Oxford University Press.

Sociedad Española de Ornitologia. 1977. *Atlas de las Aves de España (1975–1995)*. Lynx Edicions.

Telleria J L, Suárez F, and Santos T. 1988. Bird communities of the Iberian Shrub steppes. *Holarctic Ecology* 11: 171–177.

Tucker G M, and Heath M F. 1994. *Birds in Europe: their conservation status*. Birdlife International. BirdLife Conservation Series No.3.

Tucker G M, and Evans M I. 1997. *Habitats for Birds in Europe: a conservation strategy for the wider environment*. BirdLife International. BirdLife Conservation Series No 6.

Various. 1992. *Espacios Naturales Protegidos de España*. Editorial Incafo. Madrid.

INDEX OF SPECIES BY SITE NUMBER

AR = Aragón; **AS** = Asturias; **CAN** = Cantabria; **CLM** = Castile-La Mancha;
CAS = Castile-León; **CAT** = Catalunya; **E** = Euskadi (País Vasco); **G** = Galicia;
MA = Madrid; **MU** = Murcia; **N** = Navarra; **R** = La Rioja; **V** = Valencia

Accentor, Alpine
AR1–AR7, AR19, AS6,
CAN2, CLM8, CAS6,
CAS11, CAS16, CAT1,
CAT2, CAT5, CAT8,
CAT11, E2, G7, MA1,
N1–N3, R1
Avocet AR8, AR14, AR15,
CAN1, CAN7, CLM3,
CLM4, CLM8, CLM11,
CLM18, CAS2, CAS3,
CAT9, G4, MA3, MU3,
N4, V2–V4, V8–V11, V17

Bee-eater AR1, AR8, AR9,
AR11–AR15, AS6, CLM1,
CLM2, CLM4, CLM7,
CLM8, CLM10–CLM15,
CAS2–CAS5, CAS8,
CAS9, CAS11, CAT4,
CAT5, CAT7–CAT9,
MA2, MA3, MU1, MU2,
N4, N6, N7, R2–R5, R8,
V1, V4, V9
Bittern AR11, CLM3,
CAT4, CAT9, MU3, N4,
N5, V3, V5
   Little AR10, AR11, AR14,
   AS1, CAN4, CAN6,
   CLM3, CLM11, CLM12,
   CLM30, CAS15, CAT4,
   CAT6, CAT7, CAT9, G1,
   MA7, N4, N5, V2–V5,
   V9, V10
Blackbird CLM10, G3
Blackcap AR4, AS6,
CLM15, CAS1, CAS11,
E1, G7, G8, N1, N7
Bluethroat CAN2, CLM5,
CLM12, CAS1, CAS6,
CAT4, CAT9, MA1, MA2,
V2, V4, V5, V9
Brambling AS1, CAN1,
CAT9
Bullfinch AR2–AR5,
AS2–AS4, AS6, CAN2,
CAS1, CAS11, CAT1, E2,
G6, G7, N1, N2, R1
Bunting, Cirl AR2, AR3,
AR7, AR9, AS3, AS6,
CAN1, CAN4, CAN6,
CAN7, CLM1, CLM6,
CLM7, CLM9,
CLM13CAS1, CAS10,
CAT3, CAT5, CAT7,
CAT8, E2, G2, G5, G6,

G8, N1–N3, N6, R1, R2,
R5, V7, V16
Corn AR8, CLM10,
CLM11, CLM14, CAS7,
CAT3, E1, G5, MU2, R3
Ortolan AR2, AR4, AR5,
AR7, AR9, AR 20, AS3,
AS6, CLM5, CLM7,
CLM12, CAS1, CAS6,
CAS10, CAS18, CAT3,
CAT5, CAT15, MA1,
MA2, N1, R3, V1
Reed CAN7, CLM3,
CLM12, CAT9, E1, N4,
N5, V2, V3, V10, V11
Rock AR1–AR3, AR5,
AR7, AR16, AR18, AS3,
AS4, AS6, CLM5–CLM8,
CLM16, CAS4, CAS6,
CAS8, CAS10,
CAT1–CAT3, CAT5, E2,
G5, G6, G8, MA1, MA2,
MV1, N1, N3, R1–R4, V1,
V6, V7
Snow AS1, CAN4
Bushchat, Rufous V11
Bustard, Great AR8,
AR12, AR13, AR15,
CLM2, CLM11, CLM13,
CLM19, CLM21, CLM23,
CLM26, CLM30, CAS2,
CAS13, MA5, N7
   Little AR8, AR12, AR13,
   AR15, AR22, CLM1,
   CLM2, CLM4,
   CLM11–CLM15, CLM19,
   CLM23, CLM30, CAS2,
   CAS3, CAS13, CAT7,
   CAT14, MA3, MA5, MU2,
   N5, N7
Buzzard AR1, AR4, AR16,
AS2, AS6, CAN3–CAN5,
CAN7, CLM5, CLM8,
CLM10, CLM13, CLM14,
CAS1, CAS2, CAS4–CAS8,
CAS11, CAT3,
CAT5–CAT7, E2, G2, G4,
G5, G7, G8, MA1, MA2,
MU1, N1, N2, R1
Honey AR1–AR3, AR5,
AR7, AR9, AR16, AR28,
AS2–AS4, AS6, CAN3,
CAN7, CLM1, CLM5,
CLM13, CAS6, CAS11,
CAT1, CAT2, CAT8, G6,
G7, MA1, N1–N3, R1

Capercaillie AR2, AR4,
AR5, AS2–AS4, AS6,
CAN9, CAT1, CAT2, G6,
G7, N2
Chaffinch CAS10
Chiffchaff AR3, AR4, AR9,
CAN1, CLM7, CAT1,
CAT4, E2, G8
Chough, Alpine AR1,
AR2, AR4, AR5, AS6,
CAN2, CAS17, CAT1,
CAT2, E2, E5, N1–N3,
N9
   Red-billed AR1–AR7,
   AR9, AR25, AS3, AS6,
   CAN2, CAN6,
   CLM5–CLM9, CLM16,
   CLM28, CAS4–CAS6,
   CAS8–CAS10, CAT1,
   CAT2, CAT8, E2, E3,
   G3–G5, G8, MA1, MA2,
   MU1, N1–N3, N7, N8,
   R1–R4, V1, V6, V12, V16
Coot AR11, AR15, AS5,
AS6, CAN3, CAN7,
CLM10–CLM13, CAT4,
G1, G2, G4, MA3, MU3,
N4, V3, V5, V8, V9
Cormorant AR10, AS1,
AS5, CAN1,
CAN4–CAN6,
CLM1–CLM4, CLM8,
CLM2, CLM13, CAS3,
CAS8, CAT4, CAT6, E1,
G1–G4, MA3, MU3, N4,
V4, V6, V8–V10
Crake, Baillon's CLM1,
CAT4, CAT6, CAT9,
MU3, N5
   Little AR10, AR14,
   CLM3, CAT4, CAT6,
   CAT9, N4, N5, V5
   Spotted AR8, AR14,
   AR15, CAN6, CLM10,
   CLM11, G1, V5, V9, V10
Crane AR8, AR15, AR23,
CLM1, CLM3, CLM5,
CLM8, CLM11, CLM13,
CLM15, CLM20, CLM22,
CAS2, CAT4, MA4, N1,
N5, R1, V9
Crossbill AR3, AR4, AR9,
AS3, AS6, CLM19, CAS6,
CAS11, CAT1, CAT2,
CAT8, E4, MA1, MU1,
N2, N3, V6, V7, V12

288

G4, G8, MU3, N2, N6, R5, V1–V5, V9, V10

Kite, Black AR1–AR3, AR5, AR6, AR8, AR11, AR12, AR14–AR16, AS3, AS6, CAN1, CAN3, CAN6, CAN7, CLM1, CLM5, CLM 7, CLM11–CLM14, CAS2–CAS8, CAT2, CAT4, CAT8, G5, MA1, MA2, N1–N6, R1, R5

Black-shouldered CLM1, CLM2, CLM13–CLM15

Red AR1–AR3, AR5–AR7, CAN3, CAN7, CLM1, CLM2, CLM5, CLM13–CLM15, CAS2, CAS4, CAS6–CAS8, CAT1, E1, G4, MA1, MA2, N1–N4, N6, N7, R1, R5

Kittiwake CAT3, CAT9, G3, G4

Knot AR15, AS5, CAN1, CAN4, CAN7, CLM11, CAT4, CAT9, MU3

Lammergeier AR1–AR7, AR19, CAT1, CAT2, CAT10, N1–N3, R2

Lapwing AR8, AR10, AR15, AS1, AS5, CLM1, CLM2, CLM4, CLM10–CLM12, CLM15, CAS2, CAT4, CAT9, N5, V4V9, V11

Lark, Calandra AR8, AR12, AR13, AR15, CLM2, CLM4, CLM11, CLM15, CAS2, CAS8, CAT7, CAT14, MU2, MU3, N5, N7

Crested AR13, AS1, CLM2, CLM4, CLM14, CAS7, CAT3, CAT5, CAT9, G1, G2, G4, MA2, MU3, N7, N8

Dupont's AR12, AR13, AR15, AR22, CLM11, CLM21, CLM24, CLM26, CAS8, CAS9, CAS18, CAT7, MU1, N7

Lesser Short-toed AR12, AR13, AR15, CLM11, CAT7, CAT9, MU1–MU3, N7, V3–V5, V10, V11

Short-toed AR12, AR13, AR15, CLM2, CLM4, CLM11, CLM14, CLM15, CAS2, CAS8, CAS18, CAT4, CAT6, CAT7,

CAT9, MA3, MU2, MU3, N7, V1, V2, V4, V9

Thekla AR12, AR13, AR15, CLM2, CLM8, CLM11, CLM15, CAS4, CAS5, CAS8, CAS9, CAT3, CAT9, MA2, MA3, MU1, MU5 N7, R2–R4, V6

Linnet AS6, CLM8

Magpie, Azure-winged CLM1, CLM2, CLM13–CLM15, CAS3, CAS4, CAS5, CAS8–CAS10, MA2, MA3

Mallard AR8, AR10, AR14, AR15, AS1, AS5, AS6, CAN3, CLM3, CLM4, CLM8, CLM10, CLM11, CAS1, CAS2, CAT4, CAT9, G1, G2, G4, G8, MA3, MU3, N4, N5, V3–V5, V11

Martin, Crag AR1–AR7, AR9, AR13, AR24, AS3, AS4, AS6, CAN2, CAN6, CLM1, CLM6–CLM9, CLM16, CAS1, CAS4, CAS5, CAS8–CAS10, CAT1–CAT3, CAT5, CAT8, E1, E2, G4, G6, MA1, MA2, MU1, N1–N3, N9, R1–R4, V1, V6–V10

House AR1, AR4, AR11, AS1, CAN1, CLM4, CLM6, CAS9, CAS10, CAT10, G2, G5, G8, N2, N3, R2, R3

Sand AR10, AR11, AR15, AS5, CAN5, CAN7, CLM3, CLM4, CLM8, CLM10, CLM12, E1, G5, N5, N6, R5, V5, V10

Merganser, Red-breasted AS1, CAN4–CAN7, CAT9, E1, G4, G8, MU3

Merlin AS1, CAN5, CLM2, CLM11–CLM13, CLM15, CAS2, CAT9, G1, G2, G8, N7

Moorhen AR8, AS1, AS5, CAN3, CLM8, CLM10, CLM12, CAS1, CAS3, G2, G4, MA3, MU3, N4, V5, V8, V9

Nightingale AR1, AR11, CLM3, CLM4, CLM6, CLM8, CLM10, CAS1, CAS7, CAS8, CAT3, CAT4, CAT8, G1, G3, G5, N4N6, R3–R5, V2, V4, V7

Nightjar AR9, AS2, AS6, CAN3, G2–G4, G8, N1, N2, V4, V7, V9

Red-necked AR12, AR13, AR15, AR21, CLM1, CLM2, CLM15, CAS2, CAS4, CAT7, CAT14, MA3, N7, V1

Nuthatch AR3, AR9, AS6, CLM9, CLM16, CAS5, CAT1, CAT2, E2, G6, MA1, N1, R1, V1

Oriole, Golden AR1, AR6, AR11, AR24, CAN4, CAN7, CLM1, CLM3, CLM6, CLM8, CLM13, CLM15, CAS3, CAS4, CAS8–CAS10, CAS15, CAT1, CAT4, CAT5, CAT7, G4, G5, N3–N6, R4, R5, R8, V4, V7

Osprey AR8, AR10, CAN1, CAN4, CAN7, CLM1, CLM3, CLM4, CLM8, CLM10, CLM11, CLM20, CAT9, E1, G4, MA3, N4, N5, V3, V5, V9, V10

Ouzel, Ring AR1, AR2, AR4, AR5, CLM5, CAT1, CAT8, CAT11, N2

Owl, Barn AS1, CAN1, CLM2, CLM6, CAS7, CAS9, CAT3, CAT5, CAT8, E1, G1, G2, G5, G8, MA1, MA2, N6, R5, V6

Eagle AR1, AR4, AR6, AR7, AR9, AR12, AR16, AR28, AS2, AS3, AS6, CLM1, CLM4, CLM5, CLM7–CLM9, CLM13–CLM16CLM25, CLM28, CAS1, CAS4, CAS6, CAS8–CAS10, CAT1, CAT2, CAT5, MA1, MA2, MU1, N1–N3, N8, R1–R4, R6, V1, V6, V7, V12

Little AR1, AR8, CAN3, CLM2, CLM10, CLM11, CLM14, CAS2, CAS7, CAS9, CAT3, CAT7, CAT8, E1, G2, G4, G5, MA1, MA2, MU2, R3, V6, V7

Long-eared AR5, AR7, AR9, CLM1, CLM5, CLM13, CAS3, CAS6, CAS8, CAS11, CAT7, MA1, MA2, N1, N3, R6, V1

Scops AR1, AR11, CAN6, CLM3, CLM10, CLM13, CAS7, CAS9, CAS10, CAT5–CAT7, G4, MA1,